P9-DES-511

Gender Positive!

Gender Positive!

*A Teachers' and Librarians'
Guide to Nonstereotyped
Children's Literature, K–8*

by
Patricia L. Roberts
Nancy L. Cecil
Sharon Alexander

McFarland & Company, Inc., Publishers
Jefferson, North Carolina, and London

British Library Cataloguing-in-Publication data are available

Library of Congress Cataloguing-in-Publication Data

Roberts, Patricia, 1936–
   Gender positive! : a teachers' and librarians' guide to
nonstereotyped children's literature, K–8 / by Patricia Roberts,
Nancy Lee Cecil, and Sharon Alexander.
     p. cm.
   Includes index.
   ISBN 0-89950-816-2 (sewn softcover : 50# alk. paper) ∞
   1. Literature – Study and teaching (Elementary) – United States.
2. Sexism and literature – United States. 3. Children – United
States – Books and reading. I. Cecil, Nancy Lee. II. Alexander,
Sharon. III. Title.
LB1575.R63 1993
372.64 – dc20   92-56686
                                        CIP

Manufactured in the United States of America

McFarland & Company, Inc., Publishers
 Box 611, Jefferson, North Carolina 28640

Dedicated to our caring and sensitive husbands,
Jim, Gary, and Alan

Contents

Introduction

More than one hundred years ago, the battle for women's rights focused on the right to vote. Today that battle has broadened into an earnest desire for equality of opportunity for both women and men. People of every race, class, and ethnic background have become aware of the issues surrounding the equality of the sexes, and men, too, have added their voices and energy to the fray, realizing that freedom from stereotypic and demeaning roles is essential for all human beings—not just women. And while magazines, newspapers, comic strips, television programs, and certain children's books continue to portray some traditionally stereotypical situations and characters (Roberts, 1976b, 1977, 1978), they also reflect an evolving awareness of a refreshing attitude toward a myriad of possibilities in gender roles and behavior for both girls and boys, men and women. All in all, this trend is positive, signifying the concerns of an increasingly insightful and enlightened society. But while attitudes may be changing in a positive direction, they still have a long, long way to go.

Breaking the Stereotypes

Since gender stereotypic behavior is the result of multiple factors in society, the approach to the correction of such expectations is multidimensional in nature. Parents and educators can learn about their own contribution to lowered expectations and can consciously alter their thinking and behavior. Young people, both female and male, as they become aware of their own sex-typed behaviors and beliefs can, with intentional control and action basic to being human, understand and remedy their thinking and behavior about these limitations.

An example of encouragement to break from imitating limited maternal models by making aware decisions is the following, abbreviated here, from a Nike shoes advertisement. The ad, in a text that takes up two full pages in large type, recommends that "You [girls] do not have to be your mother unless she is who you want to be. . . . So if you inherit something, inherit their [female ancestors] strength . . . their resilience. Because the only person you are

destined to become is the person you decide to be" (HG, Nov., 1992). Powerful advice in the service of sensible shoes, a major need that American women,
and girls aspiring to be women in the style of this culture, could use.

Wearing sports shoes may help young women use their physical strength
to become physically resilient but what is the "sport shoe" counterpart to the
development of psychological resilience in the face of stereotypic expectations,
modeli ıg, and other reinforcers of limitations? One answer open to educators
who are librarians, classroom teachers, and parents, is bibliotherapy.
Bibliotherapy suggests a strategy to help youngsters resist pressures that nar-
row their gender role expectations and solve problems that baffle their
stereotyped notions by reflecting on alternate solutions presented and
stimulated by characters found in books. New strategies and values, modeled
by strong, nonstereotypic young females who successfully cope by being
positive, planning ahead, finding satisfaction in talents and hobbies, persisting
in the face of failure, relating to caring people, and having a sense of humor,
demonstrate dramatically the importance of a personal sense of control over
one's life and how it might be achieved (Cecil, 1989). To support the interest
of educators and others in helping youngsters see alternative ways to resist
these pressures, resilient nonstereotypic characters found in children's books
have been identified (Cecil & Roberts, 1992).

Models in Children's Literature

Finding nonstereotypic models in children's literature has not always been
easy or, depending on where one looked, possible. Publishers of basal readers
have, in recent years, claimed an awareness of the influence stories can have
on the perception of readers and have responded to criticism by correcting
some of the discrepant roles and stereotypic portrayals of females and males.
Better representation, in terms of balance of number of male and female
characters, was the beginning of righting the wrongs in children's readers
(Rupley, Garcia & Longnion, 1982).

Noting the changes described above has been encouraging, but unfor-
tunately, to be effective, we as classroom teachers, librarians, and parents
must examine basal and supplementary books, as well as other children's
literature, for stereotypic content that demeans, leaves out, or misrepresents
females and minorities and then take our own corrective action (Roberts,
1976a).

Corrective action means that we must review materials before presenting
them to students. The following is a guide to the evaluation of basal readers,
supplementary readers, and children's literature, generally. Such a review
should lead to the elimination of sexist stories and to the inclusion of stories
that are enhancing to nonstereotypic gender beliefs.

Look for:

1. *Balance.* Balance in the number of females and males depicted as main characters and in illustrations.
2. *Variety in Occupations.* Portrayals of females and males in a variety of occupations, not just the traditional. Look for the reversal of traditional gender roles.
3. *Reversal of Traditional Roles.* Portrayal of females in roles that are predominantly active, dominant and capable. Look for portrayal of males in roles that show their dependency needs in a sympathetic manner.
4. *Desirable Traits.* Portrayals of females as having predominantly desirable personality traits.
5. *Variety in Character Types.* Stories of exotic characters or special accomplishment not out-weighing stories of characters in realistic roles.
6. *Contributions of Females as Well as Males.* Stories that present the contributions to society of females as well as males [Tibbetts, 1978; and Rupley, Garcia & Longnion, 1981].

Bibliotherapy offers a powerful tool to librarians, teachers, and parents in their efforts to correct the imbalances and sexist misrepresentations to which girls and boys are subjected. This book is a guide to that effort.

How to Use This Text

This book is designed to aid teachers, parents, and librarians in their efforts to locate nonstereotypic stories for children. The authors have identified and described over 200 books whose main characters have one or more of the valued attributes noted earlier. The books selected are designed for children in the formative elementary school years (K–8), when developing a sense of competence and personal control over choices is crucial to self esteem.

The book is organized into two parts: 1) picture books that are generally used with primary children (some, with more sophisticated concepts, are appropriate with older children, as noted); and 2) multi-chapter nonpicture books that contain more in-depth treatment of the character and the plot—features that usually are meant for older children. Selections are from fanciful fiction, contemporary and folk literature, historical fiction, and biographies. To help in decision making, each book is annotated in terms of the main character and story line with the nonstereotypic aspects of the main character and story identified. Recommendations for using the book as an instructive vehicle are described in a "Target Activity" section. To enhance reflection and identification with the characters and their problems, the target activities for each story include ideas to involve children in activities such as role playing, writing, and discussions of stories as a whole class, in smaller groups, or

individually. Teacher-models with strong convictions can demonstrate through
these activities that life choices for girls and boys are not limited by gender.
These activities will aid children as they reflect, analyze, and empathize with
the characters in these stories and the problems they face.

Introducing children to a story character like Mirandy in *Mirandy and
Brother Wind*, written by Patricia McKissack and illustrated by Jerry Pinkney,
thrusts the youngsters into a dilemma that is related to a central concern of
theirs: How to pursue a goal but remain sensitive to the needs of friends who
may get in the way of one's pursuits.

In this example, Mirandy is hoping to win her first cakewalk, a dance
rooted in African American culture in which the pair of dancers with the most
flamboyant dances takes home the cake. The trouble is, Mirandy's most logical
partner, Ezel, is much too clumsy to be a partner who could help her win.
Mirandy decides to try to catch Brother Wind and have *him* be her partner.
Although everyone she speaks to tells her, "Can't nobody put shackles on
Brother Wind, he be free," Mirandy perseveres. She tries to put black pepper
on his foot prints to make him sneeze so she can slip up behind him and throw
a quilt over him. She tries to catch him in a crock bottle, but he escapes.
Finally, Mirandy traps Brother Wind in the barn. At the cakewalk, when
another girl makes fun of Ezel's clumsiness, Mirandy defends him and claims
him as her partner. She immediately regrets having done such a "tomfool"
thing, since she has caught Brother Wind for her partner. She goes to Brother
Wind and makes a wish that she and Ezel will dance with grace and style and
win the cake.

At the end of the story, the teacher's job would be to guide students in
examining why Mirandy did not give up her goal: Can the children remember
a time when they wanted to do something that seemed impossible, and
remember, too, what other people told them about the possibility of pursuing
that goal? Each child would pair-up and share her/his goal seeking experience
with the partner who would first give the reason(s) that the goal would be impossible to achieve, and then, with the partner's very best arguments, the
reasons the goal would be possible. The teacher could then compare with the
class the various goals described and discover if the goals differed along
gender lines and some of the reasons for these differences. From this com-
parison, another exercise using their best arguments for and against such
differences could be developed—thus promoting the reflection, analysis, problem solving, and understanding important to role and goal considerations
generally.

In the example of Mirandy as a young black girl who is slightly resourceful
and clever, children will find a model of "will to persevere to reach a goal."
They will also find a person who is compassionate and who learns to use experiences thrust upon her to reach her goal. In this story, instead of allowing
the experience of defending Ezel to distract her from her goal, she adjusts to

the circumstances and continues to persevere. This part of the story's essence is especially important to girls who have been socialized to value relationships above everything else (Gilligan, 1982). They can learn that achieving goals and having good friends and intimate relationships are not mutually exclusive desires. Being compassionate must not mean giving up on oneself. Children will learn to be kind to themselves and others from our modeling the conviction that both are possible for each of us.

This book is intended as a recourse for educators who are looking for resources to supplement and replace others that misrepresent or misinform children about gender roles. It is designed to be used by caring adults who are committed to helping children cope with the stereotypic messages that are frequently the norm modeled on television, in their homes, and among their friends. Enhancing children's language curricula by using quality stories and activities that expand their expectations of what is possible will better prepare them for the real and changing world they will face as adults. This text is designed to assist in that expansion.

References

Cecil, N.L. (1989). *We Have Overcome*. Dubuque, Iowa: Kendall/Hunt.

_____ & P.L. Roberts. (1992). *Developing Resiliency through Children's Literature: A Guide for Teachers and Librarians, K–8*. Jefferson, NC: McFarland & Co.

Gilligan, Carol. (1982). *In a Different Voice: Psychological Theory and Women's Development*. Cambridge, Mass.: Harvard University Press.

Roberts, P.L. (1976b). *The Female Image in the Caldecott Medal Books*. Monograph 2, Laboratory of Educational Research, University of the Pacific, Stockton, Ca.

_____. (1978). "The female image in the Caldecott medal award books." *Resources in Education*. April. ED 181467.

_____. (1976a). "Getting the message via content analysis." *Resources in Education*. Oct.

_____. "Sugar and spice and almost always nice: A study of the Caldecotts." *Resources in Education*. Jan. ED 127556.

Rupley, W.H., Garcia, J. & Longnion, B. (1981). "Sex role portrayal in reading materials: Implications for the 1980s." *The Reading Teacher*, 34, 7, 786–791.

Tibbetts, S.L. (1978). "Wanted: data to prove that sexist reading material has an impact on the reader." *The Reading Teacher*, 32, 2, 165–69.

Literature
for Grades K–3

Contemporary Realistic Fiction

1. Alexander, Sally Hobart. *Mom Can't See Me*. Photographs by George Ancona. New York: Macmillan, 1990.

    Blind author Alexander gives readers a sensitive picture of her life that is told from the view of her nine-year-old daughter. This book shows how both mother and daughter have learned to cope with living with a disability. Alexander helps with cooking, cleaning, taking the children to lessons, and helping at school. She includes some of the frustrations of blindness (fear of children catching blindness) and her sadness in not seeing what her children are seeing. Through the print of the narrative and the black-and-white photographs, the child sees the ways that Sally Alexander copes with her blindness and solves her daily problems with the help of her young daughter. 2–3.

    Target Activity: "Find Sensitivity to Others"

    Ask the students to find newspaper articles that concern a disabled group. Some articles will state the positions and points of view on issues; others will be stories about regional events; still others will be about someone identified as a disabled American. With the children, discuss:

    1. What attitudes toward the group were shown in the article?
    2. What types of news did you find that were useful for understanding more about a disabled person?
    3. In what ways could you help a disabled person? In what situations would such a person need your help?

2. Baylor, Byrd. *Hawk, I'm Your Brother*. Ill. Peter Parnall. New York: Charles Scribner's Sons, 1976.

    In the Santos Mountains, Rudy Soto wanted to fly like a hawk; he spent hours watching them and took a baby redtail hawk from its nest. Seeing the hawk caged and resentful, Rudy released the bird and watched it fly away, feeling that he was flying together with the bird in spirit. They called to one another just as one "brother" would call to another. Seeing the wild hawk fly made Rudy Soto yearn for the bird's sense of autonomy achieved by flying. To Rudy, flying was a symbol of controlling his life. 2–3.

    Target Activity: "Tests of Strength and Courage"

    Discuss the boy's sensitivity in feeling close to other living things. In another Baylor book, *The Desert Is Theirs* (Scribner's, 1975), point out the relationship of the young boy and the earth shown through the Papago Indian culture and the emphasis of sharing with the earth, not taking from it. With children, discuss more about the theme: humans can learn from the animals and plants that adapt to the sun and to the scarce water supply in the desert. How does this theme (learning from nature) relate to the other Baylor story?

Compare both books to *The Indian Heart of Carrie Hodges* (Viking Pr., 1972). In this story, a young girl learns Native American ways from an older friend and learns about herself through finding what animal she feels close to in her life. As in the Baylor books, this child tests her own strength and takes control of her life.

Discuss with children: Are tests of strength and courage different for boys than girls? How? What situations that would confront both men and women require emotional strength and courage? Have children brainstorm some situations common to both genders. Ask them to select one situation that might have to be faced by males and females. Have them write about how courage would be required to deal effectively with this situation.

3. Bunting, Eve. *The Wednesday Surprise.* Ill. Donald Carrick. New York: Clarion, 1989.

In *The Wednesday Surprise*, a range of emotions and feelings is shown. Grandmother and Anna work together, secretly, on a present for Dad's birthday. They spend Wednesday nights together reading books, and as they read the stories, they plan a surprise for Anna's father. On the Saturday of his birthday, Anna's father comes home from his week on the road as a trucker, takes a nap, and wakes up to the party preparations and his presents. After all have been opened, Anna announces one more—a present that only the two of them can give. Anna has taught Grandmother to read—and Grandmother begins to read to Dad. With sensitivity, Dad's eyes fill with tears as Grandmother reads book after book. Pre–3.

Target Activity: "Is It Okay to Cry?"

Anna takes on responsibilities and spends quality time with her grandmother to teach her to read. Father is not embarrassed by his emotions and cries with happiness when his mother reads aloud.

Brainstorm with children some other occasions that would cause people to cry. Ask them why they thought Anna's father was crying. Do they think it is good for men/boys to cry? Why or why not? Ask children to think of the last time they cried. Have pairs of children relate this experience to each other starting with the sentence stem, "The last time I cried was when _____." Instruct the listener in the pair to affirm the other child's feelings by responding, "It's okay to cry," and then relate his/her story.

4. Carrick, Carol. *Dark and Full of Secrets.* Ill. Donald Carrick. New York: Clarion Books, 1984.

Although Christopher likes the clear green ocean, he doesn't like the murky pond because he can't see what is in it. His father teases him about being afraid of sea monsters and teaches him to snorkel so that he can actually see what is in the pond. His Dad returns to shore to read while Christopher happily continues snorkeling; the boy's mask suddenly fills with water, and he panics when his feet don't touch the bottom of the pond. He is even more frightened when something—the sea monster?—snatches his leg. The dog comes out and helps tow him in to shore. That night, when the family goes for a canoe ride, Christopher looks at the dark surface of the water and realizes his fear is gone because he knows what is underneath the surface of the pond. By seeing what is in the pond and then facing his worst fears about its contents, Christopher learns that he can conquer fear by confronting it. Conquering fear by confronting it gives Christopher control over this part of his life. 2–3.

Target Activity: "It's OK to Show Your Emotions"

Bring into the classroom several containers filled with various ingredients such as cooked spaghetti, jello, or yogurt. Blindfold several class members and have them put their hands in each of the containers. Take note of any reluctance and/or hesitation. Ask for volunteers among unblindfolded class members to put their hands in the containers.

Discuss differences in eagerness to participate of those who know what is in the container as compared with those who do not. Ask children why they think what is known is less frightening than the unknown. Let them offer additional examples of this phenomenon from their own lives.

5. Caudill, Rebecca. *Pocketful of Cricket.* Ill. Evaline Ness. New York: Holt, Rinehart & Winston, 1964.

On an August afternoon, six-year-old Jay carries a cricket home as a pet who lives in a wire-screen cage in his bedroom and, in September, takes the cricket to school in his pocket because he is reluctant to leave it behind at home. Every day Jay and the cricket spring around the room, and every night the cricket fiddles in the dark. When school starts, Jay hides the cricket in his pocket and they ride to school together on the bus. Jay has an understanding teacher who allows him to share with the class, and next time he brings in something less noisy—speckled beans. Jay is a sensitive male character and his teacher is a sensitive female character. Jay has positive personality characteristics as he takes a cricket for a companion, and the teacher demonstrates her understanding of the friendship as she allows Jay to show the cricket to others in the room. Jay's understanding teacher asks him to show his chirping pet to the class. An intimate relationship of child and pet develops and is supported by Jay's relationship with his understanding teacher. The teacher shows her sympathy for the small boy's need for something familiar (and friendly) near him on the first day of school. K–2.

Target Activity: "Jay's Sensitivity to a Living Creature — A Cricket"

As you know, Jay did not want to be far away from the cricket. So, Jay decided to "write" with a mix of pictures and words (a rebus record) and tell about some of the happenings with his pet — things like the cricket's living in a wire-screen cage, his surroundings in the bedroom, his journey to school in Jay's pocket, and his debut as a chirping cricket in the classroom. Draw some of the pictures for a rebus record that Jay might have drawn. Share your pictures with others. In groups to respond to the story, the children may discuss:

1. In what way would you say that living things have needs that are the same as humans'? Different from humans'?
2. In what way would you say that living things have fears that are the same as humans'? Different from humans'?
3. Since insects don't talk as humans do, what are some of the ways that insects can communicate with one another? Communicate with humans?
4. Related to being sensitive toward the insect world, students may be asked to write a list of complaints humans might have toward the insect world and then write a list of complaints they think the members of the insect world might have toward the human world. For example, in the first list, you might write that mosquitoes bite and flies carry diseases. In the second list you might write that humans have invented sprays and insecticides.

6. Cleary, Beverly. *Ramona and Her Father*. Ill. Alan Tiegreen. New York: Morrow, 1977.

Father loses his job when Ramona is in second grade and there is less money for the family. Mother begins to work full-time and Father, worried and irritable, looks after Ramona after school. Worried about their father smoking, Ramona and Beezus begin an anti-smoking campaign. Christmas brings happier times with Beezus cast as Mary in the Christmas pageant at church and Ramona as a sheep. Further, Father announces a new job that starts January 2. Ramona faces the problems of a working mother, an unemployed father, and her father's smoking. The reader finds the problems are dealt with in a realistic and reassuring manner. Some humor. 2–3.

Target Activity: "Ramona's Anti-smoking Campaign"

Ramona takes on responsibility, worries, is reassured, and faces several problems. The fact that Father smoked turned out to be a great worry to Ramona, and so she and her brother started their campaign against smoking. Invite the students to design posters for Ramona's anti-smoking campaign.

7. Fitzhugh, Louise. *Harriet the Spy.* Ill. New York: Harper & Row, 1964.

Eleven-year-old Harriet keeps a notebook of observations about people. Other people think Harriet is exceptional, intelligent, and curious. Harriet hides in secret places, observes others, and writes her observations down in her notebook. When her classmates find her notebook, they join together in "The Spy Catcher Club." To convince her classmates to forgive her, self-confident Harriet uses her resourcefulness. But she still returns to her favorite diversion: observing others and writing about it.

Target Activity: "Observing Others and Writing"

From the school or public library, obtain a selection of articles or other information about famous photographers. (Be sure to find a fairly equal selection of male and female photographers.) Allow children to select one of the photographers to read about in other sources. Ask each child to share some of their findings with the class.

With selected photographs and questions such as the ones that follow, a teacher can encourage children to interact with illustrations of people they see and show the extent of what they discerned by writing down their observations. For the students:

1. After looking at a magazine illustration, how many different words can you use to describe what you see in the illustration? In another illustration?

2. Why do you think some people are impressed by photographs?

3. What do you believe are some of the main reasons why the photographer took the illustration in the way she/he did? Why do you suppose the photographer made this decision? How do you suppose other photographers might have been affected?

8. Gaugh, Patricia Lee. *Bravo, Tanya.* Ill. Satomi Ichikawa. New York: Philomel, 1992.

Tanya is joyous when she dances with her stuffed toy bear under the trees as she listens to the wind but is frustrated in ballet class—she can't even hear the music. With the gentle encouragement and support of the accompanist, her natural coordination comes through and she turns into a young dancer enthusiastic about being a ballerina. Pre-2.

Target Activity: "Gentle Encouragement"

With the children, talk about the way the ballet accompanist encouraged Tanya in ballet class and extend the discussion to ways other people have encouraged some of the children to feel comfortable doing something they want to do. Discuss some of the goals the children have for their careers in life.

Option: "Memory Boxes"

Memory boxes can be created by interested students. A memory box is the collection of items that represent a person's memories—e.g., memories of a grandmother who studied ballet—from a particular time period. For instance a grandmother's box can contain drawings of unusual items of the 1920s or a guessing game about the 1930s with the answers found somewhere in the box. A bibliography for further reading about intergenerational stories can be included. A song sheet or page of recipes can be written, decorated, and inserted. If desired, students may put a list of the contents inside the lid of the box for a check to account for all items. Given to a relative or a friend at a nearby senior citizens center or convalescent home, the boxes demonstrate a student's sensitivity to others.

9. Hoffman, Mary. *Amazing Grace.* Ill. Caroline Binch. New York: Dial, 1991.

Grace listens to stories, reads them, and makes them up. She likes acting them out and gives herself the best parts. When the class is going to produce *Peter Pan,* Grace wants the lead but hears a peer who shows lack of sensitivity say she can't because she's a girl and because she's black. At home, her mother and grandmother tell her she can be anything she wants to be if she puts her mind to it. Motivated by a visit to a ballet starring a dancer from Trinidad, and by her family's support, Grace's spirit makes her shine during the audition. Grace is a spirited female character who has positive personality characteristics and support from her family. She is independent, brave, and competent, and does well during her audition for a part in *Peter Pan.* K–2.

Target Activity: "What Makes You Shine?"

With children, discuss the concept of motivation, i.e., "you can be anything you want to be if you put your mind to it." Discuss the sensitivity of Grace's relatives and their support for her. Discuss reasons why the children think that visiting the ballet which starred a dancer from Trinidad motivated Grace to have the spirit to make her do well during her audition.

10. Hurwitz, Johanna. *E Is for Elisa.* Ill. Lillian Hoban. New York: Morrow, 1991.

Eight-year-old Russell, who is in the Cub Scouts and goes to cookouts, promises never to tease four-year-old Elisa again (call her crybaby). Elisa rides her tricycle and can say the alphabet, and when she accepts his challenge to jump off a chest of drawers, she breaks her arm in the jump. Elisa wants to grow up and be able to do all the things that Russell does. Russell is an active male character who is remorseful when Elisa is injured as she tries to do all the things that Russell does. Russell and Elisa have a sibling rivalry as Russell matures in this matter and is sensitive toward his younger sister. Pre–3.

Target Activity: "Repentant"

With children, discuss the meaning of the word "repentant," and elicit examples from their experience. Discuss Elisa's desire to "do all the things that Russell does" and talk about why Elisa might want to do this. Discuss "it's O.K." for boys (and men) to be remorseful and to be sensitive to girls and women.

11. Keats, Ezra Jack. *A Letter to Amy.* Ill. author. New York: Harper & Row, 1968.

Peter wants to invite Amy to his birthday party, even though he knows his friends will make fun of her because she is a girl. But Amy is clearly very special to him, as evidenced by the fact that he sends her a special invitation, when he has just asked everyone else. Peter is seen as a sensitive little boy who values his friendship with Amy; he doesn't even fold when the other boys say, "A girl—ugh!" when Amy arrives. K–3.

Target Activity: "I'm the Only One!"

Lead a general discussion with children about a time they went someplace and felt alone because they were the only girl, boy, child, American, etc. Brainstorm some words that could be used to describe how they felt. Pair children and have them role play this situation or the one with Amy and Peter. Have one child play the "different" child and the other child portray a child trying to do and say things to make the first child feel welcome.

12. Klein, Norma. *Visiting Pamela.* Ill. Kay Chorao. New York: Dial, 1979.

Carrie is a five-year-old who likes to have friends come to visit, but she has never spent time in another child's house because she is afraid of the unfamiliar: the light is different, you might not be able to play what she wants to play, or you might bump into things because you don't know where everything is. Finally, she is asked to spend the afternoon at her friend Pamela's house, and after a few minor problems, she sees that she can cope with the unfamiliar and she has a good time. How Carrie comes to terms with her fears, many of which all children harbor at one time or another, makes a heart-warming story. K–2.

Target Activity: "Facing My Fears"

Lead a general discussion about fears by sharing something you used to be afraid of, but overcame by facing it (e.g., public speaking, snakes, the dark, etc.). Brainstorm some things that the children are afraid of facing. Chart the top three fears on the writing board and ask children to "vote for" their top fear. Further refine the chart by comparing the top three in terms of gender. Example:

snakes										boys
										girls
lightning										boys
										girls
the dark										boys
										girls

Point out that everyone – boys and girls – is afraid of something and that the fear generally goes away when we confront it. Have each child turn to a neighbor and discuss how his or her top fear can be conquered.

13. Maury, Inez. *My Mother the Mail Carrier – Mi Mama la Cartera.* New York: Feminist Press, 1976.

In Maury's bilingual story, Lupita's mother is brave, strong, and a good cook. She loves outings and likes her work, carrying mail. Lupita wants to be a jockey when she grows up and sees a positive vision of life through her mother's abilities at home and at work. She yearns for a nonstereotypical occupation and, like her mother who likes her work, knows she will like her work too – being a jockey! 1–2.

Target Activity: "Nonstereotypical Jobs People Do"

Look in the newspaper for articles about jobs people do. Point out nonstereotypical jobs and discuss the abilities you think the person needs to do his/her job. Relate those character traits to gender. What jobs can females do? Males? What does it take to do those jobs?

14. Miles, Miska. *Annie and the Old One.* Ill. Peter Parnall. Boston: Little, Brown, 1971.

Annie lives on the Navajo Indian Reservation with her grandmother, called the "Old One," her father, her mother, and a herd of sheep. She helps tend the sheep and garden and goes to school. She lives a happy life until she learns from her grandmother that when the new rug being woven by her mother is completed, her grandmother will go back to mother earth. Since her grandmother means so much to her, Annie feels she must do something to prevent this from happening. She attempts to keep her mother from weaving the rug by misbehaving at school and letting the sheep out of the corral at night so as to distract her mother. Both of these ploys fail, as the teacher is merely amused by Annie's antics, and the sheep do not wander far. Annie then resorts to stealthily unweaving the rug at night, and is caught in the act by the Old One. The Old One then takes Annie aside, out into the mesa, and points out the natural evolution of seasons, time, and destiny. With this, Annie realizes that "she was a part of the earth and the things on it. She would always be a part of the earth, just as her grandmother had always been, just as her grandmother would always be, always and forever." Annie gains a deep, unspoken realization of the inevitability of earth's natural order and accepts this way of life. The next morning, Annie starts weaving the rug. Annie is very close to her grandmother and relies on her to explain life and to help her understand who she is. She cannot imagine living without "The Old One." Annie finds it difficult to accept her grandmother's aging and death. 3.

   Target Activity: "Annie Grows Up"

   Discuss what students have learned about Annie. Write descriptive traits on the board. Brainstorm some ideas about how Annie will be feeling when the rug is finished, when Annie is grown up and has children, or when Annie is an "Old One." Determine what values Annie has learned from the Old One and how she would carry them into later life. Ask children to choose one of Annie's later stages and write several sentences about what her life was like at that time.

15. Mills, Lauren. *The Rag Coat.* Ill. author. Boston: Little, Brown, 1991.

   In Appalachia, Minna, a young girl, wants a coat so she can attend school. With the recent death of her father, the family cannot afford a coat. A group of mothers who come to her house to make quilts hear of her need, and they help her with a new quilted coat. At school, she is teased for wearing "rags." She recoups and tells the other children her coat is full of stories—their stories—for each rag has come from one of their homes. The children are sorry for their taunts. Minna is a strong female character who shows her positive personality characteristics when she rebounds against the teasing of children at school. She is strong and quick in her response that the coat is full of stories. Minna is resilient and returns the children's teasing with something that interests them—the idea that her coat holds a story from their homes, represented by the material scraps sewn together. The children undergo a group character change that involves being remorseful and coming to terms with their taunts, and the story deals with the universal problem of being accepted by others at school. 1–4.

   Target Activity: "Creating a Story Quilt of Strong Story Characters"

   With children, suggest the idea of creating a story quilt for the class. Invite each child to bring a square of fabric from home and learn about its meaning.

As the children bring the fabric pieces to the classroom, take time for each one to tell the significance of the fabric (i.e. my older sister's first party dress; a shirt that belonged to my grandfather who worked on the railroad; a piece from a white scarf that belonged to my great uncle who was a gunner on a bomber in World War II). Invite children to use fabric pens to draw story sketches on the fabric. Once the squares are sewn together, display the story quilt in the classroom and take time to review the stories represented by the squares in the quilt.

16. Nash, Ogden. *The Adventures of Isabel.* Ill. James Marshall. Boston: Joy Street/Little, 1991.

Self-reliant, determined Isabel, a character created by Nash in 1963, faces bears and other bugaboos with perfect *sang-froid.* Isabel is free of agitation and cool in trying circumstances. Isabel encounters a bear and knows just what to do. She is portrayed as a rather round, bespectacled, redheaded heroine with polished nails and hair bows. K–2.

Target Activity: "Knowing What to Do"

Brainstorm with children some other circumstances that would certainly unsettle the average person, such as seeing a troll under a bridge, finding a flying saucer full of aliens in the backyard, or discovering a rattlesnake in the bath tub. Have children select a partner and act out one of these scary encounters, taking on Isabel's "cool as a cucumber demeanor," while the other partner portrays the frightening creature. Allow children to switch roles. Invite partners to perform their close encounter experience for the rest of the class.

17. Ness, Evaline. *Sam, Bangs and Moonshine.* Ill. author. New York: Holt, Rinehart & Winston, 1966.

Samantha has trouble distinguishing between what is real and what is imaginary (e.g. moonshine). When this problem jeopardizes the life of her good friend, Thomas, the difference becomes clear to her. She tells Thomas that she has a baby kangaroo (moonshine) and sends him off to Blue Rock to find it. A storm blows up and the tide comes in, stranding Thomas and Bangs, Sam's cat, on the rock. Thomas is rescued by Sam's father, but Bangs is swept away. As Sam goes to bed, she knows that her moonshine was responsible for Bangs' death and Thomas' endangerment. A scratching at the window tells her that the water-logged cat outside is indeed Bangs. Sam visits Thomas and gives him a gerbil (named moonshine), because it looks just like a baby kangaroo. 1–3.

Target Activity: "How Have You Changed?"

With children, discuss "Sam portrays a positive female role sensitive to Thomas." Sam is an active female character who matures and changes, coming to terms with her fascination for "moonshine" and her friendship with Thomas. Engage the children's discussion about ways they have changed since their last birthday.

18. O'Connor, Jane. *Molly the Brave and Me.* Ill. Sheila Hamanaka. New York: Random House, 1990.

Part of Random House's high-interest, low-readability *Step Into Reading Books Series*, this young reader's story concerns a little girl in the second grade, named Beth, who admires her friend, Molly. Molly can stand at the top of the monkey bars on one foot and doesn't mind "when Nicky hides dead water bugs in her desk." Molly is so brave, Beth muses, that Beth wishes she were just like Molly. When Molly invites her to spend the night, Beth is honored, but fears Molly will soon realize what a "wimp" she is when she gets homesick or is afraid of unfamiliar things. They go berry picking and cross a stream by walking across a log. Beth is afraid, but she tries it and falls. Molly doesn't tease her, even though Beth "feels like a jerk." Then, when Butch, Molly's dog, runs into a field of corn, the two girls follow him. They soon find that getting out is not that easy. After walking around in circles for awhile, Molly admits she is scared. Beth is amazed and takes the lead. "Don't be scared," she tells Molly. "We'll get out of here." And, using her street smartness, Beth leads Molly down the space between two rows of corn without making any turns. They soon leave the field of corn. Molly relates the incident to her parents, adding "Boy, does she (Beth) have guts!" Beth has begun to believe that she does, indeed, have "guts." 1–3.

Target Activity: "Brave People"

Have children recall all the things that Molly could do that made Beth think she was brave. Ask them if they have ever known a child who they thought was similarly brave. Why do they think Beth thought Molly would think she was a "wimp"? Do they feel that the person they feel is brave would feel the same way about them? Read the book *Earl's Too Cool for Me* (Trumpet Club, 1988) by Leah Komaiko, which also concerns a very brave child. The child telling the story thinks that Earl would probably not even want to speak to him, being as cool and confident as he is. But he finds that Earl is "just a regular guy" and wants to be friends. Ask children why they think children would be shy around someone who seems to be extra brave. Brainstorm ways they could get to know these children. Have them role play these ways.

19. Paustovsky, Konstantin. *The Magic Ringlet.* Ill. Leonard Weisgard. Maine: Young Scott Books, 1971.

An old soldier gave a magic ring to little Varyusha, telling her it had the power to bring happiness to her and health to her sick grandfather. As she was returning home through the woods, the ring slipped off her finger and fell into the deep snow. However much she dug, she could not find it. Each day, as the winter winds blew more fiercely and her grandfather's cough grew worse, she blamed herself for being so careless. One spring day when the snow has melted, she finds the ring. As she waits for the "enormous happiness" to happen, she realizes that happiness dwells within her. Varyusha learns that she must open her eyes and appreciate all the simple beauty of her own environment—spring in the woods, the birds, the flowers, and the clear sky. She realizes that how she views what she has will cause happiness. She decides not to put the ringlet on her index finger, because her happiness is within her. 1–3.

Target Activity: "Varyusha's World: A Journey"

Discuss with children the idea that sometimes we are so close to our own home, city, and surroundings that we fail to appreciate the good things that we have. Ask children to pretend that they are about to go on a journey to Russia, where Varyusha lives. Ask them to take two or three minutes to think about what they would like to tell Varyusha of the beauty in their surroundings. Tell them to visualize a favorite tree, a stream or lake, flowers in their yard, birds that they have heard, or other features of their environment of which they are fond. Then ask them to turn to a neighbor. Have a neighbor pretend to be Varyusha while the other child tells what makes him/her happy about their world. When they finish, let the children reverse roles. Such an activity allows both girls and boys to become sensitive to their surroundings in a caring manner that is too often thought of as "feminine."

20. Peavy, Linda. *Allison's Grandfather.* Ill. Ronald Himler. New York: Scribner's, 1981.

Allison's grandfather is in the hospital, dying. Erica, Allison's friend, thinks back on the wonderful times she has had visiting Allison and her grandfather on his ranch and listening to the tales of when he was a cowboy. Erica wants to ask about dying, but cannot bring herself to accept the death of this strong and lively man. The book concerns Erica's full range of emotions about Allison's grandfather and his impending death. She overcomes her fear, with her mother's help, and begins to understand death as a peaceful and natural life process. 2–3.

Target Activity: "Living History"

What Erica recalls most about Allison's grandfather are his colorful stories about his days as a young man in the rodeo circuit. Allison's grandfather had enjoyed telling his stories, and they were a way to share his past history with his granddaughter and her friend, drawing them all closer. Similarly, many children have close relationships with their grandparents and miss their stories of "the way it was in the old days" when they die. Discuss the value of the recollections of the elderly with the class.

Ask each child to select an elderly grandparent, aunt, uncle, friend, etc., whom they care about and who lives close enough to speak to (the telephone can be used for this purpose). Write a list of possible questions on the chalkboard:

What was life like when you were my age?
What things were very different from now?
What were your favorite things to do?
How did you make a living?
How did you meet your wife/husband?
What do you miss most about those days?

Ask children to tape-record the answers or take careful notes. Encourage them to share their "Living History" with the class. Ask each student to tell what the most interesting thing they learned was and how the activity has changed their relationship with the elderly person to whom they spoke.

21. Peters, Lisa Westberg. *Good Morning, River!* Ill. Deborah Kogan Ray. New York: Arcade, 1990.

Through the seasons, Katherine has a special relationship with her elderly neighbor, Carl, and she looks forward to hearing him yell at the river in a booming voice each morning; it seems that the river always answers him softly. When Carl's illness forces him to move away, all is quiet at the river. When he returns and is able to talk only in whispers, Katherine is the one to make the river talk again as the special relationship continues to grow. Katherine learns about the river and its resounding water from Carl; he is the only one who can make the river resound until she calls out for Carl when he loses his voice. K–3.

Target Activity: "Talking to the River as Drama"

Ask the children to dramatize Katherine's early morning meeting with Carl as he yells at the river to say "Good Morning." Discuss the story and some of the actions that show the sensitivity of the two characters. Engage children in suggesting ideas for dramatic play with:

1. How will you show that Katherine has a positive friendly relationship with Carl?
2. What would show that one of the characters breaks the mold of a gender stereotype?
3. In a role play, create a dramatic play scene where Katherine learns to talk to the river from Carl.

22. Polacco, Patricia. *Just Plain Fancy.* Ill. author. New York: Bantam Little Rooster, 1990.

Naomi Vlecke is a young Amish girl who sometimes questions the plain lifestyle of her community. It is Naomi's job, with her sister Ruth's help, to mind the chickens, and when one abandoned "chicken" egg hatches, she is astounded to find that the chicken is very fancy. When she hears her elders talking about a person in a neighboring Amish community who was "shunned" for dressing too fancily, Naomi worries that they will shun her beloved little chick too, so she and Ruth hide him while deciding what to do. At a neighborhood "frolic," the chickens escape from the henhouse when someone leaves the henhouse door open. Naomi bravely addresses the elders, asking them not to shun the fancy chicken. She tries to take the blame for his fancy plumage. The two-page full color painting of a peacock is then revealed to the reader. The elders explain to Naomi that "this is one of God's most beautiful creatures. He is just fancy . . . and that's the way it is." Naomi is rewarded with a new white organdy cap for raising one of the finest peacocks that the elders have ever seen. K–3.

Target Activity: "Beauty Plus"

This delightful story of a brave and resourceful Amish child has merit for portraying the pluckiness of the little girl, Naomi, but also for pointing out that it is okay to be beautiful, which is often difficult for young girls to grasp who want to be recognized for traits other than their beauty.

Have children think of some female characters in children's literature with whom they are familiar. Ask them to identify those that they feel are particularly attractive, beautiful, or "fancy." Ask them to name one other characteristic of each of these females. Are any of them brave? Kind? Helpful? Discuss which trait they think is the most important. Optionally, have them also think of someone they know who is attractive, beautiful, or fancy. Discuss other traits that belong to these people. Finally, discuss the fact that "beauty" is a gift over which people have no control, but they can choose to be helpful, kind, etc.

23. Rabe, Bernice. *The Balancing Girl.* Ill. Lillian Hoban. New York: Dutton, 1981.

In a poignant variation on a theme, this book tells the story of Margaret, a wheelchair-bound first-grader who is very proud of her ability to balance things. When she builds castles in the classroom out of cylinder spires, her nemesis, Tommy, says, "Oh, that's simple," and knocks them down when no one is looking. When the school has a carnival to raise funds, Margaret makes an elaborate domino city and sells raffle tickets for the right to be the one to push the first domino, which will create a chain reaction and collapse the whole city. Tommy wins the raffle and knocks the city down. Margaret has made more money for the carnival than anyone else, but she demonstrates considerable strength of character and compassion by making Tommy feel good about his contribution to the carnival. The book underscores the strengths that the disabled can have. K–3.

Target Activity: "Contrast Chart"

Lead a discussion about Tommy's behavior and why he acted the way he did. Ask the children if they have ever known someone who was a "bully" and what things the bully did. Ask the children to recount how Margaret reacted to Tommy's bullying and how that reaction made Tommy feel good about himself. Explain that Margaret was being a "peacemaker." Using a contrast chart, have children brainstorm some qualities that they feel describe a "bully" as compared with a "peacemaker." Example:

Bully	*Peacemaker*
1. mean	1. kind
2. tries to hurt	2. tries to help
3. angry	3. happy
4. kids don't like him (her)	4. kids like her (him)

24. Robinet, Harriette Gillem. *Ride the Red Cycle.* Ill. David Brown. Boston: Houghton Mifflin, 1980.

A viral infection in the brain left damage that affected Jerome Johnson's whole body. When his health improved, he had to learn to support his head and to crawl all over again, but his legs remained crippled and he was confined to a wheelchair. He had a dream, however; he wanted to learn to ride a tricycle. After his father buys him one, the whole family is disappointed when he cannot even move the pedals. Secretly, he painstakingly learns to ride it— and to take his first steps. His courage and pride take him farther than his parents or the host of specialists that treat him ever expected. Jerome holds onto his dream in the face of humiliating defeat and works to show others and himself that he can succeed. He learns to walk by himself, through his own persistence. 2–4.

Target Activity: "Obstacle Walk on an Obstacle Course"

That Jerome Johnson persisted and took great pride in finally learning how to ride a tricycle is a concept that is lost on many able-bodied youngsters, but they are better able to appreciate their own accomplishments if they can emphathize with Jerome's success. To help children to understand life with a handicap, set up an obstacle course in the classroom with desks and chairs. Steps to take:

1. Using a watch with a second hand, time a child's walk through the obstacle course.
2. Then blindfold the same child and time him/her again. Have the child make successive trials in an attempt to match the original time achieved without the blindfold.
3. Let all in the class participate in the obstacle path walk, both sighted

and blindfolded, until they can reach their same time when blind-folded.

4. Ask them which success they feel proudest of—with or without the blindfold?

5. Finally, ask them to write a letter to Jerome Johnson telling him what they have learned about success, perseverance, and being sensitive to others.

25. Rylant, Cynthia. *Miss Maggie*. Ill. Thomas de Dirazia. New York: E. P. Dutton, 1983.

A young boy, Nat, has heard stories about the reclusive elderly lady who lives in the log hut on his family's property; a big black snake is reputed to live with her, among other scary things. Nat initially fears Miss Maggie; he looks in her window, then runs away. One day he overcomes his fears when he finds her in trouble: in the heart of winter she is without heat. He finds her sitting on the floor of her cabin clutching a dead starling. He runs to get help for her. His family begins taking care of her and taking her with them on outings. Nat establishes a special, caring relationship with Miss Maggie. 2–4.

Target Activity: "A Letter to Miss Maggie"

Begin the activity with a discussion about rumors. Ask children if they have ever heard many people making the same unkind statements about someone and then later, although several people had said the same thing, they found the statements were untrue. Recount the rumors that were circulating about Miss Maggie. Discuss which were true and which were untrue and where such rumors may have originated. Instruct children to write a letter to Miss Maggie as if they are Nat. Ask them to include in the letter:

1. Why they peered in her windows and were frightened of her once.
2. How much they care about her now.

Option: "Research Lives and Contributions of Women Authors"

To acquaint students with the work of Rylant and other female authors, a teacher may display several books and introduce the titles with brief book talks. In the last 30 years, several authors have received the Caldecott Medal award (or the Honor award), and the titles can be grouped into two groups: a) books about intergenerational relationships and childhood experiences, and b) folk literature. In the group about intergenerational relationships are Karen Ackerman's *Song and Dance Man* (Knopf, 1988), and Jane Yolen's *Owl Moon* (Philomel, 1988). Childhood experiences are recounted in titles such as Cynthia Rylant's *When I Was Young in the Mountains* (Dutton, 1983). The folk literature group contains such tales as Ann Grifalconi's *The Village of Round and Square Houses* (Little, Brown, 1987), Margaret Hodges' *St. George and the Dragon* (Little, Brown, 1985), *Why Mosquitoes Buzz in People's Ears* (Dial, 1976) retold by Verna Aardema, *The Funny Little Woman* (Dutton, 1973) by

Arlene Mosel, *One Fine Day* (Macmillan, 1972) by Nonny Hogrogian, and *A Story, A Story: An African Tale* (Atheneum, 1971) by Gail E. Haley.

26. Schertle, Alice. *My Two Feet.* Ill. Meredith Dunham. New York: Lothrop, Lee & Shepard, 1985.

This is an upbeat story of a little girl's musing about where her feet take her, shod and unshod. Like any young child, girl or boy, this child likes to walk on special places, climb like a monkey, walk in the sand, and go barefoot, avoiding bees and glass. The story extols the virtues of feet and walking – in summer and in winter. Every child can relate to this "unisex" story. K–2.

Target Activity: "Things We All Like to Do"

Select one child to recite this story from memory. As this is being done, write on the writing board all the activities in which the child took part. Ask children to raise their hands if they have enjoyed these activities, too. Ask them to add to the list other activities that all children, not just boys or girls, tend to enjoy. Point out that there are probably more activities in common than there are activities that only one or the other would enjoy.

27. Schertle, Alice. *William and Grandpa.* Ill. Lydia Dabcovich. New York: Lothrop, Lee & Shepard, 1989.

William rides the bus by himself to visit his Grandpa, who meets him at the station. They sing and jump, Grandpa makes chili, and William uses shaving lather to make a white mustache. After supper, they share a story, look at the stars in the night, and drink hot chocolate. This book shows continuity of generations and a warm relationship between a child and a grandparent as they enjoy some of the activities of any ordinary day – preparing dinner, telling stories, and enjoying the beauty of the nighttime sky. Pre–1.

Target Activity: "True Stories"

Invite children to volunteer a story that they remember with fondness with an older person. They may ask an adult at home to tell them a story from his/her own family history that the adult remembers with fondness. If desired, each may tell a brief part of the history to a learning partner or to a small group. To record the story for part of a family's history, engage the students in writing the stories on small poster boards, preparing a decorative frame or border around each written history, and inserting colorful yarn so the history can be hung somewhere in the home. The children take their histories home and present them to someone in the family.

28. Schick, Eleanor. *Joey on His Own.* Ill. New York: Dial Press, 1982.

Joey has never gone shopping by himself. His mother asks him to go to the store and buy some bread for lunch, so he reluctantly starts off. He is frightened and the buildings seem taller than he remembers, the traffic noisier, and the neighborhood bullies meaner. When he gets to the store, he doesn't know which bread to choose; he is overwhelmed. When he brings the bread home, his mother tells him he has done a fine job, and he is proud of himself. Joey's mundane adventure is a good example of how fear of the unknown is reduced by experience with it. Joey panics when given a task he has never been asked to do before but feels triumphant when he completes it successfully. 1–2.

Target Activity: "A Special Shopping Trip"

After reading *Joey on His Own* with children, tell them they are going on a pretend shopping trip in their minds. Have them close their eyes. Lead them through the following visualization activity:

> Your mother has asked you to go and buy her a loaf of bread from the store. You have gone to the store many times with your mother, but you have never before gone to the store by yourself. She gives you one dollar and kisses you goodbye. You walk out the door and down the street. Trucks and cars whiz by you and you are a bit scared. You look both ways and, when there are no cars, you run across the street. There is the supermarket! You walk in and walk up and down the aisles looking for the bread. Finally, on the other side of the store you find the bread, but you can't remember what kind your mother wanted. Will she be angry if you buy the wrong kind? Way in the back of the shelf you see some bread in a red wrapper. Yes, you're *sure* that is the kind of bread you usually eat. You pick up the loaf and hand the dollar to the woman at the checkout counter. The woman says, "Will that be all today?" and you answer, "Yes, thank you." She gives you three pennies in change, puts the bread in a paper sack, hands it to you, and you walk out the door. You skip home and give your mother the bread and the three pennies. She smiles and thanks you.

Tell children to open their eyes. Write two columns on the chalkboard, one titled "before" and the other "after." Ask them to share their feelings before and after buying the bread. Discuss the differences in the feelings and why we feel pride when we have accomplished something we were afraid to do. Ask children to share any experiences they had where they were afraid to do something but were proud when they accomplished it successfully.

29. Seed, Jenny. *Ntombi's Song.* Ill. Anno Berry. Boston: Beacon Press, 1989.

In South Africa in a rural Zulu life setting, six-year-old Ntombi takes a first journey to the village store to buy sugar for her mother. Told by other women that a monster lives in the forest, she is frightened by a passing bus, and spills the sugar into the sand. Deciding to earn the money to replace the sugar, she dances for tourists and sings a song her mother created for her when she was a baby and receives a coin. She uses the coin to buy more sugar. 2–3.

Target Activity: "Mishaps Happen"

Look at the illustrations again so the students get a close-up view of the mishap that happened to Ntombi. Encourage them to relate the mishap in the story to one that has happened to them in their lives and to talk about solving problems. Discuss the way each solved the problem or the way each could have solved the problem or the way each would solve the problem if it happened again to them. Invite them to draw a picture of what each would have done to help Ntombi if he/she had been there when she spilled the sugar on the ground.

30. Stanek, Muriel. *I Speak English for My Mom.* Ill. Chicago: Whitman, 1988.

Lupe Gomez helps her mother who speaks and reads only Spanish. Lupe helps her with trips to the dentist and with shopping, even though Lupe acknowledges she would rather play. Speaking and reading only Spanish, Mrs. Gomez needs her daughter's help as she completes her tasks and activities in her daily life. Even though she would rather play with her friends, Lupe is persistent and stays with the job of translating for her mother. Pre–3.

Target Activity: "Showing Sensitivity to Language of Others with *A Show of Hands*"

Children can learn sensitivity to signers and speak sign language by using *A Show of Hands: Say It in Sign Language* (Harper & Row, 1980) by Mary Beth Sullivan and Linda Bourke. With the book, children will see that some people communicate by reading lips and speaking and others use sign language – a language made up of hand shapes and movements. This language is for everybody because it is expressive, beautiful when seen by others, and fun! Children may practice making the hand and finger signs for some of the letters (pp. 54–55), or practice spelling their names or sending a message to someone in the room. Reminiscent of Lupe who translated for her mother in a previous book, the book can help children translate for another student who is using only sign language.

31. Steig, William. *Brave Irene.* Ill. author. New York: Farrar, Straus & Giroux, 1986.

Irene's mother, a dressmaker, is ill and, in a fierce snowstorm, cannot deliver a ball gown that she has sewn. A series of obstacles almost prevents Irene from fulfilling her mission – the box is blown from her arms, the dress blows away, and she is nearly buried alive when she falls off a cliff. But Irene perseveres and the gown is delivered to a very grateful duchess. Irene is a plucky character who does not give up when obstacles seem overwhelming. She trudges on, thinking of her mother's face and how unhappy the duchess will be if she doesn't get her dress. She triumphs in the end, inspiring the reader. 1–3.

Target Activity: "Guess What Happened, Mother/Father?"

Tell students that Irene's mother cannot fully appreciate the errand that she successfully completed unless her mother hears every detail of that very difficult mission. Divide the students into pairs. Ask one child to play the part of Irene's mother. Encourage the child playing the part of Irene to recount the many misadventures she had delivering the dress, sharing her feelings of frustration along the way as well as her feeling of jubilation when she arrives at the house of the duchess. Allow the child playing the part of a mother/father to ad lib some reaction that a proud mother/father might have made. Then have children reverse roles. Finally, several pairs may volunteer to share their role plays for the whole class to promote an appreciation for a female heroine and a chance to try on the role of a sensitive, affirming father for boys in the class.

32. Yashima, Taro. *Crow Boy.* Ill. author. New York: Viking, 1955.

A small Asian boy, Chibi, is an isolated child at school and spends the time looking at the ceiling, his desk, or out the window. Every day he walks miles to school and notices what is around him. He has six years of perfect attendance and receives attention from a new teacher, Mr. Isobe, who recognizes Chibi's knowledge of nature and discovers that Chibi can imitate the voices of crows. Chibi does his imitations with the others in the school talent show. With this performance he earns the respect of others and is nicknamed "Crow Boy." With the help of a kindly sixth grade teacher, a lonely boy wins the admiration of his classmates. K–2.

Target Activity: "Sensitivity to Nature"

Discuss with children the idea that Chibi was taunted because he was very different from what the other children expected of young boys. On the writing board make two columns. At the top of one column, write "What some children can do," and at the top of the other column write "What Chibi could do." Help children to brainstorm some skills and abilities that some girls and boys possess that gain them recognition, such as being good at sports, being a good reader, having a good sense of humor, and so on. Could both girls and boys possess these same traits? Under "What Chibi could do," help children to recall the special abilities that Chibi possessed and his extraordinary sensitivity to nature. Ask children why they think the children in Chibi's class did not recognize these abilities as worthy of praise. Invite children to keep a notebook of sounds in their environment that they hear every day as they walk or ride the bus to school. Have them share their reflections with the class. Such an activity affirms sensitive reflecting that is too often subtly discouraged in young boys.

33. Zemach, Margot. *To Hilda for Helping*. Ill. author. New York: Farrar, Straus & Giroux, 1977.

Hilda, a cooperative and helpful little girl, receives a tin-can-top medal from her father for helping set the table at night. Her sisters, Rose and Gladys, never help, but Gladys becomes extremely jealous of Hilda's medal. Gladys makes up a prediction of doom about what will happen to the medal—it will get dirty, rust, or Hilda will lose it. Maybe (Gladys fantasizes), it will be buried under a tree. But Hilda, strong within herself, recognizes Gladys' jealousy for what it is and offers her own happy version of the medal's future; it will be buried and grow a tree with medals on it! Despite Hilda's sister's taunting, Hilda looks on the bright side of the future, retaining a positive vision. 1–3.

Target Activity: "We Are Special"

Discuss with children the fact that each is special in a unique way. List on the chalkboard all the ways in which they have at one time or another helped their families, helped in the classroom, or helped a friend. Collect tin-can tops to make medals for each child similar to Hilda's, which will say, "To _____ for helping with _____." Use construction paper for the letters and glue them on with Super Glue.™ Have each child select a task with which she/he has helped recently.

34. Zolotow, Charlotte. *William's Doll*. Ill. William Pene duBois. New York: Harper & Row, 1972.

William's father wants him to play with his train or basketball. While William likes to do stereotypically "male" activities, he also wants a doll to play with. His father, brother, and male friends are upset by this. His friends and his brother call him a "sissy" but he is defended by his grandmother, who explains that William can practice for the time when he becomes a father himself. K–3.

Target Activity: "Moms and Dads"

Ask children why they think that William was picked on for wanting to have a doll. Do they think it is okay for boys to play with dolls? Why or why not? Ask the girls in the class if they have ever played with a toy that was considered a "boys'" toy. Did they get called names when this occurred? Discuss why they think society seems to think it okay for girls to play with "boys' toys" but takes a dim view of boys playing with "girls' toys." With children's input, make a list on the chalkboard of all the things a person should know in order to be a successful mother or father. Ask children then to tell how playing with dolls will help both boys and girls prepare to play the role of parent.

Folk Literature

35. Bang, Betsy. *The Old Woman and the Red Pumpkin.* Ill. Molly Garrett Bang. New York: Macmillan, 1975.

This is a Bengali folktale that is a great story! It is about a wise old woman who outsmarts a jackal, a tiger, and a bear, all of whom she meets on her way to her granddaughter's house. The old woman is helped by her granddaughter to outsmart the animals for the trip back home, but in the end, her own wits save her. K–3.

Target Activity: "Outsmarting Danger"

Before acting out the story, discuss with children the choices this old woman had to save her life: Did she have a weapon — a gun? Was there some-one around to help her? Could she outrun the danger? (What could she do? What she could do was be smarter than the danger.) Discuss how the old woman understood the motives of the animals by appealing to their hope for a *good* meal and their greed for the *best* part.

36. Bang, Betsy. *The Old Woman and the Rice Thief.* Ill. Molly Garrett Bang. New York: Greenwillow, 1978.

This is a Bengali folktale of an old woman who has a complaint for the local ruler. Every night, someone steals her rice, and she wants to put a stop to it. On her way to the Raja, she finds scary friends who ask her to take them home with her. She does not find the Raja but returns home with her friends who find a place to be in and around her house. After that, she has no need of help from the Raja because she has these helpers who protect her rice. K–3.

Target Activity: "Hearing Voices"

Before acting out the story, discuss with children how the old woman first thought she could solve her problem (get help) and:

1. Then ask them who helped her. They will likely name the animals and objects who spoke to her.
2. Then ask them where the voices were really coming from in the story. Was it from the thinking of the old woman? If so, then who solved the woman's problem?
3. When children understand the poetic trick of giving voices to things that don't speak, they will understand that the old woman solved her own problem and that she was a *smart* old woman.

37. DePaola, Tomie. *The Legend of the Bluebonnet*. Ill. author. New York: Scholastic, 1983.

In this retold Comanche legend, a drought and famine have killed the mother, father and grandparents of She-Who-Is-Alone, a small girl. All she has left is a warrior doll that her mother once made for her. One evening, the shaman of the camp tells his people that the famine is the result of the people becoming selfish. They must make a sacrifice of the most valued possession among them and life will be restored. No one volunteers a valued possession except She-Who-Is-Alone, who offers her warrior doll. Deep in the night she makes a burnt offering of the doll, and then scatters its ashes over the fields below. Where the ashes have fallen, the ground becomes covered with bluebonnets. The Comanche people take the flowers as a sign of forgiveness from the Great Spirits. From that day on, the little girl is known as One-Who-Dearly-Loved-Her-People. The small girl gives up the thing she loves best in all the world for her people. She spends a frightening night alone on a hill offering her doll as a burnt offering to the Great Spirits, clearly a courageous act of self-sacrifice and unselfishness. 2–3.

Target Activity: "One-Who-Dearly-Loved-Her-People Is an Active Participant and Loyal to Her People"

Bring to students' minds other stories they have read or heard where the main character has unlimiting choices about unselfishness and loyalty as a basic value for people. Some of the stories show main characters with a most precious possession, e.g., Tera and her pig, Wilbur, in *Charlotte's Web* by E. B. White; Sarah and her unicorn in *Sarah's Unicorn* by Bruce and Katherine Coville; the child and his carrot plant in *The Carrot Seed* by Ruth Kraus; Dick and his cat in *Dick Whittington and His Cat* by Kathleen Lines. Have children rewrite *The Legend of the Bluebonnet*, superimposing the new character and her/his prized possessions in a famine of modern times. Tell students, "Describe the famine. Tell what your character says when (s)he offers his/her prized possession as a sacrifice to end the famine. How does your character feel? Describe the night on the mountain. What happens as a result of your character's sacrifice? How does your character feel about saving his/her people? What has your character learned from the experience?"

38. DePaola, Tomie, reteller. *The Legend of the Indian Paintbrush*. Ill. reteller. New York: Putnam, 1988.

This is the story of Little Gopher, who cannot be like other children, but who, through his art, has a special gift for his people. Little Gopher finds that his place among his people is to paint their deeds so they will always be remembered. He is lonely, but faithful and true. He is rewarded with magical brushes left on a hillside. They hold colors and allow him to paint his vision of the evening sky. Discarded, they take root and multiply and bloom in colors of red, orange, and yellow. Simple poses of the characters show the dignity of the Indians' spirit. K–2.

Target Activity: "Unlimited Option for Boys to Express a Wide Range of Feelings and Interests"

Invite children to see the ways primary colors turn into other colors with the overhead, a clear glass or plastic container, water, and drops of food coloring. Drops of red and yellow food coloring in the water in the container are swirled and the overhead projects the mingling as the colors turn into orange. Encourage children to use the colors of red, orange, yellow, and other shades to create their own visions of the evening sky or of the deeds of people. They will show in their drawings that no matter how small or young we are, our visions are important ones.

39. Esbensen, Barbara Juster. *The Star Maiden.* Ill. Helen K. Davie. Boston: Little, Brown, 1988.

This is an explanatory tale that tells the story of a flower that originated with the Ojibway (Chippewa) in the north lake country. A star maiden watches the earth and wants to make her home with the tribe, who prepare to welcome her. The rose on the hillside where she first comes to rest is too far from the village, and a flower on the prairie is too near the trampling feet of buffalo. Finally, she finds the peaceful surface of a lake and calls her sisters down to live with her where they can be seen today as water lilies. K–3.

Target Activity: "Ojibway Indian Legends Show the Valued Role of Women"

To continue a study on Ojibway Indian legends, discuss the poetic use of words in this story and the illustrations that are framed on three sides with the patterns authentic to the tribe; then read other legends showing the valued role of women and girls.

40. Gag, Wanda. *Gone Is Gone.* Ill. author. New York: Coward-McCann, 1935.

In Bohemia, a man, Fritzel, wants to do housework, and so Leisi, his wife, agrees to do his work and he does her work. He has a series of misadventures during the day and when she returns from the field, he begs her, "Please let me go back to my work in the fields and never more will I say that my work is harder than yours."

Leisi is resourceful as she returns from her hard work in the fields with the water jug in her hand and the scythe over her shoulder. She sees the cow hanging over the edge of the roof and cuts the rope. She sees the garden with the gate wide open in which the pigs and goats and geese are eating. She finds the churn overturned and the child all stiff and sticky with dried cream and butter. She sees the dog, full of sausages and looking none too well. She sees the cider all over the floor and the stairs. She notices the kitchen floor that was piled high with peelings of vegetables and littered with dishes and pans. She notices the soup kettle and two arms waving and two legs kicking and a weak bubbly gurgle coming out of the kettle. When Leisi cut the cow's rope, Fritzel dropped down the chimney right into the kettle of soup in the fireplace. Leisi agrees that Fritzel should return to his work and she to her work and says, "If that's how it is, we surely can live in peace and happiness for ever and ever."

Target Activity: "What's Gone Is Gone"

With the children all chiming in with "What's gone is gone," invite the children to accept roles, then trade roles and modify the gender of the characters, and act out some of the following situations:

Situation #1: While Fritzel/Leisi, is frying sausages he goes to get cider and returns to see the dog dashing out the door with the string of sausages flying after him. The dog gets away and Fritzel says, "What's gone is gone."

Situation #2: He/she returns to the house to see that the cider has run out all over the cellar.

Situation #3: He/she turns back to the churn in time to see his daughter climbing upon it and spilling the half churned cream and butter on the ground.

Situation #4: He/she prepares a noontime meal of soup with potatoes and onions and other vegetables and he notices the cow is slipping and sliding on the roof. Fritzel/Leisi, ties a rope around the cow's middle and drops the other end down the chimney. He/she pulls the rope through the fireplace into the room below. He/she ties it around his own middle. Just as he /she was getting ready to put the vegetables into a pot of hot water, the cow slipped off the roof of the house and Fritzel was whisked into the chimney where he dangled. He couldn't get up or down.

Situation #5: Fritzel/Leisi tugs at his legs and rescues Fritzel/Leisi, from the soup kettle. They agree to retun to their work so they can live in "peace and happiness."

For another version of this tale, read aloud Abe Gurvin's retelling with *The Husband Who Was to Mind the House* (Young Readers Pr., 1968).

41. Ginsburg, Mirra. *The Proud Maiden, Tungak, and the Sun.* Ill. Igor Galin. New York: Macmillan, 1974.

This is a Russian Eskimo tale of why the tundra is no longer cold all year. It starts in typical fashion with a beautiful maiden who does not want to marry any of the men in her village. Her father becomes very angry with her and with her mother, who tries to protect her. He calls down the wrath of Tungak, an evil spirit, a bully not unlike the father when he is angry. The maiden runs away from the demands of Tungak and marries into the family of the Sun.

When they later visit her family the season changes because they bring the sun with them. 1–3.

Target Activity: "Scary Anger"

Discuss the story with the children, emphasizing: a) how the father felt when his daughter refused his wishes for her to pick someone to marry, and what he said; b) how the daughter felt when the father was shouting and threatening; c) what she did to get away when Tungak appeared; and d) how the mother felt when her husband was threatening the daughter and when she was told to be silent and called a foolish woman. Have children draw pictures of the "scary anger" of the story showing one or more of the characters when they are yelling, frightened, or quietly angry because their feelings have been hurt. Have the titles of the pictures reflect the feelings portrayed, e.g., "Tungak frightens her" under a picture of the maiden running, and so on.

42. Grimm Brothers. *Rumpelstiltskin.* Ill. Paul O. Zelinsky. New York: Dutton, 1986.

Parents boast that their daughter has an ability to spin and are told that she must spin straw into gold or lose her head. Crying, the girl notices a creature who offers to do the spinning for her. In return, she will give him her first born child when she marries the King. When he comes to claim the child, he returns three times to give her three chances to guess his name. If at the end of the third time, she hasn't guessed his name, the child will be his. Each time, she tries to solve her problem by bargaining and by guessing the creature's name. Before the last day of the bargaining time, a maid follows the creature and hears him singing his name; she returns and tells the queen.

Target Activity: "Finding the Answer to a Riddle"

With the students, read Rumpelstiltskin's refrain from a favorite version or from Jakob and Wilhelm Grimm's "Rumpelstiltskin" in *Household Tales* (Macmillan, 1926). In this refrain, the little man cried out:

> Today do I bake, tomorrow I brew.
> The day after that the Queen's child comes in;
> And oh! I am glad that nobody knew
> That the name I am called is Rumpelstiltskin.

Option: "Active Role of Women and Girls"

Compare this book with *Duffy and the Devil* (Farrar, Straus, 1973) by Harve Zemach, where the maid, Duffy, makes an agreement with the devil, who promises to do her knitting for three years. At that time, Duffy must know his name or go away with him. When the time arrives, the squire tells Duffy what he has overheard while out hunting: a creature who sings a verse that children can repeat:

> Tomorrow! Tomorrow! Tomorrow's the day!
> I'll take her! I'll take her! I'll take her away!
> Let her weep, let her cry,
> Let her beg, let her pray —
> She'll never guess my name is . . . Tarraway!

With children, discuss switching the character roles in the story with the maid being a male and Tarraway being female. Discuss the effect such changes have on the children when reviewing the story. Discuss the effect as it relates to gender stereotyping of characters in stories.

43. Grimm, Jakob and Wilhelm Grimm. "The Wolf and the Seven Little Kids" in *Household Tales*. Trans. Margaret Hunt. London: G. Bell & Son, 1884.

Tricked by the wolf into opening the cottage door, one kid hides under the table, the second springs into bed, the third into the stove, the fourth into the kitchen, the fifth into the cupboard, the sixth under the washing bowl, and the seventh into the clock case. The wolf satisfies his appetite and swallows them all except for the kid hiding in the clock case. When mother returns, she and the remaining kid follow the wolf and find him snoring in the meadow. The mother sees something moving and struggling inside his stomach. "Ah, heavens," she says, "is it possible that my poor children whom he has swallowed down for his supper can still be alive?"

After fetching scissors, needles, and thread, the goat cuts open the wolf, and all six kids spring out still alive. What rejoicing there was! Then they embrace their dear mother. Mother suggests that the kids find some stones "to fill the wicked beast's stomach" while he is asleep. When the wolf awakens, he begins to walk and finds that the stones inside him knock against each other and rattle. He cries:

> What rumbles and tumbles
> Against my poor bones?
> I thought it was six kids,
> But it's aught but big stones.

When the wolf reaches the well and stoops down to drink, the heavy stones make him fall into the water, and there is no help to rescue him. The seven kids call out, "The wolf is dead! The wolf is dead!" and dance for joy around the well with their mother.

Target Activity: "Mothers/Fathers Protect Their Children"

With children, engage in pantomime and portray some of the actions as the story is reread: the mother takes an active role in protecting her children.

In the story, the wolf is the villain animal and the mother goat is the heroine. Discuss with the children other stories in which the wolf is the villain or in which the mother is the heroine. In this story, Mother Goat told her children, "Be on guard against the wolf; if he comes in, he will devour you all—skin, hair, and all. The wretch often disguises himself, but you will know him at once by his rough voice . . ."

Option: Invite the children to look for additional stories where women and girls are successful, and then have them read a biographical sketch about the author who wrote the story in *Something About the Author* (Gale Research) or another favorite reference source. Encourage the children to look for items in the biographical sketch that may be evidence to support the sensitivity of the author toward women and girls. The students may report their findings back to the whole group:

The story I found where women and girls were successful was:

_____ .

The story was written by _____.
In a biographical sketch about the author, I found _____.
I think this relates to the author's sensitivity about women and girls because

_____ .

An emphasis on the sensitivity of men and boys in children's books also should be introduced with other authors and stories:

The story I found where men and boys were sensitive to women and girls was:

_____ .

The story was written by _____.
In a biographical sketch about the author, I found _____.
I think this relates to the author's view about men and boys (women and girls), because _____.

44. Guirma, Frederic. *Princess of the Full Moon.* Ill. London: Macmillan, 1970.

This is a favorite folk tale told by the people of Upper Volta in Africa. People sit around the fire at night, the girls with the women and the boys with the men as is their tradition. As the tale of the beautiful princess is told, the children call out the names of each character to speak, because they have heard the story many times and enjoy anticipating what comes next. The story is a traditional tale of good disguised as ugly and bad disguised as handsome, with a foolish princess mistaking appearance for true worth. She learns her lesson, and in the end, she luckily gets both goodness and beauty and is saved from evil. 2–3.

Target Activity: "What Does 'Perfect' Look Like?"

After discussing the story's facts and all its beautiful detail, have the children draw pictures of different events. For example, the scene with the seven-headed snake or the princess playing the shepherd's flute would give them the opportunity for including some of the elaborate detail of the story in their pictures.

Discuss with them the traditional nature of the story with its moral for women that suggests that they should not be too demanding for good looks or riches in their mates because love and goodness are more important. Ask the children who they think is the traditional story teller in this culture? Is it a woman or a man? If a woman were to tell such a story, how would she tell it? Explain how a woman might change the character of the princess to a prince and the shepherd to a woman. The moral would then be for men. It would tell readers not to think perfection is the prettiest face or the richest woman but instead to think of perfection as love because of the goodness in the heart of the woman.

45. Gurvin, Abe, reteller. *The Husband Who Was to Mind the House.* Ill. reteller. New York: Young Readers Press, 1968.

This retold version of Wanda Gag's *Gone Is Gone* (Coward-McCann, 1935) challenges the normal stereotypes of "male" jobs versus "female" household work, which is thought to be easier and less stressful. The husband in the story makes a big fuss one evening, complaining that his wife never does anything. "Don't be angry," replies his wife, Goody. "Tomorrow we will change places. I'll go out and cut hay all day and you can stay home and mind the house." The husband assumes that his new job will be easy and sleeps late the next morning. What ensues is a true comedy of errors, with the pig getting loose in the kitchen, the butter churn overturning, the baby screaming and the husband spilling the water in the fireplace pot and forgetting to feed the cow. When Goody comes home, she finds the cow dangling from the roof by a rope, the result of another of her husband's mistakes. The book ends by asking the reader to ". . . guess who stayed home to mind the house from now on!", implying that the husband has a newfound respect for his wife's work *and* her ability to perform it. 2–3.

Target Activity: "A Homemaker's Job"

Ask children if any of their parents are "homemakers." Brainstorm the activities that might be done by homemakers of today compared with the old-fashioned farmer's wife in the story. Add to the list activities that would also need to be performed if there were nonschool-aged children at home, too. Discuss whether or not this job sounds easy. Why do they think the husband thought it was so easy? Did he change his mind? Do they think their fathers think what their mothers do is easy? Have pairs of children take the part of a homemaker and a spouse. Have the homemaker tell the spouse all the things he/she has done all day.

46. Jacobs, Joseph. *Aesop's Fables.* "The Lark and Its Young." London: Batsford, 1954.

A Mother Lark had a nest of young birds in a field of ripe grain. One day, she found the little birds quite excited, for they had heard the owner say it was time to gather in the grain. "Do not worry," said Mother Lark. "If he is depending on his neighbors, the work will not begin today. But listen carefully to what the owner says each time he comes and report to me." The next day, the little birds heard the owner say, "This field needs cutting badly; I'll call my relatives over to help me. We'll get them here tomorrow." The little birds told their Mother and she said, "Never mind. I happen to know the relatives are busy with their own grain. They won't come. But keep your ears open and tell me what you hear." The third day, the owner came and said to his son, "We can't wait any longer. We will hire some men tonight and tomorrow we will begin cutting the grain." When Mother Lark heard these words, she said, "Now we'll have to move. When people decide to do things themselves instead of leaving work to others, you know they mean business."

Target Activity: "Mothers/Fathers See the Nature of Others"

With students, discuss the idea that Mother Lark knew the nature of humans and kept informed about what was going on; talk about times when people have decided to do things themselves instead of leaving work for others to do. Then focus more specifically on times when women and girls have decided to "do things for themselves" instead of leaving work for others to do. Ask students to contribute their oral comments from their experiences or books they have read to help complete a matrix on a writing board:

People Who Did Things for Themselves	Evidence People "Meant Business"
_____	_____
_____	_____
_____	_____

Ask children to dictate the story and switch the role of Mother Lark to Father Lark. Record the children's dictation on a chart or the board and discuss the effect the change has on the story with the children. The children may show their "role expectations" through their discussion which will enable a teacher to make a point that "It's O.K. to switch roles."

As a culminating review, return to the list and invite the children to identify successful leaders who represent both sexes.

47. McKissack, Patricia C. *Mirandy and Brother Wind.* Ill. Jerry Pinckney. New York: Knopf, 1988.

Mirandy was hoping to win her first cakewalk, a dance rooted in African American culture, in which the pair of dancers with the most flamboyant dances takes home a cake. The trouble is, Mirandy's most logical partner, Ezel, is much too clumsy to be a partner who could help her win. Mirandy decides to try to catch Brother Wind and have *him* be her partner. Although everyone she speaks to tells her "Can't nobody put shackles on Brother Wind . . . he be free," Mirandy perseveres. She tries to put black pepper on his footprints to make him sneeze so she can slip up behind him and throw a quilt over him. She tries to catch him in a crock bottle, but he escapes. Finally, Mirandy traps Brother Wind in the barn. At the cakewalk, when another girl makes fun of Ezel's clumsiness, Mirandy defends him and claims him as her partner. She immediately regrets having said such a "tomfool" thing; she'd caught Brother Wind. She goes to Brother Wind and makes a wish; she and Ezel dance with grace and style and win the cakewalk. A beautifully illustrated book that portrays a young black girl as highly resourceful and clever, yet compassionate. 2–3.

Target Activity: "Pursuing a Goal"

Have children retell the story, paying special attention to the attempts Mirandy made to catch Brother Wind. Ask them why they feel she did not give up. Ask them to take a couple of minutes to remember a time they really wanted to do something that seemed impossible. What was their goal? What did other people tell them about the possibility of pursuing their goal? Have each child share their goal with a partner. Let the partner be the "other person" who gives them reasons why their goal is impossible. Tell them to try their best to offer arguments as to why they should continue pursuing their goal. Compare the goals of the boys and girls in the classroom.

48. Mosel, Arlene. *The Funny Little Woman.* Ill. Blair Lent. New York: Dutton, 1972.

In this Japanese tale, a little woman pursues a rice dumpling and is captured by the wicked Oni, green underground creatures who live in dark caverns. A captive, the woman must cook for them with a magic paddle that makes grains and grains of rice. Trying to escape, she leaves in a boat floating on an underground river. To recapture her, the Oni suck the river water into their mouths and leave the woman's boat in the river's waterless bed. The funny little woman has a contagious laugh though, and it makes the Oni laugh, too. Laughing, they spill all the water back into the river bed. She floats back to her home and becomes the richest woman in Japan by making rice cakes with her magic paddle. While escaping, the funny little woman looks so humorous that the Oni laugh and laugh, allowing her boat to float back to her house. 1–3.

Target Activity: "Active and Adventurous Role of the Female"

Share poems about being unselfish, about being able to break enchantments, or about ways to escape magical creatures – to show other ways to be active and adventurous. Several aspects of an active and adventurous female are discussed in humorous ways in the verses of J. Prelutsky's *Something Big Has Been Here*. For example, in "The Turkey Shot Out of the Oven," the unknown narrator promises to plan ahead the next time he/she stuffs a turkey and promises "never again to stuff a turkey with popcorn that hadn't been popped." Other poems to listen/read and to discuss are: "I Am Growing a Glorious Garden," "I Am Wunk," "A Remarkable Adventure," "My Brother Is as Generous as Anyone Could Be," and "My Family's Sleeping Late Today."

49. Rehyer, Becky. *My Mother Is the Most Beautiful Woman in the World*. Ill. Ruth Gannett. New York: Howell, Soskin, 1945.

While preparing for a Ukrainian harvest feast, six-year-old Varya gets separated from her mother in the fields. When found by rescuers, Varya describes her mother as "the most beautiful woman in the world," and all search for the mother until the child sees her rounded, "almost toothless" mother, who is beautiful in the eyes of her daughter. Separated from her mother, six-year-old Varya thinks of her mother as "the most beautiful woman in the world," and shows the girl's significant relationship with a caring "other" in her life. K–3.

Target Activity: "My Father Is the Most Handsome Man in the World"

Discuss with children why it was that Varya described her mother as beautiful when the women did not, in fact, possess typical physical beauty recognized by others. Write the phrase on the board, "Beauty is in the eye of the beholder." Discuss the meaning of this phrase with the girls and boys. Ask children to tell what words are used to describe a boy, or man, who possesses physical beauty. What traits might be more important for both females and males than physical beauty? Have children brainstorm their ideas and write them on the board. Finally, retell the story, with the children's help, and change the story so that Varya becomes separated from her *father* in the fields. Later, discuss why a father, or another significant male person, may be "handsome" to a child due to his helpful actions. What might Varya's father have done for her that would make him "handsome" in her eyes, even if physically he was not?

50. Sleator, William. *The Angry Moon*. Ill. Blair Lent. Boston: Little, Brown/Atlantic Monthly Press, 1970.

A rainbow appears and takes the young girl to the sky when Lapowinsa angers the moon. To retrieve the girl, Lupan shoots his arrows toward the moon; he notices a chain of his arrows form a ladder on which he climbs into the sky. Reaching the top, he is taken by a small boy to his grandmother's house, where Lupan receives four objects to aid in the rescue of Lapowinsa. Lupan follows the sobs of Lapowinsa to the moon's home, substitutes a pine cone in her place in a smoke hole and they begin their escape. When the pine cone burns, the angry moon pursues them. A fish eye becomes a lake to block the moon's progress, a rose turns into a tangled thicket to slow the chasing moon. A stone grows into steep mountains, and the children make their escape and return to earth to tell their story to succeeding generations. Lupan is an active character who has the positive characteristic of caring for another as he comes to the aid of Lapowinsa. Lupan is independent, brave, strong, and competent. His grandmother portrays a positive adult female role, and the story deals thoughtfully with the problem of caring for others. 2–3.

   Target Activity: "Lupan Expresses a Range of Feelings"

1. The questions/activities that follow are examples of the types which teachers and librarians can prepare to encourage children to talk about how they feel about some of the ideas related to the book before it is read or heard.

   a. Why do some people come to the aid or rescue of others? Does it always have to be a boy (man) who comes to the aid of a girl (woman)?

   b. Why is a person often punished when he/she angers others?

   c. Without using the word *angry*, write or talk about what you think the title, *The Angry Moon*, means to you.

   d. Create an "angry" research project and include these things: Make a list of words that best describe an angry person. Make a list of things that cause a person to become angry. Tell how you recognize anger. Tell what you could do to overcome anger in another person.

2. After reading or listening to the story, the students may be asked to think back to the rescue event and then write their impressions about a person who came to the aid of or rescued another person. Take time to discuss the children's work and point out examples that modify gender stereotypes. You may suggest, *Write your impressions to be put into a book for others to read and comment on.*

3. With the children, you may read these sentences about some of the things Lupan experienced in the story. After hearing each sentence, invite the students to "tell how you think Lupan felt and more about what he did" and "As Lupan was feeling this way, tell how you think the young girl felt."

   a. Lupan discovers that a rainbow appears and takes the young girl to the sky when Lapowinsa angers the moon.

b. To retrieve the girl, Lupan shoots his arrows toward the moon.

c. He notices a chain of his arrows form a ladder on which he climbs into the sky.

d. Reaching the top, Lupan is taken by a small boy to his grandmother's house.

e. At his grandmother's house, Lupan receives four objects to aid in the rescue of Lapowinsa.

f. Lupan follows the sobs of Lapowinsa to the moon's home, substitutes a pine cone in her place in a smoke hole, and they begin their escape.

g. When the pine cone burns, the angry moon pursues them.

h. Lupan sees that a fish eye becomes a lake to block the moon's progress, a rose turns into a tangled thicket to slow the chasing moon. A stone grows into a steep mountain.

i. The children make their escape and return to earth.

j. They tell their story to the succeeding generation.

4. Suppose the moon could be put on trial in a court for the crime of taking the girl away and you were the prosecuting attorney. Prepare a brief (your argument and charge of the crime) against the moon.

5. With others, make a brief handbook called *Handling Your Anger: Ten Top Suggestions for Taking Care of It Within Yourself.*

51. Yolen, Jane. *The Emperor and the Kite.* Ill. Ed Young. Cleveland, Ohio: World, 1967.

In this fanciful folk-like tale, the smallest child, Djeow Seow, rescues her father, the emperor, from his prison in a tower. Using her kite each day, the small child flies it to the barred window of the tower with its attached basket of tea, rice, and poppy seed up a rope on her kite. With it, the emperor returns to the palace, expels the criminals from the palace, establishes peace in the kingdom, and places a tiny throne for Djeow Seow next to his, where she learns from him and is ready to rule the kingdom gently and loyally when it is time. K–2.

Target Activity: "Djeow Seow Is Strong, Active, and Adventurous"

With the children, discuss the strong characteristics shown by Djeow Seow. Draw a visual display of a large kite with a long kite-tail. Along the tail of the kite draw lines radiating outward, and on each line write some of the characteristics discussed by the children. Invite the girls and boys to make their own kites and put in their own words to describe the characteristics.

Fanciful Fiction

52. Allinson, Beverley. *Effie*. Ill. Barbara Reid. New York: Scholastic, 1990.

Effie was like all the other ants in every way but one: the other ants had tiny ant voices, but Effie had a big loud voice. When she boomed "Hello!" to her friends, they would go away quickly. When her colony of ants is faced with an approaching elephant, Effie bellows, "Stop! Please watch where you step!" Not only does she save the lives of the other ants, but she also makes friends with the elephants, who thereafter tread carefully through the grass, watching their step and chatting with Effie and her friends. This charming, humorous story of a female ant's trait that could be seen as a "gift" or a "curse" is brought to life with beautiful illustrations made of plasticine. K–2.

Target Activity: "Speak Up!"

Discuss the story of Effie with the children, pointing out that her special problem was her trait of having a loud voice. Write the word "trait" on the writing board. Ask children if they have ever been scolded for talking too loudly. Brainstorm some situations where talking loudly is appropriate, such as when someone is speaking in class so that everyone can hear. Discuss when speaking loudly is NOT appropriate. Ask children if they feel talking too softly/loudly is a special problem of girls or boys. Encourage children to provide reasons for their answers.

Tell children they are going to retell the story of Effie in play form in small groups of six. One child will take the part of Effie and speak in a big loud voice. The others will take the parts of the caterpillar, spider, grasshopper and butterfly, all of whom run away because Effie speaks so loudly. The sixth child will play the part of the elephant who almost steps on Effie, but eventually becomes her friend. Each group can then share its skit with the rest of the class who can play the part of the other ants in the colony, speaking in tiny ant voices.

53. Burton, Virginia Lee. *The Little House*. Ill. author. Boston: Houghton Mifflin, 1942.

Located in the country, the little house (who develops a personality) watches the changing seasons and, when the years pass, sees the city growing closer. She is surrounded by more and more tall buildings and elevated tracks. The little house becomes shabby and seems forlorn. Finally she is moved back into the countryside where the little house can hear the birds, watch the sunrise and sunset, and see the stars at night. Pre–2.

Target Activity: "Being Sensitive to Thoughts of *The Little House:* This Must Be Life in the City"

Roads were made and the countryside was divided into lots. More houses and bigger houses sprang up. Then came apartment houses and tenement houses, schools, stores, and garages that spread over the land and crowded around the little house. "This must be living in the city," thought the Little House, who didn't know whether she liked it or not. She missed the field of daisies and the apple trees dancing in the moonlight.

Through discussion, encourage the children to be sensitive to the changes that the little house saw, and then discuss the jobs related to the changes and who probably did the jobs. Scramble the events and ask the children to sequence them. Scrambled list:

1. Cars and more cars were coming down the roads in the country. What jobs are related to this change? Who probably did the jobs?
2. Surveyors and steam shovels began to dig and make more roads. What jobs could women/men hold?
3. Trucks, gasoline stations, roadside stands, and small houses were built along the new roads.
4. Some of the countryside was divided into new lots for houses.
5. Bigger houses, apartment houses, schools, and stores were built.
6. Buses and rail systems were built.
7. The air became filled with dust and smoke and loud noises.
8. Multilevel office buildings were built.

54. Coombs, Patricia. *Lisa and the Grompet.* Ill. New York: Lothrop, Lee & Shepard, 1970.

Lisa is constantly being told what to do by her mother, father, and big sister. She is beginning to sorely resent it. When she goes outside to mull this resentment over, she comes upon (or imagines) a grompet who tells her *his* sad tales: because no one ever disciplined him as a child he has shrunk to almost nothing. Lisa takes the grompet home with her and gives it orders ("Wash your wings and face, Grompet,") as she is given orders; the orders make the grompet very happy, and Lisa becomes more agreeable about doing what she is told. She feels strong and in control even if it seems that everyone in the family is always telling her what to do. K–3.

Target Activity: "A Girl with *Sang-Froid*"

Ask the girls and boys to make a note of all the things they have reminded others to do during the week. Remind them of the time that Lisa takes the grompet home with her and gives it orders ("Wash your wings and face, Grompet,") as she is given orders. Ask them to write these things down in list form with spaces next to each in which to make check marks. Ask them to use the list for one week to try to help themselves to remind others about important matters. If they remember to remind someone about an item on the list, tell them to check the item for that day. After the week is up, ask the children to bring in their lists and discuss how they helped others using this reminder.

55. Lobel, Arnold. *Frog and Toad Are Friends.* Ill. author. New York: Harper & Row, 1970.

In this book, there are five short stories about these friends. In one story, Frog entices Toad out of his home so he can enjoy the spring day. Children enjoy Toad's reactions when Frog knocks on the door: "Toad, Toad," shouts Frog. "Wake up, it is spring!" "Blah," says a voice from inside the house. In another story, Frog finds Toad looking very sad and asks him what is wrong and Toad replies: "This is my sad time of day. It is the time when I wait for the mail to come. It always makes me very unhappy." "Why is that?" asks Frog. "Because I never get any mail," says Toad. Children enjoy the brief stories for each chapter. Children can read them separately or listen to them read aloud, and smile at the humor in the author's writing. K–3.

Target Activity: "Sensitive Male Characters"

When animals pose as people in stories, an animal can show sensitivity to others just as a child can. In these books, there is friendship between the two characters, Frog and Toad, and sensitivity and caring are shown when Frog finds that Toad is sad.

Read other stories of friendship in *Frog and Toad All Year* (Harper & Row, 1976) or in *Frog and Toad Together* (Harper & Row, 1972); discuss friendship, sensitivity, caring, and other characteristics of Frog and Toad, and list them on left-hand side of the board. Ask the students to select a different colored chalk for the two characters (such as green for Frog and brown for Toad). With a green chalk, read down the list and, opposite an appropriate characteristic, invite a student to put a check on the line where they believe Frog has that characteristic. After the students have rated Frog on the characteristics, then ask them to do the same for Toad. Engage the girls and boys in showing others in another class how to "read" the check list and how to get information about the two book characters from it.

56. Moss, Marissa. *After-School Monster.* Ill. author. New York: Lothrop, Lee & Shepard, 1991.

Arriving at her apartment after school, Luisa finds a fierce-looking purple creature towering right inside. Menacingly, the creature says, "I'm going to pluck you like a rose. I'm going to chew off your nose. I'm going to gobble up your toes." After overcoming her fear, she scolds the creature and confronts it with "I'm strong, too! Strong inside, where you can't get me!" Hearing those words, the towering monster shrinks down to a limp purple rag that she throws into the garbage. 1–3.

Target Activity: "Confronting a Problem Directly"

Some children find it refreshing to find a female character in an Hispanic inner-city neighborhood who confronts a problem directly in a picture book. Luisa displays a vibrant inner-self as she quickly confronts what she faces and "speaks out strongly."

Have a general discussion with children about some of the problems they face when they leave school—individual monsters. Write on the chalkboard or overhead the results of their discussions under the heading "Things we can do." For those who insist that they can't do anything, allow them to see that they can take small steps in facing a problem, such as Luisa's feelings of defeat, scolding and then direct confrontation, etc. Have each child choose a way to deal directly with a problem and, if they are comfortable about acting in front of others, act it out.

57. Peet, Bill. *Pamela Camel.* Ill. author. Boston: Houghton Mifflin, 1984.

Pamela the camel lives in the circus, where she is absolutely miserable. She is a scrawny, awkward animal who cannot do any tricks, so she is never part of the big show. Instead, she is relegated to the menagerie tent where the crowds stare at her and insult her, calling her "stupid" and "bad-tempered." Since Pamela can't do anything to prove her intelligence and she is becoming bad-tempered from all the hurtful remarks, she decides to run away. Traveling over the railroad tracks to avoid the highway traffic, Pamela notices a break in the rail that she realizes will cause a disaster for the next train. Bravely, she stands on the track when the next train comes along, to alert the engineer of the imminent danger. When the engineer sees the piece of track, Pamela is the subject of a wild celebration. She is brought back to the circus and billed as an heroic, intelligent, train-saving camel. This is a good story to show children that looks and talent are not everything: courage is important, too. K–3.

Target Activity: "It's O.K. to Be Me"

Show children the pictures of Pamela the camel and discuss why the crowds, without knowing how special she was, might insult her. Compare this story to *The Ugly Duckling*, by Hans Christian Andersen, and ask children to explain why the duckling, too, was taunted and made to feel he did not belong. Bring in a Barbie doll and a G.I. Joe, or similar toys. Discuss how these toys can make some children feel that they are not good enough, because they don't look as perfect as these stereotypical toys. Tell children that it is fine to look just the way they do. Ask them to think of one thing they dislike about the way they look. Have them draw this feature, or write it on a piece of paper (e.g., "I dislike my long nose."), telling them they will not share this with anyone.

Ask them to write on the paper "o.k.," and tell themselves, "It's okay to (have a long nose)."

Follow up by reading *The Ordinary Princess,* where Amy, the young princess, is not beautiful physically but attracts people for other reasons.

58. Pollock, Penny. *Ants Don't Get Sunday Off.* Ill. Lorinda Bryan Cauley. New York: Putnam's, 1978.

Anya is a brave, hardworking ant who is getting tired of working so hard and longs for an "adventure." One day there is a heavy rainstorm that washes away her nest and Anya gets more adventure than she bargained for. Anya becomes a heroine as she courageously saves the queen's life, goes back for the baby ants, and finally does a daring rescue of three lost eggs. By this time she has lost her nest mates, and the rest of the story outlines her harrowing search for her home. When she finally makes it home and the other ants immediately tell her of all the work that is to be done, Anya realizes that work is exactly what she wants to do. 1–2.

Target Activity: "Anya Remains Cool"

When the flood occurs, Anya remains cool during this trying time, and she reminds the other ants of their loyalties to the rest of the colony. When trying to get home, Anya gets stuck on a piece of gum and has to use her wits to figure out how to get unstuck.

Show children the "Map of Anya's Trip" on p. 46 of the text. Discuss Anya's ability to stay cool in a trying situation and then trying to find her way back to her ant colony. Ask children to imagine they have been in a huge flood and have traveled in a turbulent stream far away from their homes. Have them chart out, using construction paper and magic markers, an imagined voyage to make their way home. Allow the girls and boys to share their illustrations with the class when they are finished and describe their journeys.

59. Shelby, Anne. *Potluck.* Ill. Irene Trivas. New York: Orchard Books, 1991.

In this whimsical story, Alpha and Betty decide to have a potluck, so they call their friends and invite them. The rest of the text details, in delightful alphabetical order, the good foods that the girls and boys have prepared and brought — from Acton's asparagus soup to Zeke and Zelda's zucchini casserole. K–3.

Target Activity: "Potluck"

Discuss some of the famous chefs (e.g., James Beard, Julia Child, et al.) with whom you are familiar. Ask children if they believe cooking is men's work or women's work. Have they ever seen a man cook? Allow those children whose fathers cook to share their experiences. Explain that you are going to plan a potluck luncheon and that each child will be responsible for 1) finding a recipe for a simple-to-prepare food and 2) helping their parent(s) or adults in the home prepare it. Send a note home describing what you are asking the children to do (if this is a problem for some families, offer to prepare some dishes with the children in advance, in school).

Option: Invite the parents and allow the children and their guests to share their perceptions of the cooking experience with the rest of the class.

60. Thurber, James. *Many Moons.* Ill. Marc Simont. New York: Contemporary Classics Series, 1990; orig. pub. Harcourt, Brace, 1943

Princess Lenore wants the moon and the Lord High Chamberlain, the Royal Wizard, and others try to fulfill her wish. Only the court Jester is sensitive enough to her to ask her how she sees the moon. She replies that she sees it as gold the size of her thumbnail and is presented with a golden moon on a chain. The king worries about what she will say when she sees the moon outside the next evening. Only the court Jester is an interesting male character who has demonstrated sensitivity and the positive personality characteristic of asking Lenore what her view is about the moon. With this insight, the story involves coming to terms with cross-sex sensitivity and, in this situation, the perspectives of the female. Lenore is filled with her own logic about the moon, and when she sees it outside the next evening, Lenore says, "When I lose a tooth, a new one grows in its place, doesn't it?" K–2.

Target Activity: "How Do You See It?"

With children, discuss their ideas of times when they asked someone of the opposite sex what they thought of something or how they saw something. Headlines from a current newspaper can provide topics to explore in discussion. Choose examples from a newspaper and discuss the headlines that offer topics with a question, *What do you believe (think) about. . .?* In a general discussion, compare the opinions of females and males on different topics. Do males and females ever disagree on topics? Agree? Do males ever disagree on topics? Do females ever disagree on topics? What statement can the children make, then, about the opinions of females and males?

Historical Fiction

61. Birdseye, Tom. *Waiting for Baby.* Ill. Loreen Leedy. New York: Holiday House, 1991.

A small boy waits for his baby sister to be born and he thinks of all the special things they will do. They will be playmates and hug and wrestle, play games of make-believe, read stories. They will swing and ride bikes. He thinks of a sister his own age. However, when the baby arrives, the boy is delighted. He snuggles close to the infant and wans to hold her close. He is happy she is with him at last. The small boy is an active, interesting male character who has positive personality characteristics as he thinks of the times of play he will have with a sister his own age. His happiness shows as he undergoes a character change and comes to terms with the reality of the situation—getting acquainted with an infant. He portrays a positive male role by showing his delight in wanting to hold his new sister close. Pre–K.

Target Activity: "Being Sensitive to a New Baby"

1. Discuss: Suppose you did not have a baby sister and you wanted one. If you could give a list of qualities that you would want in a new baby sister or brother, what kinds of things would be on your list?

2. What do you think makes a person sensitive to a sibling of the other sex? How do you expect a sensitive person to act? When has your sensitivity been strong and you have done something to respond to your sensitivity?

3. Suppose that a sibling was behaving in a way that you thought could get her/him into trouble. If you believe you have the right to point out to the brother or sister how wrong she/he is, how would you go about showing your sibling some of the mistakes he or she is making?

4. *Display sensitivity lessons by preparing a booklet.* First, discuss, *What do people do when they are sensitive to others?* With another student as a partner, prepare an illustrated booklet with the title *How to Become Sensitive in Ten Easy Steps.*

5. "It's all in the eye of the beholder," say some people when they mean, "If you look for sensitive things, you will see them; if you look for things for which you can demonstrate sensitivity, you will find them." How did the sister appear in the eyes of her brother before the sister arrived? How did the sister appeal to her brother after her birth as an infant? How did the brother change?

62. Bulla, Clyde Robert. *A Lion to Guard Us.* Ill. author. New York: Scholastic, 1983.

This intensely readable book tells the story of a plucky young heroine named Amanda and her determination, against all odds, to stay together as a family with her beloved brother and sister, despite the grim reality of her mother's death which leaves them in poverty. Amanda also holds fast to her dream of tracking down her father, who had left the family behind. The author uses a simple prose style, developing her characters well against the backdrop of the story of the founding fathers and mothers of the Jamestown colony and the families that were left behind in England. 2–3.

Target Activity: "A Medal for Courage"

Discuss with children the word "courage." Ask children to retell, in sequence, the things that Amanda did that took courage. Read children the picture storybook *Rose Blanche* (Creative Education, Inc., 1985), by Robert Innocenti. Have children also retell the ways in which Rose showed courage. Ask children to pretend that they are on a committee to award a medal for courage to one of these two young girls. Which one would they choose? Why? Invite children to write a paragraph telling about who they would choose and why. Allow them to read their paragraphs to the rest of the class. Using a bar graph, chart the number of children who chose Rose and who chose Amanda. Discuss the difficulty children had in making their choices.

63. Byars, Betsy. *The Golly Sisters Go West.* Ill. Sue Truesdell. New York: Harper & Row, 1986.

May-May and Rose are two high-spirited, singing and dancing sisters who travel out west in a covered wagon, entertaining people and getting in and out of trouble all the way. First, they can't get the horse to go to begin their journey until May-May reveals the magic word. Next, they are preparing to give a show to a crowd of people but take so long to argue about who goes first that the audience leaves. Then May-May loses her red hat, and in another argument about who should sing first, the hat gets squashed. May-May does a sad dance, "The Dance of the Squashed Hat." Finally, the sisters hear something outside their wagon one night. They decide that their fussing has scared the prowler away. They agree never to fuss again unless they hear something outside their wagon.

Though their problem-solving skills are unorthodox, the two sisters show how, even amidst arguments, siblings can really care for one another and work together. K–3.

Target Activity: "The Golly Sisters: Next Chapter"

After reading *The Golly Sisters Go West* with children, read selected portions of *Patty Reed's Doll*, which is a more realistic account of people going west—the Donner Party's journey west. Help children to select one of the large problems faced by Patty's family, such as severe hunger, broken wagons, dysentery, and so on. Ask pairs of students to role play how the Golly sisters would have handled the chosen problem. Ask them to include a peaceful resolution to any disagreements the sisters might have had about facing the problem. Encourage the pairs to present their "next chapter" role plays to the whole class.

64.   Coerr, Eleanor. *The Josefina Story Quilt*. Ill. Bruce Degen. New York: Harper & Row, 1986.

Faith's family is traveling to California in a covered wagon in the 1850s. The little girl convinces her father to allow her to take her pet hen, Josefina, with them on the journey. Her father warns that if the hen causes any trouble, ". . . out she goes!" Josefina starts a stampede on one occasion and another time nearly drowns in a river, forcing Faith's brother, Adam, to try to rescue her. Still, Faith talks her father into allowing the hen to stay. When Josefina's cackles warn the family of robbers in their wagon one night, Josefina becomes a heroine, but dies soon after of old age. Though devastated at the loss of her pet, Faith puts her warm feelings for Josefina into a patchwork quilt that pictorially tells the story of their good and bad times together. 1–3.

Target Activity: "Story Quilt"

Hold a general discussion about the good and bad times in Faith's life. Ask children to share some of the good and bad events in their lives. Give each child twenty-five three-inch squares made from different colored construction paper. Ask them to make a small picture on each square to represent some happy or sad event in their life. Allow each child then to paste the squares together to form a story quilt on a large sheet of tag board or construction paper, using any pattern they wish. Encourage them to tell orally about their story quilt and what each patch reminds them of when they see it.

65.   Dalgliesh, Alice. *The Courage of Sarah Noble*. Ill. Leonard Weisgard. New York: Scribner's, 1954.

Based on a true incident, eight-year-old Sarah Noble travels from the Massachusetts Colony to the wilderness of Connecticut to cook while her father builds a new home for the family. "Keep up your courage, Sarah Noble," says mother as she wraps Sarah's cloak around her before the two begin the journey. When her father goes to bring the rest of the family, Sarah stays with Tall John, his Indian wife, and their children, and the words of her mother become a comforting refrain (along with her cloak) to give her strength to face the new life in the wilderness. 2–3.

Target Activity: "Courage Pages"

Invite students to consider themselves as a band of courageous people. There are many acts of courage accomplished by both sexes that each child knows about but that the others may not be aware of in their experiences. Explain that just as Sarah had courage, others, both girls and boys (women and men), must keep searching to find what makes them courageous in special situations. Write on the chalkboard the following beginning sentence starters:

> ONCE I HAD COURAGE AND I . . .
> TODAY, TO SHOW COURAGE, I WOULD . . .
> SOON, I WANT TO BE ABLE TO SHOW COURAGE AND . . .

Complete the lines with dictations from the group and encourage students to contribute ideas for the sentence endings. Encourage students to write their own sentences of courage and to illustrate them if they wish to do so. Collect the pages of courage and put them into a class Courage Book. Point out courageous acts by both sexes. Display the book so all students can read about what the others can do or hope to do in the future.

66.   Godden, Rumer. *Impunity Jane.* New York: Viking, 1954.

In this early fiction set in a nursery in London decades ago, there are rough-and-tumble boys, "tiresome" little girls (stereotypes to discuss), and a little doll who belonged in a pocket. When the shop woman sells the doll to Effie, she points out that the doll is strongly made, and says, "why, you could drop her with impunity." Effie wants to know the meaning of the word and is told "impunity means escaping without hurt."

Target Activity: "Escaping without Harm or Hurt"

The doll survives several experiences with "impunity" and escapes without being hurt. After reading the story aloud to students, ask them to identify a time when the doll "escaped without harm" and discuss what *could* have happened to Jane. Times to discuss:

1. When Impunity Jane wished she was a trotting horse, i.e., "Oh, I wish I were a little horse!" cried Impunity Jane.
2. When the doll hears bells chiming in the church and says, "Oh, I wish I were a bell!"
3. When the doll hears and sees other things: "A bugle, a horse, a bell, a shuttlecock—oh I want to be everything!" cried Impunity Jane.
4. When years go by and other young girls play with the doll and the doll's house—first, Elizabeth, then Ethel, then Ellen, then cousin Gideon. To Gideon, Impunity Jane says, "Rescue me. Don't leave me here, here where Effie and Elizabeth and Ethel and Ellen have kept me so long."
5. When Gideon puts Impunity Jane into his pocket and she is with him as he runs, swings, and climbs trees.
6. When Gideon is searched and the doll is found by bullies on the street, and Gideon says, "She can be a fireman or a porter or a driver or sailor."
7. When Gideon's guilt over stealing the doll causes him to return her to the doll house and Ellen, who is giving her toys away, gives him the pocket doll, and the doll becomes "his mascot," which means she brings him luck.

Option: "From the Past: What the girls did; What the boys did"

With children, review the activity of the children in the story to draw the contrast in the roles written by an author of the 1950s. As the children recall the events in the story, write their contributions about what they do today on a chart on the writing board:

In the Early 1900s

What the Girls Did	*What the Boys Did*
1. played with doll's house	1. ran, skated, climbed trees
2. sewed doll's clothes	2. dug a hole
3. rode horses	3. pretended a hole was a gold mine
	4. pretended a hole was a cave with fossils

In the 1990s

What Girls Do	*What Boys Do*
1.	1.
2.	2.
3.	3.

From the two charts, discuss ways that actions of girls and boys have changed from the past to current times.

67. Goldin, Barbara Diamond. *Cakes and Miracles: A Purim Tale.* Ill. Erika Weihs. New York: Viking, 1991.

In Eastern Europe in the 19th century, Herschel, blinded by a childhood illness, misbehaves at school. One night he dreams ways to make what he sees in his imaginations. In his mother's kitchen, he is sensitive to the shapes and sculpts cookies in the shapes of images he sees in his mind and helps his mother sell them for Purim. Herschel breaks the mold of a young male character who is differently abled and quite imaginative. He is creative and talented. He doesn't hold back but helps his mother sell the three-cornered pastries he makes after seeing their shapes in his mind. Pre–3.

Target Activity: "Imaginations"

1. A teacher may encourage children to reveal how they feel about certain ideas that will be found in the story and discuss:
    a. What are imaginations?
    b. How do imaginations begin?

c. Why do you think humans are capable of imaginations?

d. Describe a time when you or someone you know had imaginations and tried to tell what they thought about to others.

2. With students, a teacher may discuss certain points in the story:

a. How can you explain the powerful influence the imaginations had on Herschel?

b. How might you explain the change that came over Herschel?

c. Why do you suppose that Herschel was so sensitive to art and making artistic shapes with the dough?

d. Related to the story, discuss artists of both sexes.

68. Lawson, Robert. *They Were Strong and Good.* Ill. author. New York: Viking, 1940.

The author uses relatives in this biography to show ancestors who had to be strong and build the beginnings of our nation. A Scots sea captain, a little Dutch girl, a Minnesota girl, and an Englishman who was a preacher in Alabama are all presented as ancestors of the author. The text is brief. Lawson uses the pictures to show the persistence and perseverance of his ancestors. Details in the illustrations show "wholesomeness" of the ancestors in scenes of the Civil War, a grandmother at sea, and caring for one another. 1–2.

Target Activity: "My Ancestors"

With some of the interested girls and boys, discuss the backgrounds of adult relatives in their homes (i.e., aunts, uncles, grandmothers, mothers and fathers). Invite interested children to tell about women and girls who were strong and made a particular accomplishment, and ask all of the children to make a visual display of family trees of adults in their homes.

Their mothers and fathers
(or adults in the home)

_____   _____

(name)   (name)

Mother and Father
(adults in the home)

_____   _____

(name)   (name)

Me

_____

(name)

69. Rappaport, Doreen. *The Boston Coffee Party.* Ill. Emily Arnold
     McCully. New York: Harper & Row, 1988.

Sarah and her sister, Emma, are growing up in wartime colonial Boston.
Sarah is outraged when she is sent to get sugar and the evil Merchant Thomas
overcharges them for the sugar. Then when another customer comes in, he
takes the sugar from Sarah and sells it at an even higher price. When Aunt
Harriet announces that Merchant Thomas has locked up forty barrels of coffee
in his warehouse so that Boston will run out of coffee and he can overcharge,
the women want to do something. Sarah comes up with the idea of having a
"coffee party," like the men had when they threw the English tea into the harbor. The women and young children capture Merchant Thomas and force him
to give them the key to the warehouse. They take all the coffee and bring it
home in containers that they have brought. Instead of allowing themselves to
be victimized by Merchant Thomas' greed, the women and children devise a
plan to solve the problem and fight back. K–3.

Target Activity: "Coffee Party"

After reading the story aloud to children, reread just the dialogue to them,
telling them that they are going to act out the "coffee party." Select children
to play the roles of Sarah, Emma, their mother, Aunt Harriet, and Merchant
Thomas. Let others be women and children who help to capture Merchant
Thomas and fill the containers with coffee.

70. Rylant, Cynthia. *When I Was Young in the Mountains.* Ill. Diane
     Goode. New York: Dutton, 1984.

In this historical fiction, there are memories of Appalachia and a girl's
happy years of growing up in the mountains of Virginia. She recalls her grandmother's kisses, her cornbread, and Grandmother "shooing" away a snake
with a hoe. Repetitive phrase of "when I was young in the mountains . . ." can
be echoed by the listening children. 2–3.

Target Activity: "Early Life Experiences: When I Was Young"

Invite the students to tell about some of their early life experiences—
perhaps a memory of when a relative was brave—and then turn the experiences into a brief story with the title, *When I Was Young.* When the stories
are drafted, the students team up with partners and read their stories to one
another. While listening to the feedback from their partner, students use a
colored pencil to write down the comments and suggestions on the draft. In a
rewriting, students may choose (or not choose) to use any of these suggestions.
The students return to their desks to rewrite the stories. If desired, the stories
may be illustrated, the pages stapled together, covers designed, and displayed
in the classroom book corner. Encourage and affirm sensitive recollections
from the boys in the class.

71. St. George, Judith. *By George, Bloomers!* Ill. Margot Tomes. New York: Coward, McCann & Geoghegan, 1974.

Hannah is an eight-year-old tomboy growing up in the year 1852. Her Aunt Lucy, one of the first women to wear bloomers, is coming to visit. While Hannah's mother thinks Aunt Lucy and her bloomers are foolish and unladylike, Hannah thinks the bloomers would allow her to play more freely like the boys, and she adores Aunt Lucy. When Hannah accidentally rips her flowing skirt and is sent to her room, Aunt Lucy helps her to turn her torn skirt into bloomers. The bloomers are finished just in time, for Hannah's little brother is stranded out on the roof trying to rescue his kite. Aunt Lucy ties a rope around Hannah, and Hannah bravely rescues the little boy. After the heroic rescue, Hannah's mother relents and buys her some bloomers. 1–3.

Target Activity: "Who Are the Jobs For?"

Read children the brief summary of the women's movement provided on p. 48 of the text. On the chalkboard or overhead, make a grid to be filled in orally with the whole class:

	girls	boys	both
nurse			
doctor			
construction worker			
lumber worker			
teacher			
scientist			
engineer			
lawyer			
president			

Ask children to think of jobs that they know. Then have them discuss whether such occupations should be undertaken by men only, women only, or both, and to give reasons for their answers.

72. Shub, Elizabeth. *The White Stallion*. Ill. Rachel Isadora. New York: Greenwillow, 1982.

Little Gretchen is carried away from her wagon train by Anna, the old mare, to which her parents have strapped her. She is befriended by a wild white stallion who gently bites off the straps and sets her down. Scared and hungry, Gretchen cries herself to sleep. The next morning she drinks from a nearby stream and nibbles on grass. Remembering that her mother has always told her to stay where you are if you are lost, the child sits down to wait. The white stallion returns and tells Anna to return Gretchen to the wagon train – or so Gretchen believes. Gretchen survives her wilderness experience by not panicking, using her common sense, and remembering what her parents have told her. K–3.

Target Activity: "Surviving the Wilderness"

Ask children to imagine that they are lost in the woods with nothing to eat or drink. Encourage them to consider what Gretchen did to survive. Discuss her actions. Ask children to offer other suggestions as to what she might have done. To augment the discussion, ask children what three items they might bring on a hike to be on the safe side in case they were to get lost.

73. Wetterer, Margaret K. *Kate Shelley and the Midnight Express*. Ill. Karen Ritz. Minneapolis: Carolrhoda, 1990.

Kate Shelley, a young girl, shows her courage when she saves the lives of hundreds of people on a train racing toward a railroad bridge that, unknown to them, has been washed away during a dangerous storm. In this true story from the history of the 1880s, Kate, without concern for her own safety, struggles through a fierce storm to the railroad bridge to alert the midnight train and save the lives of others. 1–3.

Target Activity: "When I Helped Someone Else"

Invite the students to tell about some of their experiences where they helped others, and then turn the experiences into a brief story with the title, *When I Helped Someone Else*. When the stories are written as first drafts, girls and boys divide into pairs, read their stories to one another, and offer suggestions. After rewriting the stories, students may illustrate the pages, design covers, and place their stories in the classroom reading corner.

74. Wilder, Laura Ingalls. *Little House in the Big Woods*. New York: Harper, 1952.

In this historical fiction, Wilder tells of her early childhood in a log cabin on the edge of the Big Woods in Wisconsin, for she is Laura of the story. In those pioneer days, each family, living miles from a settlement, was self-sufficient. Each season brought its related work, and readers find a description of the daily doings that made up pioneer life. 3 up.

Target Activity: "Summertime"

With children who are looking forward to a summer vacation, read aloud the excerpt "Summertime" from *Little House in the Big Woods* by Wilder. As you read, ask them to listen for some of the "daily doings" that Laura and the others did during the summertime. After listening to the selection, the children may contribute what they heard and their comments may be recorded on a chart, overhead transparency, or on the writing board:

What Laura and the other boys and girls did in the summertime:

visited relatives
rode in the Big Woods
cooked dinner
visited nearby neighbors
looked at neighbor's possessions—the laces, embroideries and china from
    Sweden
nibbled cookies
shared cookies with Baby Carrie
climbed trees with Clarence
stood still while Ma curled her hair with cloth strings and then combed it into
    long curls
gathered a pan of chips to kindle the fire in the morning
received a whipping with a strap from the wall because she slapped Mary
weeded the garden, fed the calves and hens
gathered eggs and helped make cheese
listened to Pa singing and playing the fiddle
Pa chopped down a tree and found honey

Students may contrast the activities above with a second list that they contribute and discuss what children do in the 1990s:

What We Do in the 1990s

When we visit relatives:
When we go riding in woods:
When we cook dinner:
When we visit nearby neighbors:
When we admire a neighbor's possessions:
When we nibble cookies:
When we play with others:

When we want curls in our hair:
When we want a fire in the morning:
When we receive the consequence for striking a brother or sister:
When we have chores at home:
When we have evenings at home:
When we want firewood or honey:

Biographies

---

75. Aaseng, Nathan. *Florence Griffith Joyner: Dazzling Olympian.*
Minneapolis: Lerner, 1989.

Florence Griffith Joyner was the seventh of eleven children born to their mother. Her mother wanted her children to do well, so she was very strict. She did not allow the children to watch television on a week day and required them, even when they were teenagers, to be in bed by ten o'clock. But her mother encouraged her children to develop their special talents, whatever they might be.

Dee Dee, as Florence was called, showed a talent for stubborn independence early, since she could go without speaking for days when she felt like it. She loved reading, kept a diary, and knew how to be noticed because of her special style. She had a pet snake that she would wear around her neck and hair styles that made her "famous" in her Los Angeles neighborhood. But her most famous talent she discovered when she was quite young—she was a very fast runner and won her very first track competition when she was only seven!

"Flo Jo," as she is sometimes called today, is known around the world for her athletic ability at running. She has won many medals at the Olympics for excelling at track competitions. Her stubborn independence helps her work harder and harder as she prepares for races. She is still known, too, for her flamboyant style as an athlete. She has worn long painted finger nails and beautiful running suits in her races. When she is not running or preparing for races, Florence Griffith Joyner writes children's books. She always loved reading and writing in her diary, and the person she was as a child is reflected in the successful adult she has become. 2–3.

Target Activity: "You Are Special"

After reading this story with the class, discuss how Florence Griffith Joyner wasn't afraid to be someone special even when she was a small girl. Have a discussion with the group about how each of them is special. Help them see that "special" can mean being helpful, kind, a hard worker, knowing when to say "no," as well as doing your best when drawing, playing sports, reading, or when engaged in other activities. Have children develop a list on the board of the many ways they can be special. Then have them draw a picture or write a story about how Florence Griffith Joyner was special when she was a child.

Option: Ask young children to draw pictures of when they are special and have them complete a sentence for each picture that starts: I am special when I _____. Have children share their pictures, stories and sentences with the class.

76. Ash, Maureen. *The Story of Harriet Beecher Stowe.* Chicago: Children's Press, 1990.

The common sight of a slave mother having her children torn from her arms never to see them again was an event repeated over and over for three hundred years in America. People tried to end slavery, but Harriet Beecher Stowe's book, *Uncle Tom's Cabin,* let people know how it felt to be a slave and to lose a child. Stowe's book may have done more to end slavery than any other single event. Stowe lost her first child before its first birthday, and she knew what sadness a mother could feel. She and her husband risked their lives to protect runaway slaves because of the horrors of slavery. Harriet wanted to do more.

Harriet had been a thoughtful child who didn't get much attention except for her amazing memory for Bible verses. She was a good student and writer. She later became a teacher and a mother. She decided that writing a book was something she would know how to do and could do in the midst of the demands of her family. She wanted many more people to understand why slavery had to end, and this was the way she could help them understand.

This book made money for Harriet and her poor family, but what made her the happiest of all was that the people who read it were convinced that slavery should be abolished. 3.

Target Activity: "Can I Help?"

Ask the children to explain how Harriet knew that slavery was a terrible life for a slave. Have children compare Stowe's life with the life of the slave mothers. Ask the children if they know people today who live terrible lives and have them compare their lives with these other people. Have children write brief essays about these people so that others can understand that some people need help and assistance from those around them.

77. Callahan, Dorothy. *Julie Krone: A Winning Jockey.* Minneapolis: Dillon Press, 1990.

Julie Krone grew up on a farm in Michigan. From the start, she loved horses, winning her first blue ribbon in a show when she was five. Later, after her first race, she knew that she wanted to be a jockey, but it took her many years to prove to male jockeys and trainers, that she, a woman, would be a good jockey.

Her mother remembers Julie's riding a horse on her own at two. By the time she was in kindergarten, she could mount a horse by using a pulley device, and by age six, she rode several miles from her home on her own. Julie played games or went fishing with her brother when she wasn't on a horse. She didn't like or do well at school. What she did like was being outdoors, and she excelled at riding horses.

Julie's parents divorced when she was fifteen. It was a sad time for her, but since she chose to live with her mother, they became very close. Her mother encouraged her and went with her when she decided to move to a race track. Once there, Julie had to find her own job and to convince a trainer to let her become a jockey. That is the beginning of the story of her hard work to erase the word "female" from comments about her as a jockey. Her goal to this day is to be the "best jockey" of all jockeys – not just the best woman jockey! 3–4.

Target Activity: "Being Different"

Have a general discussion with the children about various activities, jobs, professions, or roles that once were thought to be for males or for females only. List their ideas on the board and ask them to identify what prevented a woman or a man from doing these jobs or activities in the past (or even today). Ask children to tell about people they know or know about who have nontraditional roles. Ask them to think about what made it possible for these individuals to go against tradition (hard work, support from a parent or other adult, determination, need, etc.).

Option: Ask the children to interview a parent, other adult, or friend about taking on roles or jobs that were nontraditional for a woman or man. Have them ask if it was hard "to be different," and what caused them to do it. Ask the children to take notes so they can report their findings to the class.

78. Greene, Carol. *Indira Nehru Gandhi: Ruler of India.* Chicago: Children's Press, 1985.

Indira Gandhi seemed destined to rule. Her parents were both activists working for the freedom of India. Indira wanted to work for India, too. She made pretend political speeches when she was just a little girl; when she was eleven, she started the "Monkey Brigade," a children's group, to run errands and help the grown-ups in the Congress party. After gaining a broad education in both India and England, Indira helped her father in his work for India. She married Feroze Gandhi, a good friend of the family, and both of them continued to work for India's freedom. After India became independent in 1947, Indira's father became its prime minister. Indira traveled all over the world with her father, learning much about politics. She became a member of the committee that ran the Congress party, and then its president. When her father died, a man named Lal Bahadur Shastri became the new prime minister. He gave Indira the job of minister of information and broadcasting. Soon after, he died, and Indira was elected the new prime minister. She was a strong leader—and one of the most powerful in the world. She helped solve India's economic problems, and formed the new country of Bangladesh. She fought many political battles. Most of all, through the respect she earned from other world leaders, she helped to make the rest of the world see that India was a great country. 3–4.

Target Activity: "Female World Leaders"

Ask the children if there has ever been a female president of the United States. Discuss reasons why this might be so. Brainstorm some qualities that children think would be necessary to be an effective president. Which, if any, of these qualities do they feel are exclusive to males? Females? Break children up into small research groups and allow them to do research on one of the following world leaders:

Margaret Thatcher	Eva Perón	Benazir Bhutto
Golda Meir	Violeta Chamarro	Corazon Aquino

Let each group make a report on their chosen leader and what each has contributed to the world.

79. Greene, Carol. *John Chapman: The Man Who Was Johnny Appleseed.* Ill. Steven Dobson. Chicago: Children's, 1991.

Johnny Appleseed is an historical recounting (with some disclaimers, e.g., "no one knows for sure," and "some say") with a setting in the wilderness of colonial America. It is the story of the pioneer John Chapman (1774–1847), and relates events from his childhood, through his experiences as "Johnny Appleseed" (given this name because he devoted his life to planting apple seeds), and on to his days as an elderly man. Pioneer, apple lover, missionary—all of these terms describe Chapman and his caring for others. Pair with Gertrude Norman's *Johnny Appleseed* (Putnam's Pub., 1960, 1–2) illustrated by James Carraway; Steven Kellogg's *Johnny Appleseed* (Morrow, 1988); Aliki's *The Story of Johnny Appleseed* (Prentice-Hall, 1978). 1–3.

Target Activity: "Appleseed Cared about Others"

Invite children to discuss Appleseed as he displays his sensitivity and caring for others. To give an image of Chapman, a teacher may read a description such as:

> Johnny Appleseed went to Ohio and wore old trousers, a
> coffee sack for a shirt, and a saucepan for a hat. He

carried a Bible and apple seeds. He was a friend to both
white settlers and to Indians, to animals and birds.

After the reading, the teacher invites the children to use the description
and to create their own original illustrations of this pioneer. After the illustrations are finished, discussed, and displayed, the teacher shows the children
the ways that Carraway and other artists have imagined Johnny Appleseed in
their books.

80. Lasker, David. *The Boy Who Loved Music.* Ill. Joe Lasker. New
     York: Viking, 1979.

In eighteenth-century Austria, in the summer palace of Prince Esterhazy,
Joseph Haydn, an Austrian composer, was the music director. Haydn loved
to put a little humor in his music. As an example, in the *Surprise Symphony*,
Haydn put in a loud chord in a slow quiet movement to "make the ladies
jump," and he solved the problem of the musicians' desired return to Vienna
with his ending of the *Farewell* symphony. The latter example was generated
when the Prince stayed at his summer palace far into the fall and did not seem
to be interested in returning to Vienna, where the musicians wanted to be.
Haydn, a great master of the symphony, composed the *Farewell* symphony
with a surprise ending, where Haydn showed that the musicians of the orchestra wanted a vacation. In the final movement, the musicians left the stage,
one by one, and blew out the candles on their music stands. Only two musicians were left, and Haydn had no orchestra to conduct. The music persuaded
the Prince to return to Vienna with his musicians and the court. 2–3.

Target Activity: "Haydn Expressed His Feelings to Others with Musical
Expressions"

With questions such as the ones that follow, the teacher can ask children
to reveal the extent of what they know about Haydn as an admirable
biographee—one who showed his sensitivity to others and demonstrated
several ways of expressing his feelings through music:

1. With children, discuss the phrase "sensitivity to others."
2. Discuss the children's perceptions about a male showing his sensitivity
   through music. After listening to a recording, ask children to suggest
   descriptive words to tell about what they hear in the music. The *Surprise Symphony?* The *Farewell Symphony?*
3. Elicit from children additional names of musicians who show "sensitivity to others."

81. Lee, Betsy. *Mother Teresa: Caring for God's Children.* Min-
     neapolis: Dillon Press, 1983.

This is the story of a Yugoslavian girl named Agnes Gonxha Bojaxhiu,
whom we now know as Mother Teresa. Agnes grew up in a very loving and

religious family. She was a happy child who enjoyed going to church and
school because she liked the stories she heard about Jesus. The priests told
her that Jesus loved little children, the sick, and the poor. She decided when
she was twelve to leave her family to become a nun. She went to India, a country with many poor people. This was a place where she thought she could show
God's love by loving others in need.

Once in India, she became a teacher, but after many years, she realized
that to serve the poor she would have to live with them and live like them.
She left the protection of the school and the church and has, since then,
served the needy, the sick, and the dying in the streets of Calcutta, India. For
many years, she has inspired people all over the world to serve poor and
desperate people. Mother Teresa has been honored with the highest award the
world can give its heroes for her selfless work with the most desperate of all
people. 2–3.

    Target Activity: "How Can I Help?"

After reading aloud about Mother Teresa, discuss how she helped other
people who were the most in need. Discuss how we can help others who are
smaller than we are, or those who seem to need a friend. Have the children
tell how they have tried to help someone in need. Have them tell how they have
been helped by a friend, a teacher, or a family member. Have them write/draw
a thank-you note for the help they have received and/or draw a picture of the
person whom they are thanking on the note. Ask them how thanking a person
who has been kind helps that person feel special. Discuss how helping people
and thanking people makes us all feel good because we know we are important
like Mother Teresa, who helps people feel important because they are not
forgotten.

82. Morse, Charles and Ann Morse. *Evonne Goolagong.* Ill. Harold
    Henrikson. Manketo: Amecus Street, 1974.

At nineteen, in 1971, Evonne Goolagong approached the center court at
Wimbledon in England. She looked happy and confident instead of frightened
as expected. In just over one hour this Aboriginal girl from a remote town in
Australia became the youngest tennis champion at Wimbledon since 1962.

As a young child Evonne learned about tennis, but she didn't learn about
her Aboriginal background. What she discovered later was that her ancestors
were the original people of Australia, and we have found out that they had a
history similar to the native Americans in the United States.

Evonne's parents and the president of a local tennis club noticed her interest and skill in tennis and encouraged her. They wondered if her interest
would continue; it did. She became known worldwide as the first Aboriginal
competitor from Australia at Wimbledon, for her athletic skills, and for the
grace she displayed against tough competition. 2–3.

Target Activity: "Our Own Special People"

Explain to the children that people are proud of women and men who come from their special group (racial, religious, ethnic, national) and have done something special. For example, Australians felt very proud of Evonne Goolagong's accomplishment. Women and Aboriginal people, groups who are not always noticed for the special things they do, were especially proud of her achievements. Ask the children to discuss people who have done something the children are especially proud of because the people are *women* and from *their special group.* Have children talk to their parents (or other adults in the home) about the women who are special to their group and why these women are considered special. Have them report back to the class.

83. Oliver, Rice D. *Lone Woman of Ghalas-hat.* Ill. Fullerton, Calif.: R. C. Law & Co., 1987.

This is the true story of an Indian woman from a tribe that lived on the island of San Nicolas off the coast of California. In 1835, this young Indian woman, from the tribe called Ghalas-hat, was moved with her people off their home island. As the boat left the island, she found that her baby was missing. She dove into the water and swam back to the island but discovered that the baby was dead. The woman, later called Juana Maria, lived alone on the island for eighteen years until she was discovered by a white man who had heard about her. This Native American woman faced difficult times alone, and the book tells us about her strength as a person, the values of her culture, and how she survived. 2–3.

Target Activity: "No Happy Ending"

Understanding the plight of Native Americans through the experience of this woman (and her story with no happy beginning or ending but with a view of our history) can help children understand that settling America was a costly affair—not only for the fighters who fought the wars—but also for families who lived here originally. Some topics for discussion:

1. Ask the children to explain why the tribe was moved.
2. Ask children what happened to the rest of the tribe as a result of this move.
3. Ask children to recount the ways this woman responded when her child was in danger and compare these ways to the responses of other mothers when their children are in danger.
4. Ask children to discuss ways Juana Maria was able to fend for herself because of her ingenuity during the long years on the island.
5. Ask children if women can be both strong and gentle and to give examples from Juana Maria's story.
6. Ask children in what ways they can compare the values Juana Maria's culture taught her with the way we are now developing a respect for nature.

Have children draw pictures of the various parts of the story by folding a paper in half and half again so that there are four places to draw events of the story. Have them write a title under each drawing.

Option: Older students, grade 4 and up, may want to compare Juana Maria's story with the story of Karana, the girl on the *Island of the Blue Dolphins,* a survival story by Scott O'Dell.

84. Powers, Mary Ellen. *Our Teacher's in a Wheelchair.* Ill. Niles, Il: Albert Whitman, 1986.

The subject of this biography is Brian Hanson. Hanson is partially paralyzed and uses a wheelchair as he teaches daycare classes. His story discusses the injury that caused the paralysis and his many accomplishments. Overcoming the problems of partial paralyzation, the preschool teacher perseveres as he teaches young children. K–3.

Target Activity: "Physically Challenged Men and Boys"

Engage children in discussing how the disabled display their creativity in coping with the challenges they face. They may take turns helping one another as they take turns being the one who "cannot get out of his/her chair" for a brief specified amount of time. The "helping" child is supportive and sharpens the pencil, picks up dropped items, gets paper and books, or assists in any way needed. Roles are reversed and the helper becomes the one sitting in the chair. Discuss: How did you feel as the helper? As the one in the chair? What can you do to help others who need assistance?

85. Roberts, Naurice. *Barbara Jordan: The Great Lady from Texas.* Chicago: Children's Press, 1984.

Barbara Jordan always wanted to be someone special, even as a little girl. She was the third and youngest daughter of parents who taught her and her sisters to behave in a way that they always would have self-respect and dignity. Barbara's father always said that if they worked hard, they could be anything that they wanted to be in life. Barbara worked hard at school, and even when she didn't get the A she wanted, she learned to work even harder.

Barbara's family was black and poor, living in the South at a time when life was not much fun for her people. Blacks were not allowed to go to the same schools as whites or eat in the same restaurants. Barbara knew that to get ahead in such a place, she would have to be well educated. When she was in high school, she decided to become a lawyer, like a black woman judge she had heard speak. She, too, wanted to help change laws that hurt her and other black people.

Barbara Jordan did become a lawyer. She also was elected as the first black state senator in Texas for almost one hundred years. She could now work to end segregation laws in the very place where they were made. 3 and up.

Target Activity: "Models to Follow"

After reading the book, discuss with children the person who inspired Barbara Jordan's decision to become a lawyer and why being a lawyer especially was important to her. Ask children to think about a person they know, have seen on television, or have read about (like Barbara Jordan) who would be a good model (and discuss this concept) for them for their adult life. Ask children to share their ideas and then each write an essay about a good model. For example, an essay may begin with, "I think of _____ as a good model for me. She/he is _____ (a lawyer, etc.). I think being a _____ (lawyer, etc.) is an important job because _____.

Option: Have each child describe why he/she thinks a particular person is a good model. Encourage other children to ask questions about this person to see if they can then guess who the model is.

86. Smith, Kathie Billingslea. *Harriet Tubman.* Ill. James Seward. New York: Messner, 1989.

Born in Dorchester County, Maryland, Harriet Tubman (1821–1913) did much to help her people. As a young girl she was a field worker and then escaped to the North. There, she decided to help others to escape from slavery. She took trips into slave territory and led more than 300 slaves to freedom, thus earning the name of "Moses." Illustrations are both in full color and black and white. During the War Between the States, Tubman was a cook, servant, spy, and scout for the Union Army. After the war, she supported schools for freed slaves in North Carolina. 2–3.

Target Activity: "Harriet Tubman: Social Activist of Her People"

Children may discuss the life of this determined and intelligent woman. Pair this story of Tubman's life as a read-aloud biography with *Runaway Slave* (Four Winds, 1968) by Ann McGovern, and discuss the ways the two authors create the excitement of Tubman's life drama.

For students' independent reading and study:

1. Read selections from books about the life of Harriet Tubman to discover: Since it was neither underground nor a railroad, find out the reasons the system for moving escaped slaves to Canada in the days before the War Between the States was called "the underground railroad." What was the meaning of "stations" in this system?

2. React to the selection in writing in a letter beginning with "Dear Harriet Tubman," in your student journal. Ask any questions you would like to ask her as well as telling your reaction to the brave deeds she performed. Include anything you think she might like to know about the way African American people are treated today.

87. Stevens, Bryna. *Deborah Sampson Goes to War.* Ill. Florence Hill. New York: Dell, 1991.

This is a biography of Deborah Sampson, who fought as a soldier in the American Revolution and suffered many illnesses and injuries. She disguised herself as a man, and no one learned of her female identity until near the end of the war.

Deborah Sampson wanted to fight for America's freedom during the American Revolution. She was strong and brave, but those traits did not count in 1781 because she was a woman. She also was taller than many men and could do the hard field work often thought of as men's work. She decided that if she dressed like a man she could join the army and fight in the war. Her secret was not an easy one to keep after she was wounded. 2–3.

Target Activity: "Keeping Secret"

After reading the story, discuss with children if they think Deborah Sampson did the right thing by pretending she was a man. Have them identify the difficulties she faced by having this secret. Ask the children if they have ever kept a secret. Ask them what their reasons were for keeping a secret. List on the board "Good Times for Secrets" and "Bad Times for Secrets." From the discussion, help children identify when keeping a secret may be dangerous because they need adult help and when it is a good idea because it will keep a good surprise. Ask children what problems they have had keeping secrets.

Option: "Deborah Disguises Herself and Fights"

Deborah had an individual personality and a different vision for her life during the war. With the children in grade three and up, the teacher encourages the girls and boys to imagine the conversation(s) that Deborah Sampson might have had with others during her enlistment as a soldier in the American Revolution. How would she keep her identity a secret? How would she talk? How would she walk? Imagine her dialogue with others as she talks about some of the major causes of the Revolutionary War and record them. Tell a partner Sampson's dialogue about:

1. The restrictive laws limited the freedom of the colonies, e.g., British soldiers were quartered in the colonists' private homes.
2. The colonists objected to paying for tax stamps and said, "Taxation without representation is tyranny."
3. Some restrictive navigation laws brought protest from merchants who wanted easier trade laws.
4. The ill-will and friction between British soldiers and colonists led to the Boston Massacre. In this event, boys pelted an English sentry with snowballs, which began the trouble; men and boys of the colony then threatened the British soldiers with clubs and stones. The British retaliated by firing on the crowd, killing 5 men and wounding 6 others.
5. Colonists dumped a shipload of tea into Boston harbor to fight against

the "Tea Act." This act let the British East India company sell its tea in America at prices so low that the local tea merchants could not compete.

6. The British attempt to seize the colonists' military stores at Concord led to the first battles at Lexington and Concord, and then to war.

88. Washington, Rosemary G. *Mary Lou Retton, Power Gymnast.* Ill. Minneapolis: Lerner, 1985.

Mary Lou Retton was only seven when she started gymnastic training. She was a child who liked to climb, jump, and run. Her parents thought that she could use her high energy to study ballet and acrobatics, which she did. Mary Lou discovered that she was very strong and could perform very difficult routines. She also discovered that she was better at acrobatics and gymnastics than ballet, because she was so powerful and muscular.

Mary Lou grew up to be a small adult like many of the top women gymnasts of the world. Her hard work as a child helped her to develop great skill by the time she was sixteen and competed in the Olympic games. This hard work paid off because she won a gold medal and was named the top woman athlete of 1984. 2–3.

Target Activity: "I'm in Training"

Have a discussion about how children can start training when they are little to have a special talent when they grow up. Write on the board what the children might want to know how to do when they grow older and the kind of training it takes. Have children write riddles to read to the class and allow others to guess for what they are training. Examples: "I swing my arms and run around (tennis, etc.)" or "My fingers are always moving (pianist, typist, etc.)." For a variation, have children act out the training instead of writing the riddle.

Literature
for Grades 4–8

Contemporary Realistic Fiction

89. Alcott, Louisa May. *Little Women.* Boston: Little, Brown, 1868.
A warm, loving, human family is shown. A daughter, Jo, is a courageous, warm and honest girl, who has a quick temper that sometimes gets her into difficulty. Jo leaves home to earn a living as a writer to help support her family. 3 and up.
Target Activity: "Honesty"
With questions such as the ones that follow, the teacher can ask students to reveal the extent of what they believe about the concept of "courageous," "warm," and "honest."

1. After listening to a selection from *Little Women,* how many different descriptive words can you use to describe Amy? Beth? Jo? and Meg?
2. Why do you think people could be impressed by Jo?
3. What do you believe are some of the main reasons that show Jo was courageous? warm? honest? Why do you think this way?

90. Bawden, Nina. *The Robbers.* New York: Lippincott, 1975.
New in London, nine-year-old Philip's life becomes difficult because the children at school tease him about his fine manners. His outlook changes when he makes friends with Darcy, whose crippled father is a canal worker. Darcy is an active female character. As a street child, Darcy lacks fine manners but is independent and competent in her unprotected world. In contrast to Darcy's life, Philip has a fine lifestyle in his grandmother's apartment. Darcy and Philip develop a friendship, and Philip matures with the realization that not everyone lives in a protected environment. 6 and up.
Target Activity: "Manners Are for Everyone"
Ask students why they think other children teased Philip, and discuss the meaning of "elegant" and his elegant manners. Have students close their eyes, and lead them through a visualization of a world where people have no manners: no one says "Please" or "thank you," but just grabs whatever he or she wants; no one says "excuse me" but just knocks each other down; no one is ever introduced to anyone or greeted by anyone. Ask students to enumerate some problems that would be caused by everyone's behaving like this. Ask the students if they think good manners are "masculine," "feminine," or "human." Invite students to answer this question in paragraph form giving reasons for their answers.

91. Beatty, Patricia. *Lupita Manana.* New York: Morrow, 1981.

Presented in this story is a moving and close-up view of the illegal immigrant situation in the United States, bringing to light what it must be like to be driven out or hunted like animals. When her father suddenly dies, thirteen-year-old Lupita emigrates from Mexico into the United States illegally. In slum alleyways, under the cover of night, in freight cars, and across the desert, gritty Lupita—dressed as a boy—learns the meaning of courage. The immigration police, who are forever on her trail, haunt her thoughts day and night. This book effectively portrays the plight of the illegal alien, but also describes in realistic detail the hope and heartbreak of poor families all over the United States. Moreover, the text is a poignant tribute to the courage and determination of young Lupita. 4–8.

Target Activity: "Lupita's Diary"

As this harrowing tale is told in the third person, children will gain a better appreciation into the main character's fears and exhilaration by trying to empathize with those feelings. Reread different excerpts from the text to children, such as the part where she is traveling by freight car, or when she is alone and very, very thirsty in the desert. Brainstorm some of the thoughts that might be going through her head at these times. Invite students to select three events that took place in Lupita's life and write diary entries as Lupita might have written them. Encourage them to select one of their entries to read to the rest of the class.

92. Burch, Robert. *Queenie Peavy.* Ill. Jerry Lazare. New York: Viking, 1966.

Queenie longs for the day when her father will be out of jail, and during the waiting time, she discovers his true nature. Queenie, very independent, throws rocks and spits tobacco but she also shows compassion for a classmate who faints from hunger. She learns that she doesn't have to fight the world because her father is in prison. She loses some of her antagonism, but she never loses the integrity of her own person. 5 and up.

Target Activity: "Discovering Someone's True Nature"

With questions such as the ones that follow, a teacher can ask children to discuss the extent of what they know about "discovering someone's true nature" and relate what they know to the book.

1. After listening to a selection from *Queenie Peavy,* how many different descriptive words can you use to tell about Queenie?

2. Why do you think Queenie was impressed by her father and longed for the day when he would return from jail?

3. What do you believe are some of the main reasons why Queenie's father was the way he was?

   4. If you were one of Queenie's friends, how would you show your sensitivity to Queenie?

93. Byars, Betsy. *Summer of the Swans.* Ill. Ted Conis. New York: Viking, 1970.

   As she moves into adolescence, Sara begins to see life as a series of "...huge and uneven steps." She finds her mood swings overwhelming, for example, and begins to worry about her physical appearance—namely that her feet appear to be too large for her body. In the middle of Sara's struggle with her own feelings of loneliness and awkwardness, Sara's brother Charlie, who is mentally retarded, becomes lost one night while leaving his home to visit some swans who have settled in a nearby pond. From the beginning of the summer when the story begins, to the end of the story at summer's end, the reader can follow Sara's growth of understanding of herself and her depth of caring for her brother. Charlie's disappearance allows Sara to come to terms with what is important in her life by facing the problem squarely, given her newfound confidence in her own abilities.

   At the beginning of the book, Sara is painfully self-absorbed. As she attempts to find Charlie she begins to have a more accepting attitude toward the things she cannot change, while beginning to appreciate the positive relationships in her life.

   The title about the swans has significance as it points to the positive vision of life that is woven throughout the book. The swans change their resting pond which attracts Charlie which leads Sara to search for him, and then to find herself in the process of looking for him. When she discovers Charlie, Sara knows that she has found more than a frightened lost brother, she has found herself and changed her self-concept from that of an ugly duckling—someone who is too tall, unattractive, and clumsy with her large feet—into one who feels more swanlike and content to be where she is instead of flying "away from everything, like the swans to a new lake." Like Andersen's story of *The Ugly Duckling,* Sara's self-concept is what changes—a change from believing she is a tall, clumsy person who is unattractive to that of a capable, self-assured young woman. 5–6.

   Target Activity: "A Week with Charlie"

   Summer of the Swans can be discussed for both content and writing style. This story of a mentally disabled brother offers possibilities for follow-up discussion: understanding of a handicapped youngster; grasp of attitudes toward this condition; examples of imagery can be reread; the development of plot and the growth of Sara's characterization are valuable elements to discuss; further, students may review the story to find evidence of the family interaction, some of the sensory experiences, to look for art ideas, to discuss different points of view, to talk about the characters' feelings, and to relate the story to personal feelings.

Option: "Help for Sara"

Discuss with students situations in which the idea of "We instead of Me" helped in resolving a problem. In her determination to find Charlie, Sara turns to Joe Melby, the boy she had despised the day before, to help her, and together they find Charlie. What is it that Sara discovers about Joe Melby that makes her realize that he is not just "a boy," but a caring person who is eager to offer help and friendship? Why do the students think Sara changed her feelings about Joe? Why do they think Joe changed his behavior? Would the boys in the class have offered to help Sara as Joe did? Why or why not? If the students had been there, what would or could they have done to help?

94. Capote, Truman. *A Christmas Memory.* Photographs by Beth Peck. New York: Knopf, 1989.

Set in rural Alabama in the early 1930s at Christmas time, in a parentless, poor home, seven-year-old Truman Capote and his friend, an eccentric elderly cousin, prepare several dozen fruitcakes and mail them to people they admire. They gather pecans from harvest leavings, buy illegal whiskey to soak the cakes, cut their own tree, and decorate it with homemade ornaments. 4 and up.

Target Activity: "Whom Do We Admire?"

Brainstorm a list of possible candidates—female and male—whom the students admire, encouraging equal representations along gender lines. Discuss:

1. Almost everyone has some kind of reputation, and it's possible that a person's reputation at home, at school, in the neighborhood, in gangs, or with friends may be different in each situation. What kinds of reputation do some of the people you admire have?
2. How does one get a reputation?
3. How does one change a reputation?
4. If you were to write a letter to someone you admire, what would you say? How would you tell them why you admired them?

95. Clymer, Eleanor. *Luke Was There.* Ill. Diane de Groat. New York: Holt, 1973.

Julius, a tough guy, cries when he returns to the children's home and finds a former social worker—his favorite—still there. Julius is an interesting hero portrayed in the different role of being sensitive enough to cry openly when he finds someone he cares about after a separation. He shows a positive personality characteristic with this sensitivity and the story deals thoughtfully with his problems.

Target Activity: "To Contrast Stereotyping"
1. To contrast the stereotyping that boys don't cry, as seen in certain regions of society, a teacher may invite the students to look for stories where boys show their sensitivity through their tears.
2. In this search, the following story, and other choices, may be located and discussed:
    a. *Mustard* (Macmillan, 1982), by Charlotte Graeber. Eight-year-old Alex and his parents grieve over the death of their beloved cat.
    b. Others:

96. Conrad, Pam. *My Daniel.* New York: Harper & Row, 1989.

Julia Creath Summerwaite (80 years old) flies to New York to visit her son's family and to take her grandchildren to the Natural History Museum. Verbal flashbacks from past to present link the story together. Summerwaite tells of her love for her older brother Daniel, his love for fossils, his search for a dinosaur, and the competitive nature of paleontologists searching for fossils in Nebraska. At the museum, the children learn of the harshness of pioneer life and the life of their Great-Uncle Daniel. Read this book aloud. 5 and up.

Target Activity: "Women, Girls, Men, and Boys – Dinosaur Hunters"
With the students, discuss some of these aspects related to the story:
Search for discoveries. Go on a newspaper search and begin to collect all the articles you can find about fossil discoveries in the United States – try to include women and girls as well as men and boys. Allow yourself several weeks and use as many different papers (magazines, reports on television) as you can find. After you have collected and mounted your fossil articles in a scrapbook, how will you respond to the following:
a. If you were to write a definition for the words *dinosaur hunter,* what would it be?
b. Find out all you can about one of our real-life dinosaur hunters and fossil-finders, and ask, "What has this scientist found? What have we learned from his/her findings?"

97. DeClements, Barthe. *Breaking Out.* New York: Delacorte, 1991.

Jerry is an active male character in high school who is sensitive to his long-time friend Grace as he helps her stand up for herself as she tries to adjust to junior high. She has frumpy clothes and doesn't stand up for herself when she is ridiculed. Jerry is competent, gets a part in a local commercial, and becomes a school celebrity. Both of the young people adjust as Jerry helps Grace develop her "spirit," and he undergoes a character change that involves coming to terms with his embarrassment of his father's being called a criminal and serving a prison term. 5–8.

Target Activity: "Sensitivity Workout: Three C's"

With students, a teacher may discuss the idea of a "sensitivity workout" before writing creatively about modifying gender roles and becoming aware of cross-sex sensitivity. A "sensitivity workout" consists of being aware of the three C's: concentration, content, and confidence about being sensitive toward others.

a. Related to concentration, writers are keen observers and they look for information, perceptions, and dreams of others. Students may discuss the information, characters' perceptions, and dreams they got from the story of Jerry and Grace.

b. Related to content, writers realize that their words must make "sense." Students may be encouraged to contribute the words from the story that make the most "sense" to them when one character was sensitive to the other.

c. Related to confidence, writers understand that they must believe that they can accomplish *something* before they can "bring it about" or make it happen. In a whole group, the students may tell their "best writing tip" to others (e.g., see things, hear things, feel things, connect with those feelings and communicate with others). After hearing one another's tips about writing, the students may discuss the idea of writing to show sensitivity to others. When students put sensitive words down on paper, they will be writing about showing sensitivity to others, but how *well* they write about being sensitive to others depends on how hard they work on the choice of words in their writing. As part of the hard work in choosing words, the students may talk about the power they have to "get rid of" the writing they have done and about their best friend being the trash can. If they are not happy with what they have written, they can discard it, and their confidence will increase by knowing they are in control of their writing.

98. Estes, Eleanor. *The Hundred Dresses.* Ill. Louis Slobodkin. Scarsdale, New York: Harcourt, Brace, 1944.

Mother Petronski learns that her daughter Wanda has told a classmate that she has one hundred dresses all lined up in her closet, even though she wears the same faded blue dress to school each day. This lie starts a daily teasing by the other girls. When the Petronskis move to the city, Wanda's father writes a note to her new teacher saying, "No more holler Polack. No more asky why funny name. Plenty of funny names in big city." Wanda leaves her old school before the winner of the drawing and coloring contest is named; Wanda is the winner with her one hundred dress designs, "all different and beautiful."

In this Newbery book, the reader feels compassion for Wanda, whom Peggy picks on each day, and for Maddie, who just stands by. Finally, Maddie realizes her conduct is as shameful as Peggy's even though Peggy has tormented Wanda more. Maddie decides she will never again stand by and say nothing when she sees another person mistreated. 4–6.

Target Activity: "Stand By and Say Something"

Invite the students to respond personally in writing to such questions as:

1. How would you have felt if you had been Wanda and been forced to wear the same dress/shirt day after day?
2. What would your reaction have been if you had moved to the big city?
3. Have you ever known anyone or read about anyone who was mistreated because that person seemed to be different from others around you? Has mistreatment happened to you? When did this happen? Who helped you when you needed help in this situation? How will you help someone—female or male—when you see this happening in the future?

99. Ferguson, Alane. *Cricket and the Crackerbox Kid.* New York: Bradbury, 1990.

Cricket is the lonely only child of yuppie parents who tries to stay on the fringes of a clique, realizing it is social suicide to be friends with the kids from a less affluent neighborhood. A new boy in class, a crackerbox kid, Dominic, is assigned to be her partner for a school project, and they become friends. They discover that family income is not a measure of friendship and happiness. Cricket rescues a new dog from the animal shelter and finds that it is Dominic's lost dog, Coty. Cricket refuses to give up the dog. The principal settles the argument by a trial: the owner of the dog will be decided by a jury of fifth graders from another class. When a verdict is reached in the trial, the winner does some problem-solving to decide which is more important—being legally or ethically right. 4–6.

Target Activity: "Partnerships"

Discuss with students the idea of forming a friendship partnership just as Dominic and Cricket did. Elicit examples from their experience and discuss the advantages of such partnerships.

100. Fox, Paula. *The Village by the Sea.* Ill. New York: Orchard Books/Watts, 1988.

While her seriously ill father undergoes heart surgery, young Emma is sent to live by the ocean with her erratic Aunt Bea. Her aunt does nothing to make Emma feel welcome or wanted, merely tolerating her presence. Surviving in this oppressive atmosphere becomes a challenge for Emma but is made easier with the help of a new friend, Bertie. Together the girls play on the beach and begin to create a village on the sand, using odds and ends they collect. One night, in a rage, Aunt Bea destroys the village. Emma is devastated by this irrational act. It is only later, after Emma reads what Aunt Bea has written in the girl's diary, that she begins to understand the woman's actions, and her hatred of her aunt dissolves.

In the beginning of the story Emma is clearly an unfortunate victim of circumstances. When she stops being angry and defensive and begins to understand her aunt's feelings, her compassion allows her to reach out and change the situation in a positive way. 4–8.

Target Activity: "Understanding Emma and the Other Characters"

Students will be placed in groups of six and assigned a particular character to study. Students will review the personality traits of their character and what is told of that character's life and try to understand the motives behind their character's behavior. Each group member will also write a question to ask of another book character (each group member will question a different character). When the groups are ready, students from different groups roleplaying the same character will sit at the front of the room *and* field questions from the rest of the class. This procedure is repeated until all character groups have been questioned. The teacher then leads a "debriefing" discussion to help children to see that understanding a person's behavior can help one to cope with it more effectively.

Option: "Emma's Family and Friends"

Invite students to consider that in all families each member has certain feelings, habits, and ways of living which the others need to understand and try to adjust to in life. Beside the name of a member of Emma's family and her friends, write some of the unique differences, and similarities, of each.

> Aunt Bea
> Uncle Crispin
> Emma herself
> Emma's new friend

101. George, Jean Craighead. *Julie of the Wolves.* Ill. New York: Harper & Row, 1972.

Thirteen-year-old Julie Miyax, an Eskimo girl, leaves her father-selected husband, Daniel, to cross the Tundra toward Point Hope, where she plans to leave for San Francisco to find a California pen pal, Amy. Lost, Julie survives because of her knowledge of Eskimo lore (setting her course by migrating birds and the North Star) and her friendship with Amaroq, the leader of a wolf pack.

This story shows the coming together of two cultures; Julie lives as the traditional Eskimo did, while her father, Kapugen, has abandoned his former way of life, married a white woman, a gussak, from the lower states, and hunts from a plane for sport rather than for food. 6–10.

Target Activity: "Survival Items"

Considering the way that students live today, they should have no use for many of the items that are listed below. The teacher asks the girls and boys to imagine that they are caught in a snowstorm in the tundra, lose their way, and feel lost and become "Marooned" on the ice and snow. There are no other human inhabitants—just Julie's Wolf Pack. Ask the students to participate in value ranking and to put the numbers 1, 2, 3, and so on in a priority order related to the items a student feels are necessary for him or her to survive in this situation.

Items for Survival

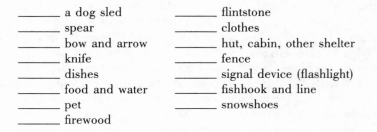

_____ a dog sled	_____ flintstone
_____ spear	_____ clothes
_____ bow and arrow	_____ hut, cabin, other shelter
_____ knife	_____ fence
_____ dishes	_____ signal device (flashlight)
_____ food and water	_____ fishhook and line
_____ pet	_____ snowshoes
_____ firewood	

102. Greene, Bette. *Philip Hall Likes Me, I Reckon Maybe . . .* Ill. Charles Lilly. New York: Dial, 1974.

Eleven-year-old Elizabeth "Beth" Lorraine Lambert is liked by Philip Hall, who is best in everything at school and who lives on the Hall dairy farm adjoining the Lambert poultry and pig farm in Arkansas. Because he likes her, he lets her do his chores every evening. Beth (with Philip's help) captures thieves, pickets the local store that sells poor merchandise, and wins the 4-H calf-raising contest. Recognizing Beth's accomplishments, Philip gets used to being second best and teams up with Elizabeth for a square-dancing contest. A member of a warm and loving black family, Beth has spirit and initiative. Humor is shown in her everyday activities. 4–6.

Target Activity: "I Reckon Maybe . . ."

With the students, the teacher discusses the ways Beth is capable, independent, and adventurous. After discussion, the teacher invites the students to start a list of names of friends and the ways they show their friendship just as Beth and Philip did. The list is titled, "I Reckon Maybe . . ."

"I Reckon Maybe..."

Likes Me (name)	Because (ways to show friendship)
1.	
2.	

103. Gripe, Maria. *Agnes Cecilia.* tr. from Swedish by Rika Lesser. New York: Harper, 1990.

Nora lives with her Aunt Karin, Uncle Andre, and cousin Dag, with constant feelings of abandonment and of being an outsider. When they move to an old home to restore it, Nora feels that a spirit from another time is trying to communicate with her. Other strange things happen. In a phone call by an old woman, she is told to go to an old doll shop in Stockholm, where she receives Agnes Cecilia, a lifelike doll. Through her friend's grandmother and great-grandmother, Nora learns about the house, a former ballet dancer, the name Agnes Cecilia, and other events that happened long ago. Doing this, Nora discovers her self and her place in the family. From her cousin, Dag, Nora learns that it is logical to presume that we have much more to understand in this world than has been proven.

In the old house, Nora's own heritage is told along with the unfolding of the mystery of the lifelike doll, whose features seem to change according to Nora's mood. The mystery includes strange events, such as Nora believing the old doll was coming to life and that she had feelings of "being there before." 6 and up.

Target Activity: "Stories from Old Family Treasures"

Ask children to talk about the objects found in Nora's room: ballet shoes, broken clock, dog's leash with the name *Hero,* and perfume. Invite deductions (such as Nora might have made) from the students: From these objects, what would their "hunches" (guesses) be about the owner? Which of these objects could only belong to a man? A woman? Which of the objects could belong to either a woman or a man?

Discuss with students the question, *What are some of the true stories about old family souvenirs* (dolls, heirlooms, mementos, pictures, toys, and other treasures) *once owned or used or played with by grandmothers or great-grandmothers?* Information can be recorded on tape or written in notes.

104. Hamilton, Virginia. *M. C. Higgins, the Great.* New York: Macmillan, 1974.

Living on Sarah Mountain near the Ohio River, M.C. sees an enormous spoil heap left by stripminers which is oozing slowly down the hill heading toward the house of his family. This place has been home to his family since 1854, when his great-grandmother Sarah, a runaway slave, found refuge on it. His father refuses to accept the danger of the landslide, and M.C. realizes he must save the family. To divert the slide, M.C. builds a wall of earth reinforced with branches, old automobile fenders, and a gravestone. Interactions with his family, the child of a family shunned by the neighbors, a strange girl, and James K. Lewis, who travels through the hills and records folksongs on his tape recorder, are shown.

In this Newbery book, M.C. overcomes great difficulties. M.C. has a warm relationship with his parents and with Luhretta. M.C. is great because of his physical prowess (he swims across the Ohio River) and because he knows the positive thing to do. He takes action to save his home from the advancing spoil heap, stops shunning a neighbor and openly acknowledges Ben Killburn (whose family members are called "witchies" because they have six fingers on each hand and six toes on each foot), and realizes that external differences are of no importance. Advanced 6 and up.

Target Activity: "I'm a Great One, Too"

With the girls and boys, discuss the meaning of the word "greatness" and its meaning in the story. Does greatness mean helping prevent a danger from occurring? Being physically strong? Knowing the right thing to do? Reaching out to make friends with those shunned by others? Realizing that what is inside is more important than what is outside? The teacher invites the students—girls and boys—to reflect upon the thought, "I'm a great one, too," and to record reasons privately in their journals as to why they should be considered great, just as M.C. Higgins was thought to be in the story.

105. Haven, Susan. *Is It Them or Is It Me?* New York: Putnam Group, 1990.

Resilient Molly copes with adolescence and forgives friends and enemies. There is some humor found in her first detention, her first kiss, her friendships. Molly's place in the crowd takes precedence over family and grades, and her wishes range from wanting a boyfriend or a new history teacher to wanting an invitation to join the staff of the school newspaper.

Persistent Molly copes with some problems that are typical in adolescence—being required to stay after school by a new history teacher, the dilemma of a first romance, and the yearning to work on the school's newspaper with friends. 5–8.

Target Activity: "Molly Has Wishes"

When the students have finished *Is It Them or Is It Me?*, they understand that Molly had wishes just as many other people do. Ask students to recall some of their wishes (Are any similar to Molly's?). Discuss Molly's wishes, write them, and then tell why they think it was or was not necessary for a particular wish to come true for Molly. Which of Molly's wishes would make her a better problem-solver?

106. Hobbie, W. D. *Bloodroot.* Ill. Holly Hobbie. New York: Crown, 1991.

Lizzie's favorite place in the whole world is a farm in New England named Bloodroot. She is excited to be spending another summer there with her Grama Ax. She and her grandmother are looking forward to spending this summer doing the things that they have enjoyed in the past—picking vegetables in the garden, biking down country roads, working on projects, taking long walks, looking for wild flowers and hummingbirds, swimming, and various other outdoor activities. They are stunned when their plans are upset because a developer is planning to buy a nearby farm and build condominiums on the land. Next, Lizzie's mother tries to get Grama Ax to leave her farm because she believes Grama Ax is too old for the hardships of New England farm life. But Lizzie and her grandmother are not folks who passively allow things to happen to them. Both are portrayed as independent and spirited females who are quite willing to fight for their beliefs. The stress of the summer's events brings the two even closer together. 5–8.

Target Activity: "Spirited Letter to the Editor"

Using a local newspaper, have students identify some civic problem that concerns them, e.g., pollution of a favorite stream or the removal of trees to build a highway. Brainstorm some alternative solutions to the problem. Have students write letters to the editor stating their opinion of the problem and offering their possible solutions.

107. Klass, Sheila Solomon. *Kool Ada.* New York: Scholastic, 1991.

With all of her family members dead, Ada is sent to live with Grandaunt Lottie in Chicago. Ada doesn't talk, can hardly read, but defends herself well in fistfights. On the inside, Ada respects her aunt and feels secure with her aunt's restraints and freedoms. She also enjoys the friendship of elderly Mr. McCoy, the apartment superintendent, who is a friendly mentor. Ada is an active female character who has positive psersonality characteristics as she comes to feel more and more secure living with her Grandaunt Lottie. She is independent, strong, and defends herself. In the story, Ms. Walker, beautiful and black, is the teacher of the class for the sixth grade problem girls into which Ada was assigned. Ms. Walker is sensitive to her and affirms Ada's capabilities and her willingness to avoid additional fights. 5–8.

Target Activity: "What a Sensitive Mentor Can Do for Me"

Discuss Ada, who is independent and strong and defends herself. Point out the friendships Ada developed with the apartment superintendent and the teacher. Elicit examples from the students' experience when they developed a friendship with another – female or male – who affirmed their capabilities as Ms. Walker and Mr. McCoy did for Ada.

108. Klein, Norma. *Mom, the Wolf Man and Me.* New York: Pantheon, 1972.

An eleven-year-old daughter, the narrator called "Scratcher," likes her unconventional Jewish life with her unmarried mother, Deborah Levine, and sometimes brags about her illegitimacy to see the reactions of others. Her best friend is Andrew, a boy (a rabbi's son) who never asks questions about her father. Mother, a professional photographer, has a nontraditional schedule, and takes her daughter on a march for women's rights and peace. They have an enjoyable relationship together, though some frank discussions lead to disagreement. Mother's boyfriend lives with them on weekends, and the daughter becomes worried about possible changes in their lives when Mother remarries. Scratcher is an active, interesting girl, involved in exciting daily doings. She has positive personality characteristics – intelligence, independence, warmth, bravery, inner strength, and competence. She is a positive female role, is ambitious, and takes pride in her achievements. Her story deals thoughtfully with the problems of her unconventional life. 6 and up.

Target Activity: "Exploring Nontraditional Roles of Characters"

With students, the teacher may explore the following:

1. After listening to an episode from *Mom, the Wolf Man and Me,* how many different describing words can you use to tell about *Father's Day at School* (chapter 1)? about watching the movie, *The Wizard of Oz,* with Mom, her mother's employer Wally, and the family (chapter 2)? about the humorous pretend-problem situations devised by her grandfather, dubbed "Mr. Jones" (chapter 3)?

2. Why do you think the daughter reacted the way she did to the argument between her mom and grandma (chapter 4)?

3. Why do you think the daughter decided to write a letter to her real father (chapter 5)?

4. Why do you think Scratcher thinks living with her Mom in an unconventional lifestyle is "nice" (chapter 6)?

5. How did Scratcher meet the Wolf Man (chapter 7)?

6. After discussing Andrew's surprise at hearing that his father would let Andrew come on the peace march in Washington, tell about a time when an adult you know did things the opposite of what you would expect (chapter 8).

7. Scratcher says that her friend Evelyn has a "lively imagination" (chapter 9). Tell others what having a "lively imagination" means to you.

8. After talking about Scratcher's habit of using funny names for some adult acquaintances, think of word associations that could create names for adults you know. For example, Scratcher realized that her Mom's boyfriend had an Irish wolfhound and was named Theodore, and so she called him the Wolf Man (chapter 10).

9. Scratcher's Grandma and Grandpa announce that they might have to move to Arizona to a climate better for Grandpa's health. Discuss ways Scratcher showed her sensitivity to her Grandpa and Scratcher's feelings about the possibility of her grandparents moving away. Then tell about a time when you learned that some of your relatives might have to move a distance away from you (chapter 13).

10. Scratcher's Mom gets into a "terrible mood," argues with her employer, Wally, and Grandma, and hardly talks with anyone. Talk with others about your idea of a "terrible mood" (chapter 14).

11. Scratcher's Mom announced that she and Theo were getting married, and Scratcher felt "horribly sick." She felt that things would change and be bad in her life — she would have a new father or a new baby brother or sister or have to move to a new place (chapter 15). After talking about Scratcher's feelings, discuss a time when things changed for the better in your life.

109. Konigsburg, Elaine. *From the Mixed-up Files of Mrs. Basil E. Frankweiler.* Ill. author. New York: Atheneum, 1967.

Eleven years old, fussy, and bossy, Claudia Kincaid runs away from her routines of home and school in Greenwich, Connecticut. With nine-year-old Jamie (her middle brother) Claudia hides out in the Metropolitan Museum of Art in New York. To help solve the problem of who sculpted Angel, the newest statue acquired by the museum, the two travel to see Mrs. Frankweiler, the former owner of Angel. In return for taping their adventure, Mrs. Frankweiler allows them to look through her mixed-up files to find the identity of the sculptor. Using the tape, Mrs. Frankweiler writes the narrative for the story and sends it along with a letter to her lawyer, Saxonberg, who is the children's grandfather. Searching Mrs. Frankweiler's mixed-up files, Claudia finds a secret that makes her different "on the inside where it counts" and returns home happy. This is humorous reading about ways the Museum is adapted for use by the two children who make it their home. 4–6.

Target Activity: "Secrets That Make You Different on the Inside Where It Counts"

With the students, the teacher discusses the idea of "secrets" and reasons why knowing certain secrets makes you feel different. Claudia, the main character, is discussed, along with the secret she finds in the files. The girls and boys are encouraged to think of "secrets" they would like to know about which are related to their lives and that would "count" (be meaningful) and make them feel happy on the inside. The teacher invites the students to write privately in their journals about these secrets.

110. L'Engle, Madeleine. *A Ring of Endless Light.* New York: Farrar, Straus & Giroux, 1980.

Sixteen-year-old Vicky and her family move to Seven Bay Island off the Coast of New England to live with her grandfather, who is dying of leukemia. At the Marine Biology Station on the island, Vicky helps a friend, Adam Eddington, with his summer dolphin project. Vicky finds she has a rapport with the dolphins and communicates with them telepathically. As her grandfather's health deteriorates, there is an emphasis on death and on accepting death as a friend to affirm the cyclic wholeness of life. To emphasize this wholeness, the words of Henry Vaughn, a 17th century English poet, are quoted by Grandfather: "I saw eternity the other night/ Like a great ring of pure and endless light."

Though emphasizing the naturalness (and beauty) of death, this is a story of pleasing family relationships that sustain the family in the difficult times. Vicky interacts with the dolphins, her parents, and her grandfather. At the station, the loving behavior of the dolphins helps Vicky keep her perspective on life. At home, Mrs. Austin sings to the family and accompanies herself on the guitar. She reads aloud from Shakespeare, and all spend time talking together in family conversations. At the hospital, Grandfather accepts death as a friend, and his words comfort the family members. 5-8.

Target Activity: "Careers in the Sciences"

Two strands of this story concern life-science–related issues: the dolphin project (marine biology) and the grandfather's deteriorating health (medicine and gerontology). To encourage interest in these areas that are too often more heavily dominated by males, have students sign up to do research about career opportunities in either field. If possible, invite a local marine biologist or health care practitioner to be a guest speaker for the class. Have children devise a list of questions for the guests concerning how they became interested in the careers.

111. Lowry, Lois. *Anastasia on Her Own.* Ill. Boston: Houghton Mifflin, 1985.

The Krupnik family is run like many of modern America's two career households, which means the traditional roles are blurred and older children are needed to keep things going. Anastasia does her part helping her frazzled mother and busy father. Things get a bit out of control when Mom has to be out of town, Anastasia gets distracted by her own new interest in dating, and Dad gets sick. This is a family of problem solvers.

Anastasia's mother is a book illustrator and, admittedly, not a good housekeeper. So Anastasia and her father make up the "Krupnik Family Nonsexist Housekeeping Schedule" to help organize the household. When Mr. Krupnik has to leave for a ten-day conference, Anastasia realizes just how difficult running a household really is. The results are hilarious. They also underscore many of the problems of the working woman who also tries to raise a family. As a refreshing change, Mrs. Krupnik makes no apologies for her housekeeping inefficiencies, and her daughter learns to appreciate her mother's complex dual role. Everyone participates in the jobs, and consequently they seem to like each other a lot! 5-8.

Target Activity: "Modern Families"

Have the students contrast how the Krupnik family lives with the ways of a traditional family. Write on the board these two family styles, and list under each how the needs of the family are met. Then ask them what kind of a family style they think they will need when they grow up. Have them write an essay on two families they see portrayed in programs on television. Are there style differences? Do the family members have realistic roles that fit modern life styles? Remind them to describe what the students do to contribute to the households. Have the class present and discuss their analysis.

Option: "Housekeeping Schedule"

After a general discussion of *Anastasia on Her Own*, ask children how the housekeeping chores are distributed in their families. Have children discuss on what basis job assignments were made. Do they think there are certain chores that are inappropriate for boys or men? Girls or women? Ask each child to devise their own personal "Family Nonsexist Housekeeping Schedule" that would make the assignment of chores, in their opinion, more gender equitable.

Option: "Research the Lives and Contributions of Women Illustrators"

With the whole group, a teacher may read excerpts from "People Behind the Books: Illustrators," by Masha Rudman in *Children's Literature: Resource for the Classroom* (C. Gordon, 1989), and show examples of the art work of several women who illustrate children's books and have been recognized for their work by winning the Caldecott Medal (or Honor award) for the best illustrated picture book in the year in which it was published. For examples, the work of Marcia Brown, Nancy Ekholm Burkert, Virginia Lee Burton, Barbara Cooney, Susan Jeffers, and Clare Turlay Newberry may be shown. Brown illustrated *Once a Mouse* (Atheneum, 1961) and *Shadow* (Scribner's, 1983). Burkert's work is found in Grimms' *Snow White and the Seven Dwarfs* (Farrar, 1972) and in Andersen's *The Nightingale* (Harper, 1968). Burton's work is seen in *The Little House* (Houghton Mifflin, 1974) and Cooney's work is found in *Island Boy* (Viking, 1988) and *Ox-Cart Man* (Viking, 1980), *Chanticleer and the Fox* (Crowell, 1958) and other titles. Jeffers has illustrated *Three Jovial Huntsmen* (Bradbury, 1973) and Newberry did the art work for *Marshmallow* (Harper, 1942) and *Widget* (Harper, 1958). Students may search for further information about a specific illustrator from *Something About the Illustrator* (Bowker) and other reference books.

112. Maclachlan, Patricia. *Arthur, For the Very First Time*. Ill. Lloyd Bloom. New York: Harper & Row, 1980.

This is a sensitive and humorous story of a boy's growing awareness. Arthur helps a large and beloved bear give birth to her litter in a rain storm and is assisted by a young friend, Moira, nicknamed "Mouse." 4–6.

Target Activity: "Becoming Aware"

Related to Arthur's feelings of love and sensitivity for the big bear, discuss with students different reasons they can think of to explain why people – both female and male – should help animals. Ideas for discussion: What do you think can happen rather suddenly that would make a person want to help a wild animal? An animal companion in the home?

To make a visual display of Arthur's feelings, students may draw a large "bear shape" on a sheet of art paper and write in the center the name Arthur. They should draw lines outward from the shape and at the end of each line draw smaller "bear shapes." Inside these, students may write these phrases or others they choose: "Arthur felt he loved the big bear when. . ."; "Mouse felt sensitive to the big bear when. . ."; "Arthur felt he was helped by his friend Moira when. . . ." Invite the students to discuss the headings with others in a talking circle group and to finish the sentences on their papers. Schedule time for the students to read what they wrote aloud to others.

113. Nelson, Theresa. *And One for All*. New York: Orchard Books, 1989.

Three friends in high school suffer tensions in their cross-sex friendship when Wing joins the Marines knowing he will be sent to Vietnam, when Sam gets deeply involved in the peace movement, and when Geraldine, Wing's sister, falls in love with Sam. When Wing is killed, Geraldine takes her anger to Sam and discovers that Sam's reason for protesting the war was to keep Wing from being killed. Geraldine portrays the theme of the story, which is about love and friendship and the effect of misunderstandings on friendships. 6 and up.

Target Activity: "Friendships"

After reading/listening to this friendship story, discuss the following:
1. Why do you think the friendship for these three might have been

harder to adjust to than it would be for other friends in their high school?

2. Certainly, Wing's joining the Marines was understood by others. But how could you explain the possibility that Sam's involvement in the peace movement helped Wing more than anyone else?

3. A lot of things "bugged" Geraldine. Tell why you think she was justified in thinking and feeling the way she did.

4. In what ways do you think Sam and Wing were alike?

5. As an activity to extend your reaction to the book, select one of the following to do:

a. Write Geraldine a letter and tell her what you think she should do now that she understands Sam's reason for joining the peace movement.

b. Wing's death changed the lives of Geraldine and Sam, and we can only guess at some of those changes by examining the things they probably had to learn as a result of the tragedy. Briefly describe some of the common everyday things (such as remembering birthdays and holiday celebrations) you believe might have changed after the news of Wing's death.

114. O'Dell, Scott. *Island of the Blue Dolphins.* Boston: Houghton Mifflin, 1960.

On the island of San Nicolas off the California coast near Los Angeles, twelve-year-old Karana survives alone for eighteen years (1835–1853) before a ship takes her to the California mainland. Karana and her six-year-old brother Ramo are left behind when their people are being removed by ship from their home island. Many of the men have been slain by Aleutian hunters. Ramo is soon killed by wild dogs, and the book tells Karana's story of survival, alone. Karana makes a fenced-in house and a cave dwelling. Karana's story is based on an actual incident. Karana's story is a survival story, a story of a human's need to love and be loved, a story of the importance of the way a human reacts to a disaster. Karana is an active and interesting female with positive personality characteristics. She is intelligent, independent, brave, strong, and competent. She portrays a positive female role, and her story deals thoughtfully with the problem of friendships with others.

With students, the teacher may discuss:

1. Karana observes nature with words such as "The sea . . . is a flat stone." What else does she refer to in nature through metaphors?

2. What is it like to be lonely? How do you describe Karana's need to love and be loved?

3. Discuss the episode on the island where Karana made the change from her present world "where everything lived only to be exploited, to a new and

more meaningful world." With students, a teacher may discuss ways Karana learned that humans could be islands secure unto themselves and yet part of humanity where all could "transgress our limits in reverence for all life."

4. After listening to an excerpt from Scott O'Dell's acceptance speech for the Newbery Medal for *Island of the Blue Dolphins* (Kingman, 1965), the students may discuss what they think he meant when he said that through the character of Karana he "wanted to say to children and to all those who will listen that we have a chance to come into a new relationship to the things around us."

5. Why do you agree or disagree that coming into a "new relationship" with the things around us would include the forgiveness of our enemies?

6. How is this "new relationship" shown when Karana saves the life of the dog that killed her brother? When Karana faces her enemy, the Aleut girl?

7. What do you think Scott O'Dell meant when he said "I believe that the hopes of civilization, unique and obscure as they are, really exist in the act of identification with our enemies."

115. Page, Valerie King. *Pi Gal*. Ill. Jacques Callaert. New York: Dodd, Mead & Co., 1970.

Prince Williams is a young boy growing up on Cat Island, an Outer Island in the Bahamas. Like many other children on the island, he longs for a chance to live a more exciting life in exotic places far beyond the island. While searching for his lost dog, he comes upon two divers who have come to the island to salvage a lost barge. Prince soon learns to dive, and the beautiful underwater life of the reef is revealed to him for the first time. After many frustrating attempts, Prince finds the barge they have been seeking, at the same time discovering he is a talented diver and deciding to pursue diving as a career. 5–6.

Target Activity: "Human Resources Book"

Invite students to consider the idea that their class is a bounty of human resources; there are many talents and abilities that each student has that perhaps the others do not know about. Explain that just as Prince Williams had to discover his talents, others must keep searching to find what makes them unique and special. Write on the writing board the following three sentence stems:

Once I couldn't *(ride my bike)*.

But today I can *(do wheelies)*.

Soon I may learn to *(win races like Greg LeMonde)*.

Fill in the lines as a group, allowing many students to contribute ideas for the blanks. Next, encourage students to write their own human resource poems, illustrating them if they so desire. Collect the poems and put them into a class Human Resources Book. Put the book on display so that all can see what their classmates can do and someday hope to do.

116. Paterson, Katherine. *Bridge to Terabithia.* Ill. Donna Diamond. New York: Harper & Row, 1977.

Jesse Aarons is a ten-year-old boy growing up in rural Virginia with what he describes as "a great piece missing" because of his fear of swinging across a high creek on a rope. He has formed an unlikely friendship with Leslie Burke, a little girl whose family has left the city for a better way of life. Leslie's life is filled with books and imagination, and together the two create Terabithia, their secret kingdom in the woods, where magical, beautiful things happen routinely through the forces of their imaginations.

Jesse admires Leslie because she not only has led him to this magical world, but she also seems to have no fears of anything. When Leslie is killed crossing the creek to Terabithia, Jesse uses all that Leslie has taught him to enable him to cope with the unexpected tragedy.

Jesse's friendship with Leslie and her family shows him a new, more positive way to live. With the death of Leslie, he brings his little sister into Terabithia, helping to assuage his pain, and he begins to share his new values with his family. 4 and up.

Target Activity: "My Special Kingdom"

Ask students to describe Terabithia, the world that Leslie and Jesse had created. Ask them if they have ever made up a fictional place. Who were its citizens and what were the rules? What was it like?

Have students form small groups and create a fantasy world, and have them assign themselves royal roles in their kingdoms. Ask them to make group decisions to do the following:

1. Who will be allowed to enter your kingdom?
2. What are the rules in your kingdom?
3. What other creatures live in your kingdom?
4. How do all the members of the kingdom get along?
5. What is magical and beautiful about your kingdom?

Students may want to draw a mural of their kingdoms. Additionally, encourage them to "discover" their kingdoms outside of school.

117. Paulsen, Gary. *The Cookcamp.* New York: Orchard Books/ Watts, 1991.

While his father is in the army in World War II and his mother is working, a five-year-old boy stays with his grandmother, who is a cook for a road-building crew in northern Minnesota. He enjoys his relationship with his grandmother and those small experiences, eating her apple pie and watching her use a thimble as she sews. The crew members take him out to work and let him ride in the big trucks. Still, he misses his mother and he is sent back to her.

Target Activity: "Homesickness"

Though every child has probably experienced a twinge of homesickness, boys often perceive that they should be able to "tough it out" and not feel such sentimental emotions. Ask the students to close their eyes and invite them to imagine a time that they were separated from their parents or guardians for any length of time. How did they feel? What exactly did they miss? How did they respond to their feelings? Have them open their eyes and write a letter to an imaginary ten-year-old boy who is away at camp, misses his mother, but feels it would not be appropriate for him to admit that he is homesick. Tell the students to encourage this ten-year-old to tell his mother how he feels.

Option: An awareness of self can emerge in spite of sex role stereotypes found in prose and poetry. Discuss incidents such as being told girls don't play baseball (because it is not ladylike) or being told that boys don't watch grandmothers sew or cook (because it is not considered manly by some). Personal experiences can be written to help each student clarify his or her feelings about an incident. The student should provide their own incidents to write about for this experience.

118. Peake, Katy. *The Indian Heart of Carrie Hodges.* Ill. Thomas B. Allen. New York: Viking Press, 1972.

Carrie Hodges is a serious and sensitive little girl who loves animals and nature. Growing up in the desert environment of Southern California, she has come to appreciate the flora and fauna around her. She is befriended by a desert-seasoned old recluse, Foster, who shares her love of nature and begins teaching her about the Indian ways and the magical relations that once existed between the Indians and the animals. Carrie is tormented when the ranchers in the valley decide to kill all the coyotes in the area because one coyote killed some sheep. She sets out on a mission to save the coyotes and learns about her own spirit at the same time.

Carrie's special relationship with Foster is highlighted in this book. Their common love of nature brings them close, and the old man teaches her all he can from his lifetime of solitary observation. 5–6.

Target Activity: "Animal Research"

Tell students that they are going to do a very peculiar kind of research. They are going to research animal "spirits" by finding out everything they can about five wild animals of their choice. Explain that they may use any resources aviailable to find out what these animals' "souls" are really like — zoologists, encyclopedias, Indian legends, video tapes, etc. When the five animals have been researched, ask students to write an essay describing which animal is closest to them in spirit and why, and how they think this is so. Finally, have pairs of students share which of the animals they feel the other child is most like and why before sharing their essay with a significant other. Provide an opportunity for students to tell about how their essay compared with their partner's feelings about which animal they are most like.

119. Pfeffer, Susan Beth. *Courage, Dana.* New York: Delacorte Press, 1983.

Dana is a self-effacing twelve-year-old who inadvertently becomes a local heroine when she rushes into traffic to save a little child's life. She becomes an instant celebrity but doubts that she is really a brave person. Her best friend, Sharon, devises a test for Dana to prove to herself that she is not a coward: an evening in a cemetery. Dana passes this test, but on the way home she observes a classmate writing graffiti on the school wall and writing someone else's initials. Dana confronts the boy, but he blackmails her by telling her that he will tell Dana's parents what *she* is doing if she tells on him. When Dana finally confesses to her parents and tells the principal who really wrote the graffiti, she realizes that it has taken more courage than anything she has ever done.

Dana learns that courage can involve choosing between right and wrong as well as being physically brave. She comes to terms with her own courageousness. 5–6.

Target Activity: "Confrontation Roleplay"

Point out to the students that the entire theme of the book might have changed if Dana had been successful in her confrontation with the boy who wrote the graffiti. Explain that confrontations about unpleasant subjects are usually difficult but that there are many in life, and our ability to handle them successfully depends on our tact, our honesty, and our ability not to back down in the face of unfair or untrue accusations. Have the students volunteer to be Dana and the graffii-writing boy replaying the scene where Dana catches him in the act of writing the graffiti. Ask the students to think of an alternative way for Dana to confront the boy so that he confesses to the principal himself. Instruct the rest of the class to watch what the two characters do and say and to be thinking of an alternative dialogue. Encourage other pairs of students to role play alternative outcomes. Discuss the relative merits of each.

120. Pitseolak, Peter. *Peter Pitseolak's Escape from Death.* Intr. and ed. by Dorothy Eber. New York: Delacorte Press/Seymour Lawrence, 1977.

On a walrus hunt in his canoe with his son, Peter Pitseolak, an Eskimo artist of Baffin Island finds himself stranded in a huge ice field that is moving swiftly out to sea. After two nights on the ice, a bluebird appears to Peter in a strange dream. The dream gives Peter courage and hope that they will find a path through the ice field and return to safety. The wind, that Peter had once feared, drives their canoe back toward Baffin Island. Peter notes in this retrospective story, "There is nothing in the world that is not good. I understood this then."

The story is told as a firsthand account by the author. He poignantly portrays his fear of never seeing his family again, which is contrasted with his renewed feeling of hope and optimism after the dream. 4–6.

Target Activity: "Obstacle or Challenge?"

A teacher may:

1. Write on the writing board the following sentence from *Peter Pitseolak's Escape from Death:* "There is nothing in the world that is not good." Ask students to share what they think Peter meant by this statement in the context of his harrowing experience.
2. Bring out the idea that some very difficult situations that we go through seem overwhelming and unfair at the time, but they often bring us new understandings about ourselves and the world, new friends, or in some other ways turn out to have been positive challenges.
3. Write on the writing board "Obstacle or Challenge?" and invite students to share some past event they have experienced that first seemed like an obstacle, but later, in retrospect, they can view as a challenge, because it turned out to have had positive benefits.
4. After all who wish to have shared orally, ask students to select one event to describe in essay format using the title, "Obstacle or Challenge?"

121. Radley, Gail. *The Golden Days.* New York: Macmillan, 1991.

Cory, an eleven-year-old foster home runaway, and elderly Carlotta, a nursing home runaway, are brought together by their needs for love, acceptance, and freedom, and start their "golden days of freedom." Carlotta, a former circus trouper, takes charge until she is hospitalized, and Cory takes over their responsibilities. Calling his social worker, Cory is reunited with his former foster parents, the Keppermans, who agree to share their home with Carlotta, too. 5–8.

Target Activity: "Exploring Feelings"

Invite students to engage in creative writing and explore the feelings about female and masculine stereotypes of strength and age. Students can take the part of Carlotta, the aging circus performer, and explore their feelings about female stereotypes of age and strength or take the part of young Cory and explore their feelings about being an 11-year-old and the strengths needed.

Option: Independent silent reading by an interested older student (grades 5–8) is a "golden silence" activity and gives times for the reader to reflect about this intergenerational story that focuses on the bravado, hesitancy, and near-misses of eleven-year-old Cory, a foster home runaway, and elderly Carlotta, a nursing home runaway, in their travels together, which they call their "golden days." After the silent reading:

1. The student may meet with the teacher for a literature response conference and come prepared to answer the basic questions of Who (were the main characters?), What (was the setting?), When and Where (did the story take place?), and Why (did the characters solve the problem(s) the way they did?).
2. Finally, ask the student to consider the unusual relationship between an elderly lady and a young boy: Upon what was their relationship based? What did Cory admire about Carlotta? What did Carlotta like about Cory?

122. Rogers, Jean. *Goodbye, My Island.* Ill. Rie Munoz. New York: Greenwillow Books, 1983.

Few selections in children's literature highlight young females who have as much knowledge and peace within themselves as young Esther Atoolik. This youngster tells the tale of her vibrant, harsh life on King's Island in the middle of the Bering Sea. This island is the Eskimos' winter home and is where Esther goes to school, fishes, and takes part in the wonderful traditions of the island. As more and more of the island people fail to return to the island in the winter, the Bureau of Indian Affairs decides to close down the cooperative store and the only school on the island. Esther realizes, with great sadness, that this will be her last year on her beloved island. The book portrays a positive view of the women on the island who are important in the decision making and who tend to be highly regarded. Another interesting character in the book is Dixon, one of the white "gussah" teacher's nephews, who comes from Wisconsin to stay on the island for a year. Excited by, but not judgmental of, the new culture, the boy asks many sensitive questions while participating fully in many new adventures. He befriends Esther, and at one point asks her, "Will you be going hunting with us?" to which Esther replies, "Women don't hunt." The question hangs in the air as both students silently try to determine why this is so. The story is a moving one of a young girl's love for a rugged existence. 4–6.

Target Activity: "A Visitor from Rigastan"

Discuss with students the meaning of "culture." Explain that there are many different cultures which all have good things to offer and much we can learn from. Relate Dixon's experience. Was he a good guest on King's Island? How did he make the people feel good about their life on King's Island? Have students select a partner and role play a visitor from the fictitious country of Rigastan coming to the United States. One child can play the visitor, who asks questions about life in the United States, while the other child plays him/herself. Tell the visitor to ask questions as if (s)he knows nothing about life here. Have visitors include such questions as, "What do children do for fun? Are there any games that boys can play but girls cannot? Why? Can girls grow up to be president in this country? Why or why not?" After the interviews, have the students discuss their answers and compare their perceptions.

123. Roy, Ron. *Where's Buddy?* Ill. Troy Howell. New York: Clarion Books, 1982.

Mike is supposed to take care of his little brother Buddy, who is a diabetic, but the child leaves Buddy with a friend so that he can go and play football, promising his little brother that he'll pick him up in time for lunch and his insulin shot. Mike comes back ten minutes late and Buddy is gone. A frantic search ensues to make sure Buddy gets his medication before it's too late. In the face of nearly debilitating fear and panic, Mike gets a grip on himself and begins rationally and logically to figure out where Buddy might be. Also, Mike shows remarkable courage when Buddy and his friend are found in a cave near the beach with the tide rapidly coming in. Mike and Buddy both learn important lessons about taking responsibility in this suspense story. 4–6.

Target Activity: "Supersleuth"

Put students in the class into pairs. Explain to them that they are going to have five minutes to decide what to do if they were faced with a big problem. Tell them the following scenario:

> Your parents are on vacation. They have left you in charge of picking up your younger sister (six years old) from the babysitter when you come home from school. You are late coming home because you were talking to your friends after school. When you get to the babysitter's, she tells you that Janey started to walk home, that you had said it was all right. You must find Janey right away! Panic sets in, but you fight it.

Give students three minutes to write down what they would do. Then allow them two minutes to share ideas with their partner. Finally, allow each pair to tell the class how they would solve the problem.

124. Rylant, Cynthia. *A Kindness.* New York: Orchard, 1988.

A fifteen-year-old boy explores his feelings when his single mother becomes pregnant and keeps the baby. When the baby arrives, the boy feels threatened because his relationship with his mother changes. The teenager is

an active interesting male character who matures and discovers a loving relationship with his new infant sister. He undergoes a character change from feeling threatened by a new sibling to coming to terms with his new feelings of
love toward the baby. This is a positive male role showing cross-sex sensitivity,
and the story deals with the universal problem of sibling rivalry. Advanced 6
and up.

Target Activity: "If It Weren't for You. . ."

Students who have siblings often have ambivalent feelings about these
siblings, and they need to know that these feelings are normal; students who
may *not* have siblings will also have ambivalent feelings about people they care
about—even their parents or teachers. After reading and discussing *A Kind-
ness* with students, read a book with a similar motif, *If It Weren't for You*, by
Charlotte Zolotow (Harper & Row, 1966). In this wistful story, a young boy
is reflecting upon all the things that would be possible if it weren't for his little
brother. "If it weren't for you, I'd be an only child and get all the presents,
I could have the whole last slice of cake and the biggest piece of candy in the
box." The boy does finally concede, however, that if it weren't for his younger
brother "I'd have to be all alone with the grown-ups." With the girls and boys
in the class, brainstorm names (general types) of some people about whom
they have mixed feelings. Discuss the observation that this is true in all relationships; people we love often also cause us problems. Start off with the
phrase, "If it weren't for you. . ." and allow the class to express some resent-
ments. For a final line encourage them to think of some positive elements that
different people add to their lives.

Option: "Sex Stereotyped Advertising"

Invite the girls and boys to collect sex stereotyped ads related to toys that
a sibling might like in newspapers and magazines. Discuss and analyze the ads
through such topics as "In what ways do the magazines and newspapers adver-
tise toys?" How do the ads show dolls? Toy cooking utensils? Housekeeping
toys? How do the ads show erector sets? Toy guns?

Invite interested students to carry the analysis of advertising further by
watching television or listening to the radio on a non–school day morning.
Students can record which products are advertised to which sex and report
back to the whole group.

125. Sachs, Marilyn. *Underdog.* Garden City, New York: Dutton, 1985.

Izzy's father has just died, and her mother died when she was four. No
one wants her. She is sent to live with an aunt and uncle who barely know her;
she is clearly an intrusion in their ultra-ordered lives. Izzy tries vainly to please,
hoping that her aunt and uncle will change their minds about sending her to
boarding school in the fall. While looking through old photos, Izzy discovers a

picture of herself, her mother, and the family dog, Gus, taken the day her mother died in a freak accident. Suddenly remembering how much she loved the dog, Izzy goes on an all-out search to find Gus, who has had a series of owners. She finally finds him and convinces her aunt and uncle to accept Gus – and her.

Most of this story concerns itself with a frustrating search for Gus. Many leads end up as blind alleys, yet Izzy continues until her goal is reached. 5–6.

Target Activity: "Izzy's Diary"

Diaries can be especially cathartic activities to students who are going through difficult and confusing times, as Izzy was. Discuss with students the fact that Izzy really had no one she could talk to about her father's death and her new living situation. Explain that sometimes writing is a good way to explore one's own confused feelings and that this would have helped Izzy. Read sections of *Diary of Anne Frank* to students to demonstrate how feelings can be written down and clarified, using a diary format. Ask students to write five diary entries that Izzy might have made. Using the writing board, brainstorm some especially low or confusing times when Izzy might have benefitted from writing down her thoughts, e.g., when her father died, when she went to live with her uncle, when she was frustrated in her attempts to find Gus, etc.

126. Singer, Marilyn. *It Can't Hurt Forever.* Ill. Leigh Grant. New York: Harper & Row, 1978.

Eleven-year-old Ellie Simon has a heart defect, and this book describes her experiences during twelve days of hospitalization for heart surgery. Ellie goes through the gamut of emotions about her impending operation – fear, mistrust of the doctors, anger – as well as caring relationships with Susan, a young nurse, and Sonia, a young patient who has already had heart surgery and who teaches Ellie all about hospital life. After the operation there is tremendous pain – more pain than Ellie had ever anticipated. But Ellie has made an important decision while being in the hospital. She has decided to become a surgeon like the one who so skillfully repaired her defective heart. In this story, Ellie struggles with overwhelming fear and helplessness during her hospitalization. She overcomes these feelings and grows as a person through the experience. 5–6.

Target Activity: "Letter to an Advice Column"

It Can't Hurt Forever tackles the natural fear a young girl has concerning her heart operation. Many fears, however, are irrational. Ask students to share some fears that they have that they would like to overcome. To open up this delicate subject, the teacher may first want to share her/his fears. Next, ask each student to pick a trusted friend for a partner. With a partner:

1.   Each student will write a "Dear Abby" letter to her/his partner describing a fear and asking advice on how to overcome it.

2. The two then switch letters and try to offer objective ideas on how to conquer the other's fear.

Because students often suffer from similar fears, yet believe they are unique in being afraid, they learn through this activity that everyone is afraid of something, and they begin to accept their own fears. Also, giving their partner advice helps them to realize they have in themselves the capacity to deal with their own fears.

127. Slepian, Jan. *Risk n' Roses.* New York: Philomel, 1990.

In her new neighborhood, Skip wants to be accepted into Jean Persico's gang. The girls have a secret club, and each must meet a challenge stated by Jean. Jean is a pest and torments old Mr. Kaminsky (who has befriended Skip's retarded sister, Angela), who has no use for the gang leader. Since she feels the rejection, Jean talks Angela into cutting the flowers from all of the old man's prize roses. Skip stops being mesmerized by Jean and decides to go her own way.

Through the pain of the problems, there is hope for Skip as a reader thinks about a strong willed peer (Jean Persico) who draws Skip and others to her (and uses them) and about Skip's hard working father, overprotective mother, and retarded sister. 5–7.

Target Activity: "Rewriting Skip's Story"

The teacher sets the stage for a discussion: Imagine that you have the opportunity to rewrite the story or parts of the story. Which parts would you rewrite? Which parts would you illustrate? How would you increase nonsexist parts in the story? The teacher allows time for rewriting and new illustrations.

128. Smith, Doris Buchanan. *Kick a Stone Home.* New York: Crowell, 1974.

Fifteen-year-old Sara, the unique heroine, is a good football player, and boys want her on their team. However, she does not date the team members, has few friends, and is still recovering from her parents' divorce of three years ago. She is unsure of everything except her vocation, which is to be a veterinarian. She comes to terms with herself and with her emotions as she faces the difficulties of early adolescence. Sara is an active interesting heroine involved in the different and exciting role of football player with a goal of being a vet. She has positive personality characteristics; she is quite sure of herself and her goal of becoming a vet. In this story she is ambitious and takes pride in her goal. The story deals thoughtfully with her problems and difficulty in her adolescent years.

Target Activity: "Sara's Goal"

1. After listening to an excerpt about Sara playing football, how many different describing words can you use to tell about what she did as a team member in *Kick a Stone Home?*
2. Why do you think some readers may be impressed by Sara's goal of wanting to be a veterinarian?
3. What do you believe are some of the main reasons why Sara had difficulty recovering from her parents' divorce of three years ago? Why do you suppose she seems unsure of everything except her career goal?

129. Snyder, Silpha Keatley. *Libby on Wednesday.* New York: Delacorte, 1990.

Educated at home, Libby goes to public middle school, where she feels she is intellectually superior to her classmates and they feel she is socially inferior to them. Libby, who takes refuge in writing, tells her story in journal entries and as a third-person narrative. Members learn of the serious problems of others in their writers' club during Wednesday meetings. Libby's portrayal is an honest characterization. 5–7.

Target Activity: "Who Acts in Emergency Situations"

Invite volunteers to contribute any emergency situations they know about from their lives or the lives of others. On the board, list some of the items which could be used to help students get out of the trouble or the emergency situation. To develop an awareness of one's self and potential in emergency situations, the students may identify those who help in emergencies, what they do, and whom the students see most often in the roles.

Ask students to picture themselves in such a situation. Discuss the items that could be useful in the emergency, and draw sketches to show how they would use some of the items to get out of the situation.

130. Stopl, Hans. *The Golden Bird.* Ill. Lidia Postma. New York: Dial, 1990.

Eleven-year-old Daniel is hospitalized with cancer. In a first person narrative, he sees three birds on the sill, one green, one blue, and one golden. The blue bird brings messages from the golden bird daily—messages that say, "Watch the tree outside your window. It may look dead to you, but if you look more closely, you'll see buds on it." Daniel discusses his death with his mother and the nurses and, lovingly and honestly, they help him face his death. Realistic scenes include the hospital, mother at the bedside, nurses caring for him, and visitors talking with Daniel. *The Golden Bird* provides a realistic yet reassuring approach for those who face the death of a terminally ill child.

Daniel comes to see death as a transformation similar to the reflowering of the cherry tree outside his window. Family love supports the story as reader sees the nature of death. 4 and up.

Target Activity: "Exploring Feelings About Crying When a Loved One Dies"

In small response groups, encourage students to consider: What did Daniel mean when he said death is a transformation similar to the reflowering of the cherry tree? Each group discusses sex stereotypes about showing feelings (it's O.K. for women and girls to cry and not O.K. for men and boys).

Creative writing will allow each student to explore feelings about being a boy and not being expected to cry or being a girl and being expected to cry.

131. Strachan, Ian. *The Flawed Glass.* Boston: Little, Brown, 1990.

On an island off Scotland, Shona MacLeod and her family face poachers and a conflict with the new American owners of the island. Shona, physically handicapped and unable to walk or talk, easily refers to herself as a piece of "flawed glass." Shona is mentally clear, but she cannot tell others her thoughts. She rescues Carl, the owner's son, from a potentially fatal accident, and they become friends. Sharing their new friendship, Carl teaches Shona to use his dad's computer, and Shona shows Carl the birds—in particular eagle hatchlings who, like Shona, also struggle for survival. Together they see other wonders of nature on the island. When Carl returns to the United States, Shona communicates with him through a computer and a modem.

Shona's struggles to walk and talk are contrasted with the ways those around her try to communicate with her. It is Carl and his knowledge of the computer that help her use her strengths. And it is Shona who sees and communicates the truth when the poachers try to incriminate her father for their deeds. 5–8.

Target Activity: "You Don't Have to Be Perfect to Be a Strong Friend"

In this poignant story, Shona and Carl are portrayed as two human beings who have particular strengths as well as weaknesses. Shona, though physically handicapped, is independent and strong and has much to offer Carl in a mutual friendship. On the board, make two columns, one entitled "Skills" and the other entitled "Personality Traits." Encourage the students to brainstorm the particular skills and personality traits that both children had that enabled them to develop a friendship. Ask each student to write a short paragraph entitled "You Don't Have to Be Perfect to Be a Friend," which will delineate their own abilities and personality traits that would make them attractive candidates for friendship.

Option: With the girls and boys, talk about the meaning of "friend" and "friendship." Explain that there are many different ways to be a friend, and review Shona's friendship with Carl in the story. How was Shona a good friend to Carl? And Carl to Shona? Invite the students to select partners and role play being friends. One student may be the "newcomer" (as Carl was to the island) and ask questions about the island while the other student stays in the role of student. Encourage the newcomer to ask questions that a newcomer might ask — about the island, what lives there, ways supplies are ordered — and so on. Encourage the newcomer to ask about girls and boys with questions such as "What do boys do on the island?" "What do girls do?"

Engage the students in making a list of activities (that both girls and boys can do) when they look at nature outside — island birds, the island, and its natural wonders, or look at learning inside — how to use the computer.

Learning Through Nature Outside   *Learning Through Computers Inside*
1.   1.

132. Vogel, Ilse-Margaret. *My Twin Sister Erika.* New York: Harper & Row, 1976.

This book, one of a series about a young German girl, Inge, and her twin sister, Erika, is a must — not only for twins, but for all young girls who must fight for their identities. Told through Inge's point of view, the story powerfully relays the sisters' struggle with friends and family, who constantly compare them or confuse them with each other. Inge shares her feelings about identical clothing, cherished items, and deep secrets. Just when they seem to be developing their separate identities, Erika dies. The death is handled in a sensitive, poignant way that allows the reader to experience vicariously Inge's feelings of loss and her courage in confronting her pain. Inge begins to discover a new place for herself and a new importance in her mother's life; the bond helps her to overcome her grief. 3–6.

Target Activity: "Older Siblings"

Ask students for a show of hands as to how many have older brothers or sisters. Ask these students to share if they have ever felt they were being compared with these older siblings. How does it make them feel? Ask students to divide a piece of paper into two columns, and at the top of one column, have them write "I am . . ." and at the top of the other column have them write "My sister/brother is. . ." Encourage them then to think of as many similarities and differences as they can between themselves and their siblings. Urge them to confine their list to personality traits and qualities, rather than physical features. Note: for those students who have no older siblings, have them choose a younger sibling, cousin, or friend of the family with whom they have been compared.

Folk Literature

133. "The Town Mouse and the Country Mouse." *Aesop's Fables.* Sel. and Ill. Heidi Holder. New York: Viking, 1981.

The Country Mouse invited his cousin, the Town Mouse, to dinner and gave him the best food. The Town Mouse disliked the food and said, "How can you stand such food? Why don't you go home with me?" When they arrived in the city, the Town Mouse gave him nuts, dates, cake, and fruit, but the Country Mouse saw a huge creature dash into the room with a terrible roar. He made up his mind to go home and said, "I'd rather have common food in safety than dates and nuts in the midst of danger."

Target Activity: "A Different Perspective of Gender Roles: Changing the Character's Gender"

With students, a teacher discusses the idea of substituting a female character for a male character in this fable (and others) and then asks the listeners to describe the effect on the story and on the listeners/readers. In a whole group, the students may discuss: What is the effect of the story/fable on an audience when they hear a version that has a gender change of the main character? After the discussion of some of the stories that follow, students may join with a partner and write their thoughts about the effect of the changes from their points of view:

1. The shepherd boy becomes a shepherdess in "The Shepherd's Boy and the Wolf," with the moral "Liars are not believed, even when they tell the truth."

2. The Mother Lark becomes Father Lark in "The Lark and Its Young," with the moral that "When people decide to do things for themselves instead of leaving such work to others, you may know they mean business."

3. The miller becomes the miller's wife in "The Miller, His Son, and the Ass," with the moral "When one tries to please everybody, she pleases none, not even herself."

4. Fables from *Gold's Gloom, Tales from the Panchatantra* (University of Chicago Press, 1925), edited by Arthur Ryder, can also be introduced in this manner: A female crow becomes a male in "The Crow and the Partridge," with the moral "Be yourself if you want to be your best."

5. Fables from *Eastern Stories and Legends* (Dutton, 1920) by Marie L. Shedlock may be selected: A man who enters a wheat field can be changed to a female character in "A Persian Fable: The Seeds and

the Wheat." Discuss the moral: "How should she who did not sow
have any right to the wheat that grew from it?"

6. Fables from *The Fables of La Fontaine* (Viking, 1954) by Marianne
Moore, translator, are a sou..ce for discussion: A dairy maid can be
changed to a dairyman in "The Dairy Maid and Her Pot," with the
moral: "Don't count your chickens before they are hatched."

134. Brett, Jan, reteller. *Beauty and the Beast.* Ill. New York:
Clarion, 1989.

Threatened by death by an angry beast, a merchant promises the beast
that one of his daughters will come willingly to save his life. Beauty comes to
the beast, refuses his offer of marriage, and dreams of a handsome prince who
says, "Do not trust too much to your eyes." Visiting her father and delaying
her return to the beast, she dreams of the beast dying and wishes herself back
at the beast's palace. She searches for him and finds him near death. Sprink-
ling water over his face, Beauty revives him and says, "Oh, Beast, how you
frightened me! I never knew how much I loved you until just now, when I
feared I was too late to save your life." Again he asks her to marry him, and
she says, "Yes, dear Beast." Suddenly in Beast's place stands her long-loved
prince of her dreams, and Beauty and the prince live happily ever after.

Target Activity: "Having a Gentle Nature"

Beauty is able to see the true nature of Beast—she knew he was really gentle in spite of his ferocious looks and his dreadful voice. Beast is gentle when
he says, "I cannot refuse you anything you ask, even though it should cost me
my life. But remember your promise and come back when the two months are
over, for if you do not come in good time you will find your faithful Beast
dead." She realizes the importance of keeping one's promise. 4 and up.

Target Activity: "Being Sensitive to Others"

To show that the characters were sensitive to one another, a teacher may
ask the students to identify excerpts about Beast and Beauty from different versions and compare the words from such titles as:

de Beaumont, Madame. *Beauty and the Beast.* Translated and ill. by Diane
Goode. Bradbury, 1978. 4–6.

Hutton, Warwick, reteller. *Beauty and the Beast.* Atheneum, 1985. 4–6.

Lang, Andrew. "Beauty and the Beast." *The Blue Fairy Book.* Longmans,
Green, 1948.

135. Colum, Padraic. "Mary Ellen Kate." *A Boy in Erin.* New York:
Dutton, 1929.

In this Irish folktale, suitable for telling before St. Patrick's Day, a just
reward for obedience is bestowed by the fairies. Mary Ellen Kate is told by a

fairy to hand shamrocks to a man in a coach on the bridge and say, "Daniel O'Connell, the fairy people of Ireland will not go against you." But Mary Ellen Kate has trouble finding the right road and the right bridge and is sixty years late to do the bidding.

Target Activity: "Helping Others Shows Sensitivity and Caring"

Since Mary Ellen Kate helped the fairies, she received a gift for her service and was told "the next time you're at the well in the pasture field, lift up the flagstone . . . and you'll find a little pan of gold."

With the students, a teacher may discuss that being sensitive and caring for others can be as valuable as a "pan of gold" and ask the students to mention characters in other tales who were sensitive and caring about others — female and male. As the students dictate their suggestions, a recorder/scribe may write the words on the board in a word map arrangement.

Folk Tales   **Contemporary Fiction**

_____   _____

**Sensitivity and Caring
Are as Valuable as
a Pan of Gold**

Biographies   **Fanciful Fiction**

_____   _____

Historical Fiction

_____

136. Goble, Paul, reteller. *Beyond the Ridge.* Ill. reteller. New York: Bradbury Press, 1989.

An old woman goes from her deathbed to the world beyond the ridge, pulls back to the world where her family mourns her, and then goes forward to where she is reunited with all of her loved ones who have gone before her. In the illustrations, some of the students may notice the contrast of the sorrow and pain of the grieving family and the joy of the elderly grandmother as she travels beyond the ridge. The story focuses on the Plains Indians' perception of passing from life to death — it is a change of worlds — that continues life's cycle. 4 and up.

Target Activity: "Beyond the Ridge"

With the students, the teacher discusses this selection of folk literature and the strength of the elderly grandmother. Read some of the Native American poetic chants and prayers in this living-dying story and locate words or phrases that point to the need for a person — female or male — to be strong.

137. Goble, Paul, reteller. *The Girl Who Loved Wild Horses.* Ill. reteller. New York: Bradbury Press, 1978.

A girl goes down to the river at sunrise to watch the wild horses, rests in the meadow, and then sleeps. A thunderstorm rumbles and the girl joins the horses, running away from a lightning flash and a gathering storm; she finally goes to live with them.

Once students understand that many Indian tales are handed down from a time when the distinctions between animals and humans were blurred, they should realize that in the early beginnings of these tales listeners accepted that animals and humans could understand one another or "speak the same language." Thus, there is no distinction between animals and humans interacting in some of the ancient Original Native American tales or in this one, a story of an Indian girl's attachment to horses. The girls and boys need to realize that certain features from the early beginnings of these tales still exist in the stories, e.g., that animals and humans still understand one another. Indeed, in this story, the animal character is very sensitive and caring toward a human character. 5–6.

Target Activity: "Animals and Humans Were as One People and Both Could Be Sensitive and Caring"

Before reading the story to the students or before their independent reading, the teacher should remind students that in many of the Indian tales the distinctions between animals and humans were not differentiated and that in some tales the animals and humans were as one people and could speak the same language and understand one another. Thus, it is no surprise when a human goes to live with or marries an animal in some of the ancient Indian tales. Remind the students of the Indians' belief in the beforetime, when the world was newly made by Old Man Above and when animals lived together as people. Discuss the point of view shown by this story and the ways it may differ in the points of view held by some children in the class.

Next, read another story to show that distinctions between animals and humans were not made in these early tales; read *Buffalo Woman* (Macmillan, 1984) by Paul Goble. In this tale, a young hunter marries a female buffalo in the form of a beautiful maiden. When his people reject her, he must pass several tests before he is allowed to join the Buffalo Nation so that he can be with her. Discuss the vocabulary of *buffalo, Calf-boy, Chief of the Buffalo Nation, tipi,* and *Straight-up-person.*

138. Grimm, Jakob and Wilhelm Grimm. "The Elves." *The Complete Brothers Grimm Fairy Tales.* Edited by Lily Owens. New York: Avenel, 1981. 5–6.

This is the familiar story of an old tale, also known as "The Elves and the Shoemaker." It is the tale of the little people who helped the shoemaker and his wife. The little people made shoes for the couple every night until the couple gave them a gift of beautiful clothes. Then the elves disappeared and were never seen again. Other versions include *The Elves and the Shoemaker* (Clarion, 1984), by Paul Galdone; *The Elves and the Shoemaker* (Four Winds, 1975), by Freya Littledale with illustrations by Brinton Turkle; "The Elves," in *Household Tales*, by Jakob and and Wilhelm Grimm, trans. Margaret Hunt (London: Bell & Son, 1884); and *Favorite Tales from Grimm* (Four Winds, 1982), retold and illustrated by Mercer Mayer.

Target Activity: "Theme of 'Good Elves Helping Good Humans' in Folk Tales"

With students, discuss a common folk, theme as one in which good extra-natural beings, without any reference to the sex of the good beings (elves, fairies, and so on), help good humans without asking for a reward and sometimes objecting to any kind of payment. With the students, role play an interview with an elf (female, male) from the story as a character from the past and then with a shoemaker (female, male) from contemporary times, a modern character. In the interview, the two characters may discuss:

> *concerns:* about keeping up one's skills, i.e., "every stitch was in the right place, just as if they had come from a master-workman (work person)."

> *dreams:* about financial security, i.e., the shoemaker was "soon in the way of making a good living and in the end became very well to do."

> *perceptions:* of way a gift will be received, i.e., "they took up the pretty garments and slipped them on, singing, 'What spruce and dandy boys (girls) are we/No longer cobblers we will be."

> *social issues:* giving something back to one who helps, i.e., "Those little men (women, people) have made us rich and we ought to show ourselves grateful." Discuss changing the term *boys* to *girls* and the term *men* to *women* and the effect of the change on the story.

Invite the students to trade roles and repeat the interview experience and then engage other students to participate.

139. Grimm, Jakob and Wilhelm Grimm. *Rapunzel: From the Brothers Grimm.* Retold by Barbara Rogasky. Ill. Trina Schart Hyman. New York: Holiday House, 1982.

Twelve-year-old Rapunzel is shut up in a high tower by a witch, Mother Gothel, in punishment for her father's theft of her rampion plants. Hearing Rapunzel's singing and overhearing Mother Gothel's command to "let down your hair," a prince sees a pair of golden yellow braids tumble down from a tiny window in the tower. The prince calls out the command, climbs the tresses, and steps through the window. The prince asks for her hand in marriage, and

Rapunzel asks for a skein of silk each day to make a ladder for her to descend. Mother Gothel discovers the prince, cuts off Rapunzel's hair, and confronts the prince. When the prince falls from the tower he is blinded by his fall into a thorny thicket. After a year, the prince finds Rapunzel, banished, and living in wretchedness with her baby twins, a boy and a girl. Not able to see, he is drawn toward her by her singing, and when she sees him she weeps with joy and embraces him. Her tears fall on his eyes and in a moment they are healed. The prince takes them away to his kingdom where they all live happily for many a long year. See also other versions, such as Wanda Gag's early translation of "Rapunzel" in *Household Tales* (Coward-McCann, 1936).

Target Activity: "The Untold Part of the Story"

With a group, discuss parts of the story that are untold about the strength and resourcefulness of the character, e.g., in what ways did Rapunzel have to be skilled to use a skein of silk each day to make a ladder for her to descend? In what ways did Rapunzel have to be strong to live in "wretchedness" during her banishment? In what ways did Rapunzel have to be strong to care for the children? Engage students in creating a word web around the words, "The Untold Part of the Story:"

"The Untold Part of the Story"

140. Hooks, William H. *The Ballad of Belle Dorcas.* Ill. Brian Pinkney. New York: Knopf, 1990.

This conjure tale of the Gullah people tells of brave Belle Dorcas, who is what was known as a "free issue" person, or the child of a slave master and a slave woman. Though free issue people generally married other free issue persons, in order to take advantage of the relative freedom of which they could partake, Belle Dorcas loved Joshua, a slave, and no one else would do. Pressured to marry one of the free issue young men, Belle goes on a hunger strike and lets her mother know that she would rather starve than marry someone other than Joshua. Her mother soon relents and allows Belle to marry Joshua, and they happily move to the slave quarters. When their old master dies, a new master takes over the plantation; he cares only for money and decides to sell his strongest slave, Joshua. Belle frantically runs to Granny Lizard, known for her magical spells, to get help for Joshua. Granny Lizard asks Belle, "Can you give up Joshua to keep him?" Without thinking, Belle answers "yes" to the strange question. She is given a "conger" bag to place around Joshua's neck. On the night before Joshua is to be sold, Belle secretly slips the conger bag around Joshua's neck, and he turns into a cedar tree. Belle flees back to Granny Lizard, who gives Belle yet another conger bag that changes the tree back into Joshua every night. The master searches for his slave, but to no avail. Belle Dorcas and Joshua spend every night together until they grow old and Belle dies. 4–6.

Target Activity: "Eliminate Granny Lizard"

Ask children to relate the events in *The Ballad of Belle Dorcas.* Discuss the magical powers of Granny Lizard and the conger bags. Can people really be changed into trees? Why were these people so drawn to the idea of magic? Ask children to suppose that the story of Belle Dorcas was true, but that there was no Granny Lizard around to cast spells. How might they keep Joshua from being sold? Encourage children to rewrite the story, this time eliminating Granny Lizard and describing how Belle Dorcas manages to remain with her husband using her own resourcefulness.

141. Huck, Charlotte. *Princess Furball.* Ill. Anita Lobel. New York: Greenwillow, 1989.

When a beautiful motherless princess grows up, her father, the king, promises to marry her to an ogre in return for a fortune. To avoid the detested idea of marrying the ogre, the princess asks for a dowry that no one can fulfill: a coat, made of the skins of a thousand different kinds of wild animals, and three dresses. One dress was to be as "golden as the sun," the second as "silvery as the moon," and the third as "glittering as the stars." Her father, however, brings her the dresses and coat, and the princess runs away. Wrapped in her fur coat to warm her in the snow, and carrying her three dresses, her mother's golden treasures (tiny spinning wheel, a ring), and seasoning for soup, she goes off into the forest and falls asleep in a hollow tree, where she is found by another king's hunters and their white dogs. Taken back to a castle, she works as a servant to the servants. When the new king gives three gala affairs, the princess wears her three dresses, and the new king falls in love with her and declares, "I cannot live without you." They are married and live happily ever after. 4–5.

Target Activity: "Ways Princess Furball Solves Some Problems"

With students in a discussion group, a teacher may invite the girls and boys to give examples of ways the princess solved some of her problems:

* Princess Furball solves the problem of an unwanted marriage by escaping from it;

* at the castle, she uses her mother's golden talisman and the seasoning for the soup to reveal her cleverness and, finally, her identity to the king.

Option: "Problem Solver"

After reading the story with the students, the teacher discusses the problems of the main character that are shown either in the print or the pictures. The students should be invited to think of their own words to describe the problems faced by the princess.

142. Jacobs, Joseph. "Molly Whuppie." *English Fairy Tales.* New York: Putnam, 1892.

Molly Whuppie is the youngest of three lassies and the most clever. She and her sisters are captured by giants. She switches the straw ropes from her and her sisters' necks and puts them around the giants' large necks. She takes their gold chains and puts them on herself and her sisters. When one giant destroys the others, Molly and her sisters run until they come to a great house, where the king asks her to return to get the giant's sword, the giant's purse, and the giant's ring. After her adventure, she marries the king's younger son and never sees the giant again.

Target Activity: "A Refrain of Defiance"

With the students, chant the refrains at appropriate parts of the story:

Giant's refrain: "Woe worth ye, Molly Whuppie! never ye come again."

Molly's defiant refrain: "Once yet (twice yet, never more), Carle, I'll come to Spain."

143. Jacobs, Joseph. "Tamlane." *More English Fairy Tales.* New York: Putnam, 1894.

Janet was the daughter of Dunbar and in love with Tamlane, son of Early Murray. Tamlane disappears and returns to tell her he was in Elfland; he is now a knight of the Queen of Elfland. Strong, brave Janet can save him. To save Tamlane, Janet must stand by Miles Cross with holy water in her hand and draw a circle around herself. When Tamlane rides by, Janet must spring upon him and hold onto him until he turns into a red hot iron. Janet then needs to put him into the pool and throw her green cloak over him, and then Tamlane will be free.

Target Activity: "Changes—Modifications in the Male Role"

With the children, discuss the main idea found often in folk tales, the idea of a journey-return pattern, and discuss this variation—the idea of a heroine who rescues a boy stolen away by a fairy queen. In this situation Janet, the girl, is the one who rescues the young man. She is faced with the changes—modifications in the male role—created in Tamlane by the spells of the Elfland creatures. Invite children to draw a version of events in this fairy tale, such as when Janet pulls Tamlane to the ground, when the elves try their spells on Tamlane, and when they first turn him into various objects. The students may consider drawing some of the following:

* frozen ice
* roaring fire
* an adder
* a dove
* a swan
* a red hot iron

Ask the students to recite together the words of the Queen of Elfland when she departs:

> She that has borrowed young Tamlane
> Has gotten a stately groom,
> She's taken away my bonniest knight,
> Left nothing in his room.

Invite interested students to look for other "journey-return" patterns with women and girls as the heroines and ask them to report their findings back to the whole group. When the reports are given, initiate a chart that represents the findings and discuss what can be learned from the chart:

Stories We Found

Journey-Return Patterns	**Heroines**

144. Kaye, M. M. *The Ordinary Princess.* Ill. New York: Doubleday, 1984.

In a wonderful twist on the usual fairy tale theme, Amy is a young princess who is given the bittersweet gift of "ordinariness" by her fairy godmother; that is, she is not a stereotypically beautiful princess, but is rather plain looking, with freckles, straight brown hair, and a decidedly clumsy demeanor. She is not interested in the array of princes whom she is supposed to marry, nor are they interested in her. Despondent, she finally runs away to get a job in the kitchen of a neighboring kingdom where she can be unnoticed. While Amy does not possess the usual traits one associates with a princess, she captivates the reader with her resourcefulness and plucky personality. 4–5.

Target Activity: "Fairy Tale Twist"

Ask children to explain how this fairy tale differs from traditional tales. Guide them to the realization that this major character not only looks differently, but acts differently than most female characters in a fairy tale. Have them consider the main female character in *Snow White and the Seven Dwarfs, Cinderella,* and *Sleeping Beauty.* Brainstorm, in two columns, what is similar

and dissimilar about these female characters, focusing on 1) physical characteristics and 2) personality. Invite children to select one of these fairy tales to
rewrite, with the main female character possessing physical and personality
traits similar to Amy's.

145. Lewis, Naomi, reteller. *Stories from the Arabian Nights*. Ill. Anton Pieck. New York: Henry Holt, 1987.

This is a long novel of tales, some with humor. It is Scheherazade's scheme
to keep her head on her shoulders and to please a mad king. At first her stories
focus on "rare and curious" objects (and the characters are objects, too) that
can be desired or destroyed. Later, some of the stories are about real devotion
and lasting love.

Whether with the help of magic or without it, the characters solve their
problems in the tales. Consider some of the characters: a flying ebony horse,
a tortoise who is a gourmet chef, a Magnetic Mountain that smashes ships, and
a Jinni who becomes a flea in order to wake a sleeping princess. 4 and up.

Target Activity: "Cinderella's Cousins"

The teacher discusses some of the versions of Cinderella to compare with
one story in this book. Some other versions are:

Cole, Babette. *Prince Cinders*. New York: Putnam, 1988. (male Cinderella)

Davenport Films, Rte. 1, Box 527, Delaplane, VA 22025. *Ashpet: An American Cinderella* (video), 1990.

Huck, Charlotte. *Princess Furball*. Ill. Anita Lobel. New York: Greenwillow, 1989.

Martin, Rafe. *The Rough-Faced Girl*. Ill. David Shannon. New York: Putnam, 1992 (Algonquin tale).

Ask students to specifically think about:

1. how the story changes with a male Cinderella (Prince Cinders).

2. how the story changes with a resourceful, competent Cinderella
(Scheherazade, Ashpet, Princess Furball).

3. how these characters compare with the original, passive Cinderella.

146. Penney, Grace Jackson. "How the Seven Brothers Saved Their Sister." *Tales of the Cheyenne*. Boston: Houghton Mifflin, 1954.

In this tale from the Cheyenne, the role of women is revealed as brothers
are changed into the seven stars, the pleiades. Double-Teethed Bull, strongest
of all the buffalo, took Red Leaf and ran away with her, and the brothers built
four strong corrals, to provide a safe place for their sister when they rescued
her. Moskois rescues Red Leaf, and when the buffalo charge the corral,

Red Leaf and her brothers climb a tall tree reaching into the sky. There they become seven stars with the girl as the head star, and the little one, off to one side by itself, little Moskois, who still keeps guard over her.

Target Activity: "Rewrite Scenes from Traditional Tales"

First, with the students, a teacher may assign parts in a reader's script and let the females read the male parts (and vice versa) in the tale. A reader's script can quickly emerge with the help of the students. In partners, students may rewrite some of the traditional scenes and reverse the male and female roles. If desired, pairs may act out or read aloud both dialogues. With the whole group, the partners should discuss the effects of the changes with members of the audience.

147. Rappaport, Doreen. *The Journey of Meng.* Ill. Yang Ming-Yi. New York: Dial, 1991.

Based on an ancient Chinese myth, this story tells of the superhuman efforts of a dutiful wife, Meng, to locate her husband, who has been forced to work on the building of the Great Wall of China. At first, her efforts are determined, but unrealistic and almost futile. When the crows teach her to fly, she can overcome the distance but not the fact that her beloved husband has already died. Determined to honor him, she bargains with the Emperor for a funeral ceremony and national mourning. He complies in order to have Meng for his own wife. When the ceremonies are completed, she spurns him and jumps into the sea. The story of this spunky woman is a lovely antidote to many of the traditional fairy tales, where the young woman always does exactly as she is told and accepts her lot in life without question. 3–4.

Target Activity: "Taking Control of One's Life"

After reading this folk tale, read the story of *Cinderella* to the children. Then place two column headings on the writing board, "Control" and "No Control." Have the children retell first the story of *The Journey of Meng* and then Cinderella, discussing whether each action shows that the female character has control over her own life or is merely controlled by the events, as Cinderella was. When children clearly see Meng as a strong character and Cinderella as more of a romantic "victim," ask them to tell which character they would rather be, and why.

148. SanSouci, Robert D. *Larger Than Life: The Adventures of American Legendary Heroes.* Ill. Andrew Glass. New York: Doubleday, 1991.

This beautifully illustrated collection of "larger than life" folk heroes contains four expected male heroes—John Henry, Old Stormalong, Strap Buckner

and Paul Bunyan—but it also contains the delightful Slue-Foot Sue, a big
brawny girl who "could do the work of ten men." She attracts Pecos Bill, who
falls in love with her and marries her. Bill is also impressed by the way Sue
can lasso a huge catfish and ride the fish bareback. After the two are married,
Bill reluctantly lets Sue ride his horse, Widow Maker. Widow Maker bucks Sue
into the sky so high "she had to duck to keep from hitting the moon." When
Bill rescues Sue, she is angry and feeling foolish, and then Sue leaves Bill.
When she hears how sad Bill is without her, she travels on a catfish and goes
looking for him. When Sue decides the West is getting too "tame" for her and
Bill, the two set off together to Australia, Argentina, and Africa in search of
more adventure. 4–6.

   Target Activity: "A Tall Tale"

   After reading "Slue-Foot Sue and Pecos Bill" to students, discuss the
features of the story that were "larger than life." Ask students to give some examples of exaggerations that they might use, e.g., "I'm so hungry I could eat
a horse" or "I caught a fish that was this big (show hands far apart)!" Also read
John Henry: The Steel-Driving Man and *Paul Bunyan and Babe the Blue Ox.*
List the facets that are larger than life in these stories. Tell children they are
going to write a tall tale about a modern-day girl who does courageous and
incredible things. Brainstorm what they think the girl looks like, her personality, and other attributes, as well as some possible feats she could perform.
After students have written their rough drafts, allow them to share them with
a peer editor-partner. After incorporating the editor's suggestions, invite
students to read their tall tales to the rest of the class.

   Option: "Reverse Tall Tale Roles"

   As students listen or read various tall tales, encourage them to discuss
what the actions in the tall tale would be like if the roles were reversed, e.g.,
the main character was a woman or girl rather than a man or boy, and vice
versa. Several versions of tall tales are available for this role reversal activity:

Reverse the Roles in Tall Tales

Role of Baseball Player
Fleet-Footed Florence (Doubleday, 1981), by Marilyn Sachs, has two sports
    rivals who marry and live happily ever after in a nonsexist baseball story
    infused with tall tale humor.
Role of a Farmer
Johnny Appleseed (Morrow, 1988), by Steven Kellogg, is a biographical retell-
    ing of this pioneer's contribution now considered a folk legend.
Role of a Cowpuncher
Bowleg Bill: Seagoing Cowpuncher (Prentice, 1957), by Harold W. Felton, is tall
    tale nonsense about a cowboy who solves his problems in a unique manner.

Pecos Bill (Whitman, 1937), by James C. Bowman, shows Pecos Bill as the tall tale hero of the Wild West.

Pecos Bill (Mulberry Bks., 1992), by Steven Kellogg, tells how Bill invented cattle drives, lassos, and rodeos.

Role of a Lumber Worker

Ol' Paul, the Mighty Logger (Holiday, 1949), by Glen Rounds, is told with earthy, exuberant zest.

Paul Bunyan (Morrow, 1984), by Steven Kellogg, offers many details in doublepage spreads.

Paul Bunyan (Harcourt, 1941), by Esther Shepard, is a substantive edition of these tales.

Role of a Riverboat Worker

Mike Fink (Little, 1957), by James C. Bowman, is a story of the legendary boatman and his adventures.

Mike Fink: A Tall Tale Retold (Morrow, 1992), by Steven Kellogg, tells the story of the King of the Keelboatmen; he floated cargo downriver to New Orleans, wrestled former king Jack Carpenter, and faced H.P. Blathersby and his powerful steamboat.

Role of a Railroad Worker

John Henry: An American Legend (Pantheon, 1965), by Ezra Jack Keats, retells this familiar tale.

Role of a Sailor

Tall Tales of Stormalong: Sailor of the Seven Seas (Prentice-Hall, 1968) by Harold W. Felton.

John Tabor's Ride (Atlantic, 1966), by Blair Lent, is a tall tale based on a New England legend about a shipwrecked sailor with exaggeration, fantastic situations, and salty marine terms.

John Tabor's Ride (Knopf, 1989), by Edward C. Day, is an account from an 1846 book of whaling adventures kept as a seaman's journal; it is Tabor's story as he told it to a young seaman. When Tabor was young and on his first whaling voyage, he complained about everything, wanted to go home, and annoyed his mates. One night, Tabor got the ride of his life on the back of a huge whale. They went down the Mississippi, through the oceans, and then back to the ship. Afterward, John was known to stare out at the ocean at night as if something fearful were out there.

Role of a Sign Painter

Mr. Yowder and the Train Robbers (Holiday, 1981), by Glen Rounds, is about the self-proclaimed "World's Bestest and Fastest Sign Painter" and his run-in with robbers and rattlers.

Role of a Steel Worker

"Joe Magarac" is found in *Heroes in American Folklore* (Messner, 1962), by Irwin Shapiro, along with stories about Casey Jones, John Henry, Steamboat Bill, and others.

Fanciful Fiction

149. L'Engle, Madeleine. *An Acceptable Time.* New York: Farrar, Straus, Giroux, 1989.

In this sequel to *A Wrinkle in Time,* Meg's teenage daughter, Polly, travels back in time three thousand years. In this prehistoric period, she finds herself in a peaceful land with a tranquil Indian tribe, the people of the wind. She fights a war, gains great wisdom, and faces a dilemma of staying in that time period or going back to her own troubles in her period in history. 6 and up.

Target Activity: "Polly's Dilemma"

With the girls and boys, a teacher may discuss Polly's role as a heroine in a science fiction setting:

1. *Consider Polly as a time traveler.* Polly traveled back in time to 3000 years ago. Draw a picture or a model of the first time she saw some of the people of the wind, a peaceful prehistoric tribe.

2. With students, a teacher may discuss, *Why do you think the author would choose unusual names for the Indian people in the story?* The students may tell what they think is added to Polly's story by the use of such names.

3. Polly stands out very distinctly in the story and her portrait can be "painted" with words instead of with a brush and paints. Students may develop a word painting for Polly to tell how she looked and dressed, her likes and dislikes, her habits and behaviors, the language she uses, and what others feel about her.

4. An interested student may write a brief dramatic script about an episode when the student thought Polly was the most interesting in her role as a positive female character. In the sketch the student may want to add information about people and events related to Polly, such as Polly's dilemma either to stay in the prehistoric time period or to return to her own troubled times.

5. As a review, a teacher may show the students some of the character elements for Polly on a character map on a writing board and show excerpts from the book. Invite students to fill in part of the map when a chapter is finished. As examples, students can include the problems, goals, attempts, and outcomes related to Polly during the visit with the peaceful Indian people.

dilemmas   **goals**

Polly

attempts to solve   **resolutions**

6. Students can create a slide show about Polly after the story is read aloud. Showing what life would be like for Polly if Polly decided to stay in the prehistoric period may be of particular interest to some students.

7. With students, a teacher may discuss Polly's time-travel adventure in this science fiction story and the built-in criticism of war involving the peaceful people of the wind. Older students may discuss any analogy in the practices of war by Nazi Germany with the war in the story.

8. Discuss Polly's individualism.

9. Discuss the power of Polly's love and the power of her love to change things.

150. L'Engle, Madeleine. *A Wrinkle in Time.* New York: Dell, 1976.

Meg (a high-school freshman) and her precocious five year old brother, Charles Murry, with their friend Calvin O'Keefe, embark on an interplanetary mission to rescue their father, Mr. Murry, a scientist who had been conducting his space/time experiments and who has been missing for over a year. During their travels they find that the entire universe is in a battle between God and the Black Thing, an annihilation force of the cosmos. Eventually, they are brought to Camazotz, a planet similar to Earth. It is dominated by the forces of the Black Thing, the evil in the cosmos. It is a planet of complete conformity. Those who deviate from the rigid behavioral standards are subject to the reprocessing. Camazotz is under the control of "It" a large brain which has a rigid and emotionless intelligence. The children struggle against It, they rescue Mr. Murry, and subsequently escape. Meg is an active interesting female character who has positive personality characteristics as she comes to the rescue of her father. She is independent, brave, strong, and competent. Calvin and Meg have a friendship as Meg matures and undergoes a character change that involves coming to terms with her weaknesses and making them her strengths. Calvin and Charles both portray positive male roles, and the story deals with the universal problem of good versus evil. 5–6.

Target Activity: "Female Role in Science Fiction"

With the students, a teacher may engage the girls and boys in one or more of the following:

1. *Consider Meg as an imaginative scientist.* Meg sent the discovery of a tesserect to the U.S. Patent Office in Washington, D.C. The tag she attached to the drawing was lost by the Postal Service. Draw a picture or a model of Meg's discovery, a tesserect, the instantaneous faster-than-the-speed-of-light method of space and time travel in the fifth dimension.

2. With students, a teacher may discuss, *Why do you think the author*

would choose unusual names for the time travel and the planet in the story? The students may tell what they think is added to Meg's story by the use of such names as:

"It"	tesserect	Camazotz
Black Thing	Cosmic force	reprocessing
annihilation		

3. Meg stands out very distinctly in the story, and her portrait can be "painted" with words instead of with a brush and paints. Students may develop a word painting for Meg to tell how she looked and dressed, her likes and dislikes, her habits and behaviors, the language she uses, and what others feel about her.

4. An interested student may write a brief dramatic script about an episode when the students thought Meg was the most interesting in her role as a positive female character. In the sketch the students may want to add information about people and events related to Meg, such as Meg's desire to find her missing father or ways she worked with Charles and Calvin.

5. As a review, a teacher may show the students the character elements for Meg on a character map on a writing board to show who the book is about. Invite students to fill in part of the map when a chapter is finished. As examples, students can include the problems, goals, attempts, and outcomes related to Meg during the rescue of Mr. Murry.

problems   **goals**

Meg Murry

attempts   **outcomes**

6. Students can create a slide show about Meg while the story is read aloud. Showing what life might be like if Meg and others were all required to act the same may be of particular interest to some students.

7. With students, a teacher may discuss Meg's fantastic adventures in this science fiction story, then the built-in criticism of a society that is an anti–Utopian society, and finally the evils of conformity and intelligence without patterns. Older students may discuss the analogy in the totalitarian practices of an earlier Nazi Germany with the story's society.

8. Discuss the idea of Meg's individualism versus rigid conformity.

9. Discuss the power of Meg's love and the power of emotion to change things and compare this power to an intelligence without emotions.

10. Discuss the messages that the story is sending to a reader, i.e., the aesthetics (the beauty of the language used and emotions expressed) and the effervescent (the literary elements).

151. Lindgren, Astrid. *Pippi Longstocking.* Ill. Louis Glanzman. New York: Viking, 1950.

Pippi is the strongest girl in the world and sleeps alone in a house all by herself. She can lift her horse onto the porch of the house. She sleeps on a bed with her feet where her head should be and decides to attend school because she doesn't want to miss the vacation days. 4–5.

Target Activity: "More About the Strongest Girl in the World"

With the students, a teacher may invite the girls and boys to arrange a display of other books about Pippi and give book talks about episodes.

Interested students can follow up with more reading in *Pippi in the South Seas* (Viking, 1959) and *Pippi on the Run* (Viking, 1971).

152. Lunn, Janet. *The Root Cellar.* New York: Scribner's, 1983.

Twelve-year-old Rose goes down into the root cellar on an old farm in Canada. When she leaves the root cellar, she finds herself in the setting of the 1860s, and the farm is prospering. The people of the time period are engrossed in the American Civil War. Rose travels to find a boy who has not returned from the war. 4–6.

Target Activity: "Female Characterization in Historical Fiction"

With students, a teacher may discuss the extent to which the students think the character is believable by using a sentence starter such as:

I think Rose is a believable character in this story because _____.

153. McCaffrey, Anne. *Dragonsong.* New York: Atheneum, 1976.

On Pern, the third planet of Rukbat (a golden star), a young girl fights for her dream to become a harpist. Because her father believes that such a desire is disgraceful for a female, he forbids her to play her music. Menolly runs away and makes friends with the dragons, who move by teleportation. She learns that she does not need to hide her skills or fear her desires. 5–6.

Target Activity: "Fear No One and Nothing"

With students reading/listening to excerpts from the sequel, *Dragonsinger* (Atheneum, 1977), a teacher may discuss the feelings of Menolly when she realized that she had no need to fear anyone or anything:

". . . no need to run or hide. She'd a place to fill and a craft that was unique to her" (p. 264). In addition, the students may talk of experiences from their lives or experiences of someone they know where a person had dreams and someone "was an obstacle" to the person's desires to follow that dream.

Interested students will want to know of the third book in the series, and read more about Menolly in *Dragonquest* (Atheneum, 1981).

154. O'Brien, Robert. *Mrs. Frisby and the Rats of NIMH.* Ill. Zena
Bernstein. New York: Atheneum, 1971.

In an experiment at the National Institute of Mental Health, some rats
receive steroid injections (which increase their intelligence and lifespan) to see
how this affects their ability to learn, and the rats escape from a laboratory.
They arrive at a farm outside of Washington, D.C., where Mrs. Frisby and her
children live. Mrs. Frisby, a widow, fears that her home in the garden will be
discovered when the farmer plows in the Spring. Her son, Timothy, is too ill
with pneumonia to move, and she seeks help. The owl sends Mrs. Frisby to
the rats who live under the rosebush with the words, "You must go, Mrs.
Frisby . . . to the rats under the rosebush. They are not, I think, like other
rats."

When Mrs. Frisby goes to the rats for help, she finds they are different
from others. She learns that the rats had known her late husband and that
they had escaped with him from a laboratory named NIMH. The rats can read,
use machines, and talk about establishing a self-supporting rat community.
They have been reading the books in the library of an empty house and prac-
ticing writing. They help Mrs. Frisby move her home, and she in turn helps
them: she warns them of government exterminators on their way to kill the rats
with poison gas. After being at the Institute and studying humans, the rats are
determined not to make the same mistakes that humans do, but they fall
into immoral behavior, too. The rats build their own community on the farm
(stealing electricity, food, and water) but finally leave to build a rat society in
a valley far away from civilization and humans. Almost all the rats escape to
the hidden valley where they intend to give up stealing and farm the land.
4–6.

Target Activity: "Modifying Gender Stereotypes of the Rats of NIMH"

With the students working together in pairs, ask the students to modify
the roles of the characters in the story. Is it a female or male role that
shows:

1. persistence in the face of failure
2. perseverance
3. problem-solving
4. feeling of autonomy
5. sense of humor
6. skills, abilities, hobby, or talent
7. courage
8. sense of control over life

155. Rodda, Emily. *The Pigs Are Flying.* Ill. Noela Young. New
York: Greenwillow, 1986.

Young Rachel has been ill with a cold and sore throat for several days; she is getting bored and tired of staying inside. She wishes something exciting would happen for a change. Suddenly it does. She finds herself riding on a unicorn into a land where it rains pigs and the intensity of a storm is measured in UEF's, or the unexpected event factor. Rachel is taken in by an elderly couple who tell her that she is what is known as an "outsider." They reassure her that she can find her way back to her own world if she wants to badly enough. She is told of another "outsider" who once worked in the town and eventually managed to go back to his home. Rachel talks to several people and follows the young man's path until she, too, finally figures out how to get back home. While Rachel is at times bewildered by the strange world in which she finds herself, she manages to fight back her tears and painstakingly figures out how to return to her family. 4–6.

Target Activity: "An Outsider Looking In"

Lead a general discussion of how it feels to be an outsider. Let students share their experiences in this regard. Give them the following scenario: "You are a group of ten-year-old girls who would like to get into a boys' basketball game during recess, but they don't want to let you in. You know you are as skilled as they are." Allow a small group of girls and a small group of boys to role play this scenario, instructing the girls to try to convince the boys to allow them to play. After the role play, invite the other students in the class to offer alternative suggestions as to how the girls could get into the game.

Option: "The Insider Goes Out"

Tell students to imagine they are going to the land Rachel visited, where pigs fly and where they will be "outsiders." Ask them to imagine that they meet one child their own age who asks to return with them. Have children write a short story about their adventures with this "insider" child, including the following details:

1. What will you tell the child about "our land"?
2. What about our land does the child find exciting? frightening? unusual?
3. Have the child experience a thunderstorm. What will the child think?
4. Tell how the child feels about being away from her/his family.
5. What special way must the child return to her/his world?

156. Van Allsburg, Chris. *The Polar Express.* Ill. author. Boston: Houghton Mifflin, 1985.

One Christmas Eve late at night, a boy boards a train, the Polar Express, that takes him to the North Pole. When he meets Santa, Santa offers the boy any gift he wants, and the boy asks for one bell from the harness of a reindeer. Santa gives him the bell, but on the train trip home, the bell is lost. On

Christmas morning, the boy unwraps a small gift and finds the bell inside. He shakes the bell and it makes a beautiful sound for him and his sister to hear. The boy's parents admire the bell but express their concern that the bell is "broken." It seems that only true believers can hear the sound of the bell. 4–6.

Target Activity: "Have the Bell Ring for You"

With the students, a teacher may discuss the thought: Think carefully about a belief you have that makes this "bell ring for you." What belief do you have that you want to write about in your journal?

157. Williams, Margery. *The Velveteen Rabbit.* Ill. William Nicholson. New York: Doubleday, 1970.

Becoming real, a stuffed rabbit toy realizes that this transformation happens when one is loved for a long time. The rabbit and the toy horse discuss their lives, and the rabbit asks the wise old Skin Horse what it means to be "real"; the Skin Horse tells him that "Real isn't how you are made. . . . It's a thing that happens to you. When a child loves you for a long, long time, not just to play with, but really loves you, then you become real." The horse goes on and tells the rabbit that other toys have become real when they become shabby (but this does not matter) because the toy is real to the child who loves the toy. Having been with his boy master in the nursery for a while, the rabbit is thrown out after the boy recovers from scarlet fever. With the help of a fairy, the toy becomes a real rabbit in reward for his service, faithfulness, and love. 4–6.

Target Activity: "The Rabbit's Feelings"

Have the students draw an outline of a rabbit in the center of a sheet of art paper and make thought bubbles radiating in lines away from the outline. Write, *The Velveteen Rabbit*, on the outline of the rabbit. On each of the radiating lines, the students will write a word to represent the feelings of the rabbit (sad, scared, brave, strong, loving). At the end of each line, the students will draw large dialogue (or word) bubbles and in them write the specific thoughts or quotes from the story that support or give evidence of the feelings the students selected. Divide the class into smaller groups and ask them to make the same kind of visual organizer for another character in the story. Regroup together as a large group and ask one volunteer from each small group to tell about their character to the whole group.

Historical Fiction

158. Avi. *The True Confession of Charlotte Doyle.* New York: Orchard Books, 1990.

Charlotte Doyle is a 13-year-old, 19th century young lady from an upper-class family, who finds herself alone on a ship crossing the Atlantic. Thus unfolds a gripping adventure story bordering on the edge of reality. Charlotte finds herself supporting the captain of the ship only to align herself later with the crew during a mutinous three-month crossing. The story beautifully underscores the young girl's remarkable courage and her unlikely friendships. Though the story generally is quite accurate in its portrayal of society in the early 19th century, Charlotte stands out as a very freethinking early "feminist." 4–6.

Target Activity: "Charlotte's Diary"

To fully resonate with the strong thinking of this unusual young lady, students can be asked to invent a diary that might have been kept by Charlotte as she went on her eventful voyage across the Atlantic. Ask them to try to show how Charlotte must have felt—scared, frustrated, triumphant, proud, etc.—as she faced some unusual hardships. This activity provides a special opportunity for boys in the class to project themselves into the mind of a most courageous young girl.

159. Bergman, Tamar. *The Boy from Over There.* Trans. from Hebrew by Hillel Halkin. Boston: Houghton Mifflin, 1988.

On a kibbutz in a children's house in 1947, several wait for their families. Rami's father returns with Avramik, the boy from over there, but Rina's father is never among the returnees. Other students misunderstand Avramik and make fun of him. When Avramik becomes a hero during the first Arab-Israeli war, the others begin to accept him. 4–6.

Target Activity: "Feelings of a Newcomer"

After this book is read, help the students develop a visual organizer with the title of the book in the middle of a page and then a space for the boy's feelings at the end of lines radiating outward from the title. In a circle at the end of each line, write a starter for the students to complete orally or in writing. Starters include: 1) When he returned with Rami's father, Avramik felt... 2) When the students misunderstood him, Avramik felt... 3) When the others made fun of him, Avramik felt... 4) When he became a hero, Avramik felt.... Discuss each particular feeling. Invite the students to make a four-page minibooklet (one sheet folded into quarters) called "Fellings," where the students write and draw about their feelings and give reasons why they felt that way at that particular time.

160. Blos, Joan. *A Gathering of Days: A New England Girl's Journal, 1830–1832.* New York: Charles Scribner's Sons, 1979.

Beginning her diary, thirteen-year-old Catherine Cabot Hall tells about things that touch her life. Since the death of her mother four years earlier, Catherine has been in charge of the household and of caring for her eight year old sister, Mattie, and her father. Catherine writes about the meals she cooks, her recipes, what she learns at school, what stories she hears from other family members, and what games they play. When her father marries a widow from Boston, Ann Higham, Catherine meets her new stepbrother. After reading news advocating the abolition of slavery, Catherine and her friend Cassie Shipman provide food and a quilt for a runaway slave. Her last entry is on March 8, 1832, when she leaves her farm in New Hampshire to help friends after the birth of their child. As a note of authenticity, two letters written by Catherine to her great-granddaughter (1899) are included.

Catherine's positive outlook on life is reflected in her recorded thoughts. Noting that the barn and house where Catherine lived have been restored and still stand, the author supports this positive vision and states that her intention was "to reconstruct life as it was when the house was new." 6 and up.

Target Activity: "Catherine's Daily Writing"

Encourage students to record events from their lives in a daily writing journal. Just as Catherine did, students may write about the meals they cook or eat, the recipes, what is learned at school, what stories are heard from other family members, and what games are played. Invite students also to share any hardships they have encountered and how they feel they adjusted to them. Do they, too, have a positive vision of life?

161. Blos, Joan W. *The Heroine of the Titanic.* Ill. Tennessee Dixon. New York: Morrow Junior Books, 1991.

Molly Tokin was a person ahead of her time. Born in 1867 in Hannibal, Missouri, she found the atmosphere too restrictive for her adventurous spirit. Leadville, Colorado, was more to her liking, and it was there that Molly became one of the most talked-about society women in all of nearby Denver. She got her initial fame singing in concert halls and then married a very wealthy man. Finally, she showed her true colors when, as a passenger on the doomed *Titanic*, she used her courage and resourcefulness to save her own life and that of the other passengers in her lifeboat. This story, a blend of fact and fiction, is illustrated with vibrant water colors that add to the impact and drama of the text. 4–6.

Target Activity: "An Interview with Molly"

Discuss with students the courageous way Molly solved the problems in her life, even when the solutions were very different from unsolicited advice she received. Ask students to pretend Molly were alive today; they could interview her about a world problem or a personal problem that they have. As a group, brainstorm one problem, such as air pollution, and ways Molly would respond to such a problem, using dialogue. Then allow students to select a problem to pose to Molly in an interview situation. Have the students write up the interview and share it with a friend or small group.

162. Brink, Carol Ryrie. *Caddie Woodlawn.* Ill. Trina Schart Hyman. New York: Macmillan, 1973.

Caddie Woodlawn is *not* your stereotypical prairie girl growing up in the 1860s. Caddie's adventurous and active qualities are to be admired by both girls and boys. Growing up in the early days in the Midwest, like Laura Ingalls Wilder, Caddie certainly livens up her family with her mischievous pranks, her daring visits to Native American camps and her fist fights in the one-room schoolhouse, but we also see her warm and humorous relationship with her delightfully three-dimensional family. The book also contains sensitive illustrations that older students will enjoy. 4–6.

Target Activity: "Comparing Caddie and Laura"

Students who have already read *Little House in the Big Woods* and *Little House on the Prairie* will find Caddie Woodlawn to be a very different female character than Laura Ingalls Wilder. Read or review one of these two books from the series so that students can compare the two characters, using a Venn diagram:

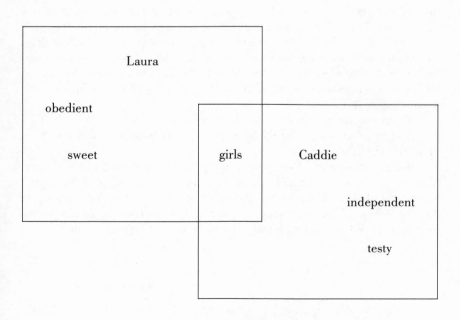

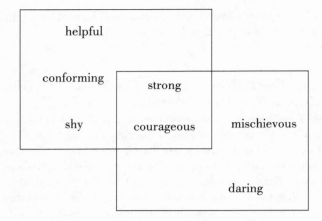

163. Coblentz, Catherine Gate. *The Blue Cat of Castle Town.* Ill.
Janice Holland. New York: Longmans, Green, 1949.

This legend is based on a true event in Castle Town, Vermont, where all
the craftsmen who sang their own song created beauty in their work and gained
contentment. Thomas Royal Dake, the carpenter, created a pulpit that was
known as the most beautiful in the state of Vermont. Another, a young girl
named Zeruah Guernsey, made a carpet so beautiful and unusual that it now
is displayed in the Metropolitan Museum of Art. Among the many designs in
the carpet is one blue cat. Others found contentment in their work, too: John
Gilroy, the weaver, made twin white linen tablecloths, and Ebenezer South-
mayd created his pewter work. According to this Vermont legend, the blue cat
of Castle Town enables the town to sing its own song of beauty in work and
contentment. 4–8.

Target Activity: "Beauty and Contentment in Work"

Appreciating beauty should be encouraged in both boys and girls as is
made clear in this legend.

Ask the students to discuss their interpretation of this trait of resiliency:
developing a hobby or talent. To them, what is the meaning of the legend
where the blue cat of Castle Town enables the town to sing its own song of
beauty in work? The students—boys and girls—can respond to a sentence
starter, e.g., What "singing a song of beauty in work" means to me:

_____ .

164. De Angeli, Marguerite. *The Door in the Wall.* New York:
Doubleday, 1949.

Robin, a young boy, is crippled by a strange disease, and he goes to live with some monks when the black plague hits London. With perseverance and the help of the monks, he learns to become independent, develops his abilities, and is able to save the town where his parents live. 4–6.

Target Activity: "Understanding Robin"

To identify with and understand Robin and his traits, present a character display to the students. To draw the character display on the board, draw a large circle and print the name *Robin* in the center. Draw lines outward from the circle and at the end of each line draw smaller circles. Write the words the students contribute in the small circles and add more as needed. Through discussion with the students, create the display with adjectives and descriptive words that the students have contributed. Then focus the discussion on the way the author has developed the character of Robin to show his perseverance. Reread the parts that show Robin's actions to help the listeners gain a better understanding of perseverance.

165. Felton, Harold W. *Mumbet.* Ill. Donn Albright. New York: Dodd, Mead & Co., 1970.

This is the true story of a courageous black woman in the late 1700s. As a slave, she had a comfortable life with the Ashley family. But because she valued freedom she approached a young lawyer, Theodore Sedgwick, and asked him to help her become free. In 1781, Elizabeth Freeman won her freedom in the courts of the state of Massachusetts. It was the first time anyone of her race had dared try to achieve freedom that way, but Elizabeth had been told that the constitution said that all were "born free and equal," and she knew that included her. After the successful trial, she joined the Sedgwick household, where her talents with the students and in the kitchen earned her the affectionate nickname, Mumbet. 4–6.

Target Activity: "Why I Should Be Free"

After reading *Mumbet* with the class, use the chalkboard or overhead projector to cluster the ideas students have about the word "freedom." Ask them if they are free to do anything they wish to. Ask them to select one thing that they would like to do that they are not allowed to do because they are too young, because their parents cannot afford it, etc. Have them select a partner to be their "lawyer." With their lawyer, have them build a case for why they should be allowed to do their selected activity. Allow each pair to "present their case" to the rest of the class, who will offer arguments against the present case.

Option: "Which Argument Is Stronger?"

A jury, consisting of nine class members, may decide whose arguments are stronger, while a judge, selected by the teacher, presides.

Option: "Exploring Cases"

With students, consider the following: 1) Give students reasonable cases in a set of 6 or so; 2) Explain the terms associated with the legal profession (for example client); 3) Emphasize the reasonableness of arguments; 4) Focus on order; 5) Consider 3 in a group roleplaying a client, a defense attorney, and a prosecuting attorney; 6) Use graphics on the board with the heading of argument and counter argument, and write down their arguments with students also recording the information; and 7) Exchange papers among groups and then ask groups to try to counter argue the arguments on paper.

166. Greenfield, Eloise and Lessie Jones Little. *Childtimes: A Three Generation Memoir.* New York: Crowell, 1979.

From the late 1800s to the 1940s, three generations of black Americans tell their early life experiences. Each of the book's three parts "catches up to the past," and each is focused on the "threads of strength" of one generation: a grandmother, mother, and daughter. Greenfield and Little's conclusion tells us of the "great sadness" and "great joy" in the lives of these women with these words: "It's been good, stopping for a while to catch up to the past. It has filled me with both great sadness and great joy. Sadness to look back on suffering, joy to feel the unbreakable threads of strength. Now, it's time for us to look forward again, to see where it is that we're going" (p. 175). 6–8.

Target Activity: "Stop and Tell Your Story: A Childtime Is a Mighty Thing"

Share with students the hope of the authors, Greenfield and Little, and their words about other students stopping and telling the story of their time and place. "Maybe years from now, our descendants will want to stop and tell the story of their time and their place in this procession of students. A childtime is a mighty thing" (p. 175).

Invite students to write about a time and place in their "childtime" and early life experience that they judge was a "mighty thing" (made an impression, changed their views, solved a problem, established an important friendship or relationship, created a better aspect of life) in their lives.

167. Hunt, Irene. *Up a Road Slowly.* Chicago: Follett, 1966.

After the death of her mother, ten-year-old Julie Trelling goes to live with her strict Aunt Cordelia, a teacher in a one-room country school. Years later, when her father remarries attractive Alicia, a high school teacher, Julie refuses to move into town with them and commutes to high school with a neighbor boy, Dan Trevort. Told in first person by Julie, the reader discovers that Julie matures through the ten-year period of the narrative, wants to be a writer, admires poems by Edna St. Vincent Millay and Sara Teasdale, has personal reactions and feelings about a classmate (mentally retarded Aggie Kilpin), and agrees to marry Dan Trevort after they both finish college. 5–8.

Target Activity: "What Poetry Do You Admire?"

Just as Julie wants to be a writer and admires poems written by Edna St. Vincent Millay and Sara Teasdale in this Newbery book, some of the students may want to be writers and will admire poets, too. Which poets/poetry do they admire? Engage students in making poetry books shaped like large pockets to relate to the phrase "put a poem in your pocket," and invite them to write the poems they admire on the pages. The left-hand page can be reserved for an illustration that relates to the poem, while the right-hand page has a written copy of the poem.

168. Hurwitz, Johanna. *Anne Frank: Life in Hiding.* Ill. Vera Rosenberry. Philadelphia: Jewish Publication Society, 1989.

Tells of her life before Anne goes into hiding as well as her days in hiding. With seven other people, Anne went into hiding for two years in a secret annex of an office building in Amsterdam; they were eventually found and imprisoned by the Nazis. The book ends with an explanation of her death, for none who lived in the annex survived the war except Anne's father. Appropriate for students who are not yet able to read Anne's diary found by her father on his return to their hidden annex after the war. Includes a time line, map, and list of related books. 6 and up.

Target Activity: "Remembering Anne Frank"

After the students listen to or read this book (less difficult than the diary), engage them in listening to another point of view, that of the Dutch woman who helped hide the Frank family. To supplement the Anne Frank story, read selections from Miep Gies' book *Anne Frank Remembered* (Simon and Schuster, 1987) to show life in Amsterdam during the Nazi occupation and to present more characterizations of strong people of the times. Advanced 6 and up.

169. Hurwitz, Johanna. *The Rabbi's Girls.* Ill. Pamela Johnson. New York: Morrow, 1982.

Carrie is one of six daughters of Rabbi Levin in a story that is a rich account of a stressful year in the life of the family, as told through Carrie's eyes. When her youngest sister is born, many of the women in the neighborhood worry that her father will be disappointed that this sixth child is not a son, but Carrie notices the Rabbi's huge smile when told he has another daughter and realizes he thinks girls are just as important as boys. She learns resilience from her father when the baby becomes gravely ill. "If God is good," Carrie asks him, "Why does he make bad things like sickness and people getting angry at one another?" Gently and wisely, her father explains that life is both bitter and good. In both happy and sad times, the Rabbi's wisdom and strength are shared with Carrie as she must face prejudice and hard times in the early years of the twentieth century. The story is important because it shows Carrie's courage, but also because it shows the sensitive and tender way the Rabbi raises his six daughters. 5–6.

Target Activity: "Daughters in Other Cultures"

Ask students why they think Carrie's neighbors thought the Rabbi would be disappointed with another daughter. Encourage them to share stories that they have heard in their own family about the birth of sons and daughters. Divide students into research groups. Have them select a country, such as China, India, or Saudi Arabia, and investigate how families in those countries feel about the birth of girl and boy babies. Have them hypothesize some reasons why boys may be favored over girls. Discuss whether the reasons were valid and if they think such preferences persist today.

170. Innocenti, Roberto. *Rose Blanche.* Mankato, Minn.: Creative Education, Inc., 1985.

Rose Blanche is probably one of the most poignant and courageous characters in historical fiction. An ordinary-looking young blonde German girl, she wants to know what is happening to the students who have been taken off the streets and transported away by soldiers. She follows the jeeps to a concentration camp outside of town and comes face-to-face with the reality of the Holocaust. Though so many ignored what was happening, Rose Blanche confiscated food from home and brought it to the camp, sneaking out of school early every day. The allied forces finally come into the town. There is much uproar and confusion. Rose Blanche heads for the concentration camp to see the students she has been feeding, and in the haze of the shadows and the fog, she is shot. 5–6.

Target Activity: "Heroines"

Write the words "heroine" and "hero" on the writing board. Ask students to define the words and then give examples of what one would have to do to be given this title. Use a word map to help the discussion:

What Is It?

A person who does
something brave

What Is It NOT Like?		*What Is It Like?*
cowardly		brave
afraid	hero	
selfish	heroine	courageous
		fearless

What Are Some Examples?

Rose Blanche	firefighters	Martin Luther King

Tell students you are going to play a game called "heroines." On 3"×5" cards, put the names of famous women who have done brave things and could be considered heroines, one per card. Tape one card to each child's back. By asking questions that could only be answered by "yes" or "no," have students try to determine the identity of the heroine on their card.

Some possible heroines include:

Elizabeth Kenny	Indira Gandi	Golda Meir
Sally Ride	Anne Frank	Harriet Tubman
Susan B. Anthony	Marie Curie	Barbara Jordan
Barbara Bush	Corazon Aquino	Margaret Thatcher
Mother Teresa	Eleanor Roosevelt	Other Heroines

Allow students to do research about the heroines with which they are unfamiliar.

171. Kherdian, David. *The Road from Home: The Story of an Armenian Girl.* New York: Morrow, 1979.

Veron Dumehjian, the author's mother, is the center of this life story told in first person. Author's note, a map showing Veron's travels, and two quotations open the book. In one opening quotation dated September 16, 1916, the reader finds that the Turkish government has decided to destroy, completely, all the Armenians living in Turkey: "An end must be put to their existence, however criminal the measures taken may be, and no regard must be paid to either age or sex nor to conscientious scruples." In a second quotation, the reader finds an order given by Hitler in 1939 which demands the extermination "without mercy or pity, men, women, and students belonging to the Polish-speaking race...."

While Veron's first seven years were happy ones, it was in the eighth year that there was an order for the deportation of Armenians living in Turkey

(1915). Within three days, Veron and her family (her parents, sister, brothers, grandfather, and uncles) left their home in western Turkey in a horse-drawn wagon. By 1919, Veron's family was dead, and she returned from her four year exile. During a Greek attack on Turkey, Veron was injured and hospitalized. Recovering, she traveled to visit her Aunt Lousapere in the city of Smyrna. In 1922, the Greeks evacuated the city, taking Armenians considered enemies of the Turks. In Greece, Veron lived with other Armenian refugees until the announcement of her engagement by her fiancee's family in 1924. She traveled with his family to America and married Melkon Kherdian. Hardships, sorrow, frightening experiences. 6 and up.

Target Activity: "Historical Interview"

The hardships experienced by Veron Dumehjian were horrendous, but by no means unique. Ask the students to interview a grandmother or other elderly person with whom they are acquainted who lived through an especially frightening political upheaval, such as the Nazi occupation in Europe or the intended eradication of the Armenians by the Turkish government. If the older person is willing, have the student tape record answers to such questions as "What are the most frightening times you remember? What are some happy memories you have of this time? How did you manage to keep a positive attitude in spite of the sorrow you experienced?" After the students have presented the information gleaned from their interviews, hold a general discussion comparing (and contrasting) the lives of the interviewees with Veron Dumehjian.

172. Laurgaard, Rachel K. *Patty Reed's Doll: The Story of the Donner Party.* Ill. Elizabeth Michaels. Provo, UT: McCurdy Historical Doll Museum, 1981.

Here is a tale that has been skillfully pieced together from journals, letters, and reminiscences of the survivors of the Donner Party, and it portrays a realistic picture of the experience of the pioneer children. One such child, Patty Reed, was noted for her dignity and maturity in the face of the extreme hardships of the westward journey. The tale is told through the eyes of "Dolly," the wooden doll that Patty Reed took all the way from Springfield, Illinois, to Sutter's Fort. Dolly is privy to the nights around the campfire, the ceremonies of the Native American tribes, the trek across the lonely desert, and the last bitterly cold, hungry days in the Sierra Nevada Mountains.

Besides documenting the astounding bravery and courage of Patty Reed, the book also shows the strength of the pioneer women, who, while hungry, cold, and concerned for the safety of their husbands, were unselfishly meeting the needs of their children: "Mother, my eyes burn so," Patty said while walking across the salt desert. "I know, darling. Close them and take my hand," responds her mother, in typical fashion.

All students will gain new respect for the contributions of the women and girls who were also the brave pioneers of the West. 4–6.

Target Activity: "Oregon Trail"

After showing students the path of the Donner Party from Missouri to California on the map, ask the students to recount some of the obstacles that pioneer men and women had to face on their journey. Have students simulate the Donner Party's ordeal using the computer simulation "Oregon Trail" (MECC). This graphic and highly motivating simulation has students face such hardships as hunger, broken wagon wheels, snake bites, frostbite, and typhus, to name a few. Students must also make decisions about food rationing, stopping to rest, buying supplies, and what route to follow. When all have experienced the simulation, have them write a log of their journey through the eyes of a dog, a doll, or some favorite toy.

173. Lowry, Lois. *Number the Stars.* Boston: Houghton Mifflin, 1989.

By 1943, 10-year-old Annemarie Johansen was accustomed to the Nazi soldiers who had been on every corner of Copenhagen for three years as she walked to school with her little sister and her best friend, Ellen Rosen. Like the lack of meat and butter, the soldiers were a nuisance of the war. That all changed, however, when Annemarie's Lutheran family learned the Nazis were about to relocate Denmark's 7,000 Jews, including the Rosens, who lived in the same apartment building. Annemarie discovers what courage is and that she has it. One night Ellen comes to live with her as a sister, and the older Rosens are hidden by the Resistance. Late that night, Nazi soldiers awaken them and demand to know where the Rosens are. Before the girls get out of bed, Annemarie breaks Ellen's gold chain and hides her Star of David. After searching the apartment, the Nazis ask why one daughter has dark hair. Quickly the father goes to the family picture album and rips out three baby pictures, carefully obscuring the dates of birth. Annemarie's older sister, who is dead, was born with dark hair. With this invasion into their home, the girls realize the Nazis are no longer just a nuisance.

The next morning, Annemarie's mother takes the three girls on the train to her brother's house at the sea. Uncle Henrik, a bachelor fisherman, is a member of the Resistance. After a carefree day at the beach, a hearse arrives with a casket, and strangers come to mourn a dead great-aunt. Annemarie suspects there was no such aunt and questions her uncle privately in the barn.

That night, the Nazis show up and demand they open the casket. Annemarie's mother quickly agrees, saying she had wanted to see her aunt one last time, but the doctor told her to leave it shut because of the typhus germs. The Nazis leave. That night, the Resistance slips the mourners out to Sweden. 4–6.

Target Activity: "Bravery in Face of War"

Point out to students that the destructive force of war has been with humans in all time periods and that humans have persevered. To emphasize this idea with books showing similar situations but in different time periods, a teacher takes students back in time to discover the destructive force of war and its effect on people from other time periods. To balance this negative force, call attention to the heroes and heroines who also emerge from such desolate eras. Have students scour newspapers and magazines for stories of exceptional valor that men and women have shown in war time, such as the bravery of those selfless persons who helped the Jews escape in World War II.

174. Matas, Carol. *Lisa's War.* New York: Scribner's, 1987.

This book is based on true experiences with a setting in Copenhagen. Lisa and her brother, Stefan, Jewish teenagers, fought with the organized Resistance movement against Jews being sent to camps. Lisa and Stefan warned friends and neighbors to flee to coastal towns to escape to neutral Sweden in the fall of 1943 before a roundup of Danish Jews by the Nazis. In Denmark, Lisa persevered and helped the Resistance movements. She "dropped" anti–Nazi literature on streetcars and, with her friend, Suzanne, took on life-threatening jobs for the Resistance. 6 and up.

Target Activity: "Lisa Saved Others from Danger"

With this book, a reader needs maturity to understand that sometimes acts of violence are needed to save oneself or others from danger. The story emphasizes heroics of battling against enemies, the tragedy of war, life-threatening situations, and severe problems people have during wartime. Since these acts are not unique to any one war, other books discuss these happenings in other time periods. Related to saving others from danger, consider reading short excerpts aloud from *Across Five Aprils* by Irene Hunt (Follett, 1964; Civil War Era) or from *Johnny Tremain* by Esther Forbes (Houghton Mifflin, 1943; Revolutionary War Days). With information from the excerpts, students can record the happenings during times of war:

Saving Others from Danger

_____

_____

In Revolutionary War	In Civil War Era	In World War II
_____	_____	_____

175. Meltzer, Milton. *Rescue: The Story of How Gentiles Saved Jews in the Holocaust.* New York: Harper & Row, 1988.

Gentiles risk their lives to save Jews in Europe from death. From archives of the Yad Vashem and other libraries in New York, Meltzer gathers his facts about the humanitarian acts by individuals and gentiles in different countries. Exciting and true stories of the heroic and compassionate people who sought to rescue Jews from the Nazi captors create a tribute to their courage. 6 and up.

Target Activity: "Compassionate Heroes/Heroines"

With the students, the teacher discusses the meaning of compassion and heroes (heroines). Students dictate words related to compassion, heroes, and heroines, and the teacher lists the words on the board. With discussion, words are grouped into categories to show relationships. Words in the categories are then rewritten in a word web with "Compassionate Heroes/Heroines" as the center of the diagramming:

ways

| ways to describe | bravery courage valor | ways of honoring heroism | medals rewards trophies | examples of heroism | saving someone risking your life putting others first |

Compassionate Heroes/Heroines

176. Moore, Robin. *The Bread Sister of Sinking Creek.* Ill. New York: Lippincott, 1990.

Maggie Callahan, a fourteen year old, travels with a packtrain from Philadelphia into the Pennsylvania mountains in 1776. Finding her aunt gone, Maggie becomes a hired girl for the McGrew family and helps Mrs. McGrew with the chores, the baby, and with twelve-year-old Anna who is deaf. Maggie has a family legacy—sourdough starter—which she calls spook yeast. The people of Sinking Creek trade for Maggie's bread. The book has a history of sourdough bread, recipes for starter, and simple as well as complicated bread recipes. Don't miss the tall tales told during a Christmas party. 5–8.

Target Activity: "Maggie's Strength—Solving Problems"

Hand to the students duplicated sheets that show a visual display for "Maggie's Ways to Solve Problems." In the center of the sheet is a large circle with the heading "Solving Problems" and lines radiating outward from the circle. At the end of each line is a smaller rectangle in which the students will write information as they hear it again or reread the story. The students fill in the rectangle with information about the ways that Maggie solved her different problems. They write about one problem in each rectangle. Invite the students to trade papers for a partner-check of the information. Return the sheets to the original owners and use them as a basis for a discussion of the story.

177. Reit, Seymour. *Behind Rebel Lines: The Incredible Story of Emma Edmonds, Civil War Spy.* New York: Harcourt Brace Jovanovich, 1988.

Emma posed as a man (one of four hundred women) to fight in the Civil War. She enlisted and was a nurse in field hospitals under General George McClellan. She served as a spy for the Union forces and changed her appearance and personality several times to preserve her anonymity. Pair with *The Secret Soldier* by Ann McGovern or *I'm Deborah Sampson* by Patricia Clapp. Both are about the Revolutionary War heroine, Deborah Sampson. There is a bibliography included for those interested in finding out more about women and their part in the Civil War—there were other women who posed as spies during that conflict. 4–6.

Target Activity: "Emma Edmonds"

To show the changes in appearance and personality of Emma Edmonds, duplicate two outlined profiles on a sheet of paper. Show the students the profiles that have no describing words. Tell the students that Edmonds had to change her appearance and personality several times to keep her anonymity. Ask the students to generate a list of words from what they read to describe Emma and then one of her personalities. Of course, they may add some of their own descriptive adjectives to the list. Compare the lists in the group discussion. Engage students in giving reasons for some of their word choices as you emphasize the traits of resiliency.

178. Rinaldi, Ann. *A Ride into Morning: The Story of Tempe Wick.* New York: Gulliver, Harcourt Brace Jovanovich, 1991.

The times were interesting: on December 18, 1777, the Continental Congress proclaimed the first Thanksgiving celebration ever decreed by a "national" authority for all 13 states; it was a day of "solemn thanksgiving and praise" for the "signal success" of the American defeat of the British at the battle of Saratoga; a new food arrived in New England from England that was the only vegetable they ate raw and which was to become a Thanksgiving tradition: celery; and Mary, the fourteen year old cousin of beautiful Tempe Wick, tells Tempe's story of hiding her horse in her house to protect him from mutinous soldiers. Tempe becomes bitter, confused, and overwhelmed by the war and her family responsibilities. Author notes that authentic letters of soldiers provided the details for the story. Advanced 6 and up.

Target Activity: "Things Have Changed"

Select a quotation from history as an introduction to a discussion on sex stereotyped behavior. As an example, consider these words from Dr. John Gregory to his daughters found in *A Father's Legacy to His Daughters* (1774), and engage students in discussion about the ways things have changed in society for girls and women:

1. "Be careful even in displaying your good sense. It will be thought you assume a superiority over the rest of the company."
2. ". . . if you happen to have any learning, keep it a profound secret, especially from the men, who generally look with a jealous and malignant eye on a woman of great parts and a cultivated understanding. . ."
3. ". . . when a woman speaks of her great strength, her extraordinary appetite, her ability to bear excessive fatigue, we (men) recoil at the description, in a way she is little aware of. . ."

Option: "Constitution of our Classroom"

Engage students in discussing ways to write a constitution—with equal rights for both females and males—for their classroom. A constitution (a basic set of rules by which a group is governed) provides for a form of government, limits powers of the government, and assures the rights and liberties of all of its citizens.

179. Speare, Elizabeth George. *The Witch of Blackbird Pond.* Boston: Houghton Mifflin, 1958.

This riveting novel portrays an independent-minded sixteen year old girl, Kit Tyler, who is orphaned and decides to leave her native island of Barbados to live with her maternal aunt, Puritan uncle, and two female cousins. Up until moving to this close-minded Puritan community in the colony of Connecticut, Kit has been educated and encouraged to lead an active life. She chafes under the narrow-minded authority of her aunt and uncle. Looking for emotional support, Kit enters into a friendship with an older woman, who is rumored by the community to be a witch. Eventually Kit, also, is suspected of being a witch. The author does a phenomenal job crafting the community's peer pressure and ostracism of those considered unconventional. The role of the female in Colonial days, as well as the integration of religion and politics, is dramatically illustrated in this stirring book, as are Kit's strong values. 6–8.

Target Activity: "Going Against the Crowd"

Discuss with students how Kit went against popular conventions with her freethinking behavior. What factors contributed to making her a person who would do and think for herself? Refer children to other young girls in literature who think for themselves and/or take unpopular stands, e.g., Esther in *Plain Girl* (Harcourt Brace, 1956) or Julilly in *Runaway to Freedom* (Harper & Row, 1977). Ask them if they have ever done something or thought something that was very different from their friends' thoughts or deeds. (Perhaps share an instance from your own life to begin the personal discussion.) How did they feel deviating from the norm? How did their friends react? How did they feel about sticking up for what they believed to be "right"?

180. Staples, Suzanne Fisher. *Shabanu.* New York: Knopf, 1989.

Eleven year old Shabanu lived in contemporary Pakistan with her nomadic family in the desert. Her parents betrothed her to a middle-aged man, and she faced the dilemma of obeying her family or obeying her desire for her own well-being. Shabanu faces her inner turmoil, is courageous, and finds signs of caring and warmth in her family. 6 and up.

Target Activity: "Shabanu Was Courageous"

With students, discuss ways they currently face their problems. Elicit times when they have faced a dilemma similar to the one Shabanu faces – that of obeying the family or obeying a desire for one's own well-being.

181. Wild, Margaret. *Let the Celebrations Begin!* Ill. Julie Vivas. New York: Orchard Books, 1991.

In a stirring story that brings to light some of the horror of the Nazi concentration camps, this author has created a celebration of the human spirit. It is 1945, and the survivors in this Nazi concentration camp include little children who have never had a toy or lived in a real home. Now it is rumored that the war is almost over, and courageous Miriam and her friends are organizing a party for the women and children living in Hut 18. They dream they will have their celebration whenever the soldiers can come to free them. Miriam and her friends dream of chicken but realize that is out of the question. She does decide, however, that it is in her power to see that every child receives a toy. As one of the older children, she has fond memories of a doll and a beloved stuffed animal from her home long ago, but many of the younger children have never even seen a toy. So Miriam and some of the women collect scraps of material, lint, and any rags that they can find. They start sewing whenever they can do so without being caught. Their determined purpose gives them strength to overcome the extreme hardships of the camp. 4–6.

Target Activity: "My Favorite Toy"

Ask children if they have ever known a child who has never had a toy. Have them close their eyes and visualize their favorite toy – now or in the past. Tell them to open their eyes and draw their toy. Finally, invite them to describe orally their toy to the rest of the class, without sharing their pictures, pretending the class consists of children similar to those in Hut 18, who have never before seen a toy.

182. Yolen, Jane. *The Devil's Arithmetic.* New York: Viking/Kestrel, 1988.

In a story of transformation, Hannah, weary of hearing her Jewish relatives tell of the Holocaust, wishes to be somewhere else. Her wish is granted when she steps out into the building hallway and into a small village in Nazi-occupied Poland—she has become the villager, Chaya, whose name means "Life." Chaya experiences the Holocaust. On a cattle car with her family and friends, she is branded and stripped, and she is shaved at the concentration camp. When Hannah finds herself again at her family's apartment, she appreciates her relatives for who they are and what they know. Advanced 6 and up.

Target Activity: "Hannah Appreciates Her Family"

With the girls and boys in small groups, the teacher asks the students to think of their family members, what they do, and what they know. The information—contributions made by the family members to the community—is discussed in the small groups. Next, the students should discuss the ways they can show their appreciation for their family members for who they are and what they know.

Biographies

---

183. Cain, Michael. *Mary Cassatt.* Ill. New York: Chelsea House, 1989.

This biography, one of fifty titles in the American Women of Achievement Series, describes the career of Mary Cassatt, generally regarded as one of the finest painters of the Impressionist Era. Although her father—and society in general—strongly discouraged women of her time and class from pursuing a career, Mary Cassatt persevered. She studied at a highly regarded Pennsylvania art school and eventually left for Europe, where she studied the masters. Edward Degas, ten years her elder and an established artist, saw her work and realized she was a kindred spirit. He asked her to join a defiant group of artists who were breaking away from the way art was made at the time. Risking her career, she joined these rebels and continued to experiment with Japanese-inspired prints and portraits of mothers and children. By the time she died in 1926, she was considered a critical and commercial success for her vivid colors and textures. Through her prolific career she had changed society's views about art and women. 4–6.

Target Activity: "Going Against the Tide"

Mary Cassatt was uncomfortable and resentful of the art establishment's rigid conservatism. She needed to express herself more freely but knew that to go against the establishment might bring an end to her career. Ask students to think of a time when they wanted to do something or wear something or say something but felt it was different from what most others did or wore or thought. Invite children to write a paragraph about the event and how they felt about their difference of opinion, ending the paragraph by telling how they resolved the situation. Did they go along with everyone else or do what they really wanted to do? Why or why not?

184. Crofford, Emily. *Healing Warrior: A Story About Sister Eliza-beth Kenny.* Ill. Steve Michaels. Minneapolis: Carolrhoda, 1989.

Kenny was an Australian nurse who developed the "Sister Kenny" method of treatment for infantile paralysis (polio). During World War I, Kenny was in the Australian Army and set up a clinic in Townsville, Queensland. Receiving funds, she set up the Elizabeth Kenny Institute in Minneapolis, Minn. Kenny's adventures in the Australian outback are mentioned along with her qualifications and some of her medical successes. Personal interviews also are sources for some of the information. Notice the bibliography which clearly labels primary and secondary sources.

Concerned with the treatment of students who had polio, Sister Kenny found that the immediate application of hot packs to relieve the muscle spasms, followed by gentle massage and exercise, usually kept the child from becoming crippled. 4–5.

Target Activity: "Events Important to Women and Girls"

For those interested further in this subject, Kenny wrote her autobiography, *And They Shall Walk* (Prior 1952). Invite a librarian in to talk to the students about ways to locate a book that was published long ago. If available in one of the collections of a state's library, read some of the excerpts from Kenny's own words.

For those interested further in events important to women and girls, present these diversified role models and their accomplishments. Encourage research by the students into women's contributions and achievements:

Diverse Role Models	*Contributions and Achievements*
Elizabeth Blackwell	First woman doctor in the United States, born February 3, 1821, in England.
Emily Howell	First female pilot for a commercial airline in the United States on February 5, 1973.
Susan B. Anthony	Famous American suffragette, born on February 15, 1820.
Others:	

185. Douty, Esther M. *Charlotte Forten: Free Black Teacher.* Champaign: Gerrard, 1971.

Charlotte Forten was from an African American family from Massachusetts. Being born in the North in 1837, before the Civil War and the freeing of the slaves in the South, she was fortunate to be part of a free black family. This family consisted of her grandparents, her aunts and uncles, her cousins, and a brother. They all were highly educated professional or business people. They also had many well known white friends and other free Northern blacks as friends. All of the people who gathered in her house at various times were very interested in helping the slaves of the South to be set free. Charlotte was most impressed with escaped slaves she met who were hidden by her family and their friends.

Since the schools where she grew up after her mother's death were segregated, Charlotte was, for the most part, educated at home by her aunt. Since she had no school mates, she read and wrote in a journal a great deal. She also attended meetings of the Female Anti-Slavery Society with this aunt. By the time she was eighteen, Charlotte was a teacher, but she continued to write in her journal. She wanted people to know and remember stories of the heroic slaves who fought for their freedom and their friends who helped them in this fight. 4 and up.

Target Activity: "Keeping a Journal"

Discuss with the students how Charlotte Forten's journal writing helped her remember the important stories of the struggle of individual people to be free and to free the slaves at the time before the Civil War. Ask students to keep a journal of special things that they know about, read, or see that they might want to remember later that they could write in a journal now. These events could be as usual as: a description of a good game with friends, a party at school, a good book they read, or an idea they would like to remember. Request ideas about sources from them.

Option: Have the students interview an adult family member or friend about a special woman they knew as a child. The students can write the story down and/or draw a picture about the person to show to the adult who shared the story. They can tell the class the story.

186. Frank, Anne. *Anne Frank: The Diary of a Young Girl.* New York: Doubleday, 1952.

An autobiography and account of the changes in the lives of eight people who hid for two years in a secret annex of an office building in Amsterdam and who were finally found and imprisoned by the Nazis. After the war, the diary was found by Anne's father, the only one of the eight to survive. 6 and up.

Target Activity: "Tribute to Spirit"

Other books are tributes to the amazing spirit shown by students in true accounts of their survival: *The Endless Steppe: Growing Up in Siberia* (Crowell, 1968) by Esther Hautzig tells of the author's five adolescent years in a slave labor camp in Siberia; *The Upstairs Room* (Crowell, 1972) by Johanna Reiss tells the author's own experiences of hiding with her sister in an upstairs room for two years when their town was occupied by German soldiers; and Reiss' sequel is *The Journey Back* (Crowell, 1976) which tells of the after-effects of war on her family. For the view of a child who did not know her grandmother was Jewish, read Ilse Koehn's *Mischling, Second Degree: My Childhood in Nazi Germany* (Greenwillow, 1977). Koehn describes her childhood of participation in the Hitler Youth movement and points out she would have been labeled an enemy of the Third Reich if the fact of her grandmother's ethnic origin had been known. 6 and up.

187. Galichich, Anne. *Samantha Smith: A Journey for Peace.* Minneapolis: Dillon Press, 1987.

Samantha Smith was an American girl like a lot of other girls her age. She was busy with softball games, roller-skating, reading, and other interests. She also liked to watch television. What she discovered watching the news reports was that the United States and the Soviet Union had many nuclear bombs that could destroy the earth. She also discovered that these two countries seemed to be talking more about war with each other than about peaceful solutions to their problems.

Samantha decided to do something about this frightening situation. In 1982, she wrote Yuri Andropov, the new Soviet leader, about her worries. Samantha was ten years old at the time, and before she was eleven she discovered that her letter had been received and had been printed on the front page of *Pravda*, the most important newspaper of the Soviet Union. Not long after that, she received a reply from Yuri Andropov himself. This was the beginning of an important relationship between Samantha, her home town in Maine, and the Soviet Union, a country whose students also want peace. 4 and up.

Target Activity: "How Can I Make a Difference?"

Discuss with the students how Samantha, even though she was a young girl, thought she could make a difference. Ask the students what problems they think need to be solved in America today. Have them try an experiment to see which of our leaders will respond to letters from them about their concerns. Guide their efforts to write and send these letters. Help the students understand that writing letters is an important way to inform the people we elect to office about what we are thinking, even if they are not always able to reply.

188. Geary, Robert. *The Elephant Man*. London: Allison & Bushy Ltd., 1983.

This is the true story of Joseph Merrick, a boy who managed to triumph over the worst fate could do to him. He grew up so facially distorted and physically ugly that he was known as the Elephant Man. Everyone ran away from him or laughed at him until, by accident, he was rescued from his torments, and it was revealed that inside his disfigured body was a brave and gentle human being. Even though Joseph Merrick had to live with the cruel ravages of a disfiguring disease and the taunts of unkind strangers, he was courageous enough to win many friends with his sensitivity to nature and his gentle ways. He triumphed over his disease by showing others how the person he grew up to be was more important than his crippled body and distorted face. 6 and up.

Target Activity: "If We All Looked Alike"

Ask students to consider how life would be if everyone looked exactly alike. Make two columns on the chalkboard, one labeled "advantages" and the other "disadvantages." Solicit some ideas from the students about the positive ramifications of having everyone look the same; do the same with negative ramifications. Then ask students to decide for themselves which of the two columns provides stronger arguments. Finally, ask them to write a position paper on the advantages and disadvantages of everyone looking alike, as Joseph Merrick might have written it, using the following format:

If We All Looked Alike

There are many advantages I can think of to living in a world where everyone looks alike. These include _____

_____ .

There are also many disadvantages to living in such a world. For example,

_____

_____ .

Considering both the advantages and disadvantages of a world where everyone looks alike, I feel _____

_____ .

189. Ghermann, Beverly. *Sandra Day O'Connor: Justice for All*. Ill. Robert Masheris. New York: Viking, 1991.

Tells of an influential, controversial woman who was the first woman Supreme Court Justice. The book also tells of her stands on important and controversial issues. Compare this one with other biographies, such as *Justice*

Sandra Day O'Connor (Messner, 1985) by Judith Bentley or *Equal Justice* (Dillon, 1985) by Harold and Geraldine Woods. Younger readers will want to find Carol Greene's *Sandra Day O'Connor: First Woman on the Supreme Court* (Children's, 1982). She overcame obstacles stemming from the fact that she was female and that she tried to balance a career and a family life. 5–6.

Target Activity: "First Woman on the Supreme Court"

In a small group with a discussion facilitator and students: Discuss the various ways you found in which the authors of different biographies of O'Connor gave you the idea that she overcame obstacles caused by the fact that she was female. What traits of resiliency do you think are needed by a Justice of the Supreme Court? By a female Justice of the Supreme Court?

Option: Find out all you can about how a person goes about being appointed a Justice of the Supreme Court of the United States. In addition to using the encyclopedia, you might write to the clerk at the Supreme Court. What does the title "Justice" mean? How long does a Justice hold office on the court? What kinds of cases do the Justices make judgments about?

190. Giff, Patricia Reilly. *Mother Teresa: Sister to the Poor.* Ill. Ted Levin. New York: Viking/Kestrel, 1986.

Agnes Bojaxhui was born in Skopje, the capital city of Macedonia, in the early 1900s. Nikola, her father, was a patriot who was working to unite Albania; her mother, Drana, was a quiet Catholic teacher who wanted her students to grow up "strong and serious." When Nikola died suddenly, religion was the link that kept the family together. Drana, Agnes, and her brother and sister spent many hours in church and in working for the poor. Young Agnes was sure God was calling her, telling her what to do. She traveled to Ireland to join the Sisters of Soreto. She later was shipped to India, her "mission" country, where she became Sister Teresa. Although Sister Teresa was assigned to teach in a pleasant Catholic school, she longed to work with the poor. She began spending more and more time in the Moti Jheel Slum caring for "the poorest of the poor." As it was the time of World War II, there were violence and rioting in the streets; Sister Teresa was taking a risk by going into the streets, yet she prevailed. In the years ahead, Sister Teresa continued to work with the poor, with students and with lepers – those that no others would touch. She founded a sheltered community, Shanti Nagar, for the victims of leprosy. Sister Teresa soon became famous around the world. Requests came in from all over the world for her to come and help. She traveled from convent to convent, from country to country, and prizes began to pour in. In 1979, she won the Nobel Peace Prize, although she responded, "I am unworthy." Mother Teresa, as she is now known, continues with her work. Millions of poor and sick await her assistance. 4–6.

Target Activity: "Helping the Homeless"

Discuss with the students the course of Mother Teresa's life. Why did she continue to live among the poor when she could have chosen a life of relative comfort? Ask students to bring in magazine and newspaper articles about the poor in this country. Have them brainstorm a list of things they can do to relieve the suffering of the poor and homeless in the community.

191. Goodall, Jane. *My Life with the Chimpanzees.* New York: Minstrel Books, 1988.

Jane Goodall grew up in a well-to-do English family and could have lived an easy, privileged life. Instead, her dream was to spend her life in Africa studying animals. At twenty-six, she first entered the forests of Africa to study chimpanzees in the wild. On her expedition, she braved the dangers of the jungle and survived encounters with wild animals in the African bush. She documented her adventures with chimpanzees, and the discoveries she has made about them and their relationships to us have gained her worldwide recognition. Jane Goodall's autobiography gives an amazing account of a person pursuing a dream and not giving up. She attributes the positive happenings in her life to "good fortune," but also she says that ". . . the other kinds of good things are those you *make* happen through your own efforts. . . . I refused to give up, even when it seemed very difficult."

Target Activity: "Letter to Jane"

Ask students to share what they would choose to be if they could be anything they wanted to. Discuss the improbability of Jane Goodall's dream. Ask the students why they think she succeeded in realizing her dream against impossible odds. Ask students if they can think of other famous people who succeeded against great odds, e.g., George Washington Carver, Maria Tallchief, Helen Keller, Greg LeMonde, etc. Tell students they are going to write a letter to Jane Goodall, or another famous person who was mentioned. Have them include the following in the letter:

1. Why they admire the person.
2. How the world is a better place because the person succeeded.
3. Their own ambitions in life.
4. Questions they would like to ask the famous person about succeeding.

192. Howe, James. *Carol Burnett: The Sound of Laughter.* Ill. Robert Masheris. New York: Viking/Kestrel, 1987.

Carol Burnett grew up being shuttled between her grandmother (who was on welfare and lived in a one-room apartment) and her parents—both alcoholics—who divorced when she was very young. Though she felt she was far from beautiful, she longed to become a great actress and spent much of her time at the movies or putting on plays. She learned that by laughing at herself she could help others to laugh at themselves, and eventually she became one of America's favorite comediennes. The book recounts her determination to succeed, her rise as a comedienne, and her struggle to like and accept herself.

Carol Burnett's early home life was not often funny. But she put to use her mother's favorite saying, "Comedy is tragedy plus time," to create her comedy. She believed it was better to laugh than to cry, and she helped her audiences to see that, too. 4–6.

Target Activity: "Making a Good Situation Out of a Bad One"

Discuss with the students how Carol Burnett used laughter to make unhappy situations into positive ones. Read to students *Alexander and the Terrible, Horrible, No Good Very Bad Day* (Viorst, 1981). Taking the events one at a time, brainstorm some ways Carol Burnett might have made these bad situations into hilarious comedy routines. Divide students into groups of three or four and allow them to pick favorite events from the book for humorous sketches.

193. McMullan, Kate. *The Story of Harriet Tubman, Conductor of the Underground Railroad.* Ill. Steven James Petruccio. New York: Dell, 1991.

Born in Dorchester County, Maryland, Tubman worked as a field hand when she was a young girl. She escaped to the North and decided to help others to escape. She took trips over the Underground Railroad to slave territory and led slaves back to freedom, earning herself the name of "Moses." Tubman, an American antislavery leader, was one of the greatest fighters for freedom, rescuing over 300 slaves. 4–5.

Target Activity: "The Tubman Scene"

With students, discuss the writing of a script for a brief scene using the character of Harriet Tubman.

Working in groups, the students should consider the task: Write a dramatic script for a "scene" between Harriet Tubman and one of the rescued slaves. In your script you will want to include important information about the people and events.

Option: Introduce the book, *Take a Walk in Their Shoes* (Dutton, 1989) by Glennette Tilley Turner and illustrated by Elton C. Fax. The skit titled "The Douglass 'station' of the Underground Railroad" may be performed without permission if not given for profit and so is appropriate for use in the classroom. Here's the scene:

One November night just after the 1850 Fugitive Slave Act became law, Tubman (with a $40,000 reward out for her) and eight fugitive slaves arrived at the Douglass home in Rochester, NY (a mansion on a hill across from the

Potomac River). A narrator announces Tubman's quiet knock at the door and Douglass' greeting; they enter, warm themselves at the fireplace, eat, and sleep. Tubman recounts their trip through the snow from Wilmington, Delaware, and how they escaped slave catchers' dogs by hiding in water and riding to Philadelphia in a wagon with a false bottom. Douglass and Tubman, who wants to leave immediately to cross the lake to Canada, discuss a plan for getting the fugitives safely into Canada. The scene ends with, "The coast is clear. Let's go."

194. Meltzer, Milton. *Betty Friedan: A Vote for Women's Rights.* Ill. Stephen Marchesi. New York: Viking Penguin, 1985.

This biography of the remarkable woman who spearheaded the women's movement documents her life from childhood as an awkward, plain-looking Jewish loner to her current career as author of *The Second Stage*, which addresses problems of combining work, marriage, and children. Her life has been dedicated to the struggle for women's rights; when a reporter asked her how she would like to be remembered, she replied, "As the one who said women are people." After giving up a job as a reporter, Betty Friedan got married and had three children. Though she greatly enjoyed raising her three children she had a vague, uneasy feeling that something was missing in her life. She began to call this feeling "the problem that had no name." She hired a housekeeper and began to do research on other women who had felt as she did and, after five years of searching and writing, published *The Feminine Mystique*, which became a huge success and changed the lives of countless middle-class women who had wondered what was missing in their own lives. She later started The National Organization for Women (NOW) and became its first president. 4–6.

Target Activity: "Women Who Made a Difference"

When Betty Friedan was a college student at Smith College, the book tells us that Betty wondered why she never studied the great American women of the past: Margaret Fuller, Elizabeth Cady Stanton, Lucy Stone, Susan B. Anthony, and Charlotte Perkins Gilman. Have children select one of these women and research them, using trade books and encyclopedias. Have them give first-person reports on their chosen person, telling what the person did that would make her worthy of study.

195. Neimark, Anne E. *One Man's Valor: Leo Baeck and the Holocaust.* Ill. with photographs. New York: Lodestar, 1986.

After Hitler's rise to power, Leo Baeck, the chief rabbi of Berlin, helped many Jews, especially the children, to escape from Germany. He continued to defy Nazi tyranny while imprisoned in the Theresienstadt concentration camp, an ordeal he miraculously survived. This book is one of several in Lodestar's Jewish Biography series. Bibliography for further reading and index. Advanced 6 and up.

Target Activity: "Struggles for Freedom"

Discuss: Struggles for freedom by women and men like Baeck are continuing today, and some evidence of this is found in news articles.

Engage the students in a newspaper search to find all the examples they can about people's causes and struggles for freedom. They can be stories about an individual or about a group. After many articles have been found, discuss the following: In a free country, how is it possible that so many people (from the news articles) find that they have to go to great lengths (sometimes to the Supreme Court) to get the freedom that they are after?

196. O'Connor, Karen. *Sally Ride and the New Astronauts.* New York: Franklin Watts, 1983.

This book provides in-depth information to augment what the news magazines and television shows have given. It shows how Sally Ride prepared herself to fulfill her dream by earning a doctorate in astrophysics and by undergoing the special training required for this job. "I wanted to be an astronaut as a child," Sally tells a reporter, "but I thought it was impossible." 4 and up.

Target Activity: "Fullfilling a Dream"

The teacher discusses the book with the students and the way that Sally Ride prepared herself to fulfill her dream of being an astronaut. Review some of the text to find evidence of traits or resiliency such as persistence, overcoming obtacles, and so on.

Discuss with the students: What are some of the "impossible things" you have thought about in your life? How does it make you feel when things look "impossible" to you? What could you do to turn the impossible into something possible? How would you try to do this?

197. Rosenburg, Maxine B. *My Friend Leslie: The Story of a Handicapped Child.* Photographs by George Ancona. New York: Lothrop, Lee & Shepard, 1983.

Leslie, a kindergarten child (ages 5–8), has auditory and visual handicaps. There are an understanding teacher, a best friend, and some responsive classmates who encourage Leslie to do as well as she can. With the help and support of others, Leslie becomes the best reader in the class, and her interpretive skills inspire sustained applause from her appreciative classmates. 4–6.

Target Activity: "A Typical Day"

Engage the students in thinking about a typical day on a weekend and the things they do that could be difficult with an auditory and visual handicap. Ask them to make a list of what is done from the time the student gets up in the morning to the time the student goes to bed.

For each of these activities, the student should have two columns. In one column, the student will write all those things for which a person needs to be able to see in order to do them, and in the other all those things for which a person needs to be able to hear.

What I Do During the Day

Where I need to hear	**Where I need to see**
1.	1.
2.	2.

When this is accomplished, invite the students to write a brief paragraph about how he/she would spend the time during this same day in the very same place if the student had the auditory and visual handicaps that Leslie did. Discuss: How did this paragraph change any of your ideas about this girl's ability to cope? opinions? feelings? ways of thinking?

198. Schroeder, Alan. *Ragtime Tumpie*. Ill. Bernie Fuchs. New York: Joy Street/Little, 1989.

Showing an urban black community, this fictional biography tells the life of Josephine Baker, a dancer famous in Europe early in the 20th century. As a young girl, Josephine (Tumpie) picks fruit from the yard and gathers coal fallen off the hopper cars at the railroad tracks. At night, she goes with her mother to hear ragtime music and to dance to the drums in the honky-tonks. One day, she wins a dance contest sponsored by a traveling peddler and receives a shiny silver dollar. This reward shows how dance enriches one's life.

After winning the dance contest, Josephine Baker follows her interest and becomes a famous dancer in Europe. 4–5.

Target Activity: "How Are Girls/Boys Supposed to Act?"

First, develop lists of ways girls are supposed to act and ways boys are supposed to act. Next, discuss how the students feel about these as do's and don'ts. Carry the discussion further and analyze the story for hurdles that Tumpie faced as a woman growing up in her time period. Relate the discussion to modern times and analyze what goes on in the classroom that could/could not be stereotyped behavior. How many girls always volunteer to be recorders/scribes/secretaries? To be the ones to care for the plants? What suggestions do the students have to remove such stereotyping?

199. Schur, Maxine. *Hannah Szenes: A Song of Light*. Ill. Donna
     Ruff. New York: Jewish Publication Society, 1990.

As a teenager, Hannah Szenes leaves the stifling anti–Semitism of
Hungary in 1939 for a new life in Palestine. In 1943, she parachutes back into
Nazi-occupied Yugoslavia to save the lives of Jews. Captured and tortured, she
defies the Nazis only to be executed in the closing days of the war. An inspira-
tional story of a young woman's bravery. Advanced 6 and up.

Target Activity: "Impact of Hitler's Policies"

For those students (advanced 6 and up) interested in the subject, there
is Albert Marrin's book, *Hitler* (Viking, 1987). Hitler's life is inseparable with
Hitler's war so it is not surprising that, after describing the dictator's childhood
and youth in Austria, Marrin describes the campaigns of World War II.
Through the history of events he points to the influence of Hitler as a dictator,
his irrationality about his racial policies, and his responsibility for major
military decisions. The book emphasizes facts that young readers should know
about the impact of Hitler's policies on the lives of people, the controls he exer-
cised, and the horrors of the Second World War. In addition to its insight into
the nature of totalitarianism, the book is a valuable addition to a collection on
the subject since it includes maps, photographs, bibliography, and index.

Option: "Parachuting to Save Lives"

To help students internalize the bravery of Hannah Szenes, take them
through a visualization exercise. Have them close their eyes and verbally lead
them through donning their parachutes, jumping from a plane, and landing
in a forest in Yugoslavia. Have them imagine conversations between Hannah
and the Jews she is trying to save. Allow them to experience vicariously how
Hannah must have felt when she was captured by the Nazis. Finally, invite
students to open their eyes and share their reactions to the visualization.

200. Sills, Leslie. *Inspirations: Stories About Women Artists*. Ill.
     Chicago: Albert Whitman, 1989.

These biographical stories show art works and the intensity of the vision
of such artists as Georgia O'Keefe (striking flower studies); Frida Kahlo (sym-
bolic self-portraits); Alice Neel (sad-eyed children); and Faith Ringgold (in-
tricate cloth pictures). The narratives explain how each artist was influenced
in the direction she chose and why each was so committed to art.

The colorful artwork from talented artists attracts anyone browsing
through this collective biography. 4 and up.

Target Activity: "Self Expression Despite Sex Role Stereotypes"

Invite the students to explore further their awareness of self in spite of sex
role stereotypes through ways that give them self-expression in art works.

Option: "Portraits with Words"

Invite students also to create portraits of the artists with words. Discuss some of the details that could be used in making these pictures with language, e.g., using information about: 1) what children's reactions and feelings to a work of art are; 2) artists' likes and dislikes; 3) choices or subjects of art works; and 4) unusual behaviors or habits or artistic media techniques.

201. Trull, Patti. *On with My Life.* New York: Putnam, 1983.

In Patti Trull's autobiography, we learn that cancer and amputation of a leg are not more traumatic than the unthinking reactions of those around you. Patti is equal to both types of pressure, and the result is her satisfaction in working as a therapist to young cancer patients. A trauma of any kind is debilitating, and the reactions of others to the trauma are painful, too. Both types of trauma cause stress and pressure and a person needs perseverance to overcome these obstacles. 5 and up.

Target Activity: "On with My Life"

Just as Patti stood up to the traumas in her life, so can students stand up to their traumas. With the students, the teacher invites the girls and boys to consider a time when they faced a debilitating trauma (or knew someone who did). Writing reflectively in their journals, the students are to consider their thoughts about the stress the traumas caused and what a person needs to do to overcome these stresses and pressures.

202. White, Ryan & Marie Cunningham. *Ryan White: My Own Story.* New York: Dial, 1991.

White tells of his struggle, how he acquired AIDS, his legal battles, and his dealings with the press, along with details about his personal life.

This one speaks to the strength of White's spirit and the importance of understanding one who has AIDS. 5 and up.

Target Activity: "Making Lemonade from Lemons"

Ryan White could easily have given up when he learned he had AIDS; lesser people would have been tempted simply to feel sorry for themselves, particularly when they found themselves ostracized by their community and school, as Ryan did, through no fault of his own. Instead, Ryan chose to use his unfortunate situation to go around the country and impart information about the disease. In a general discussion with students, compare Ryan's struggles and triumphs with those of Patti Trull (*On with My Life*, Putnam, 1983) and her bout with cancer that led to a career as a therapist. Have students brainstorm some other characters in life or in fiction who experienced difficult traumas and who succumbed to them. Ask each student to select one of these situations and rewrite an event in the person's or character's life so that the struggle results in some positive understandings or occurrences.

203. Zola, Meguido. *Karen Kain: Born to Dance.* New York: Franklin Watts, 1983.

This is an easy-to-read biography of Karen Kain and will appeal to the student interested in ballet. The book follows the well-known Canadian in her career, from her decision to become a professional to her best moments when she is a Juliet and a Giselle and an Odette-Odile. Music mentioned. A student reads about the hard work and dedication needed in developing dancing skills. 4–6.

Target Activity: "Born to . . ."

The biography of Karen Kain certainly will appeal to all those students interested in ballet, but there is also a larger principle in the book: all talents and skills require hard work and dedication to develop. With the students, brainstorm some careers about which they are interested and write them on the writing board. In small groups, have students select one of the careers and either: 1) research the professional route necessary to enter this profession, or 2) interview a person who is currently in the career or who was in the career. Ask one student in each group to be the spokesperson to tell the rest of the class about what one must do to become a member of that profession.

Extended Activity Units
for Grades K–3

Selected Books

204. *Crow Boy* by Taro Yashima. Ill. by author. New York: Viking, 1955.

Focus on Modifying Gender Stereotypes: Chibi breaks out of the typical perceptions that children may have about a young boy at school. This young boy is sensitive to his environment, respects school, participates in the talent show, and has perfect attendance.

Overview: A small boy, Chibi, feels out of place at school for five years; in the sixth grade, a new friendly teacher likes Chibi's drawings and handwriting and spends time talking to him. At the talent show, Chibi imitates the voices of crows and the teacher explains how Chibi learned the calls, leaving his home for school at dawn and arriving home at sunset every day for six long years. Chibi is honored for his perfect attendance at school for six years and receives the name "Crow Boy." 2–3.

New Vocabulary: Chibi, cross-eyed, forlorn, imitate, Mr. Isobe, perfect attendance, zebra grass

Materials: writing paper, pencils, crayons, art paper.

Motivation: (linking prior knowledge; "into" the reading activities).

1. Ask students to think of ways to describe a small boy at school. Ask them to sketch their descriptions. As a contrast, show the illustrations where Chibi was sensitive to his environment and list their ideas on the board. In small groups, ask them to tell their classmates why they drew their sketches the way they did. Back in the whole group, discuss their descriptions further.

2. Ask children to think if they have ever changed their minds about a person—female or male—after getting to know him or her. Encourage them to share incidents that made them change their minds about the person.

3. Write the words *Crow Boy* on the board. Have students turn to a partner and discuss, "One thing *Crow Boy* makes me think of is. . . "

Purpose for Reading or Listening: "You are going to read (hear) a story about a young boy named Chibi who was called stupid and slowpoke by the other children at school but he was very sensitive to his environment and noticed things around him. Read (listen) to find out how others at school change their minds about Chibi after the talent show."

Discussion Questions: (through the reading activities).

1. Describe how you think Chibi learned to imitate voices of crows: How do you think he felt?

2. How do you think Chibi felt when others nick-named him "Crow Boy"? What might *you* have said or done at the talent show?
3. How did the new teacher get acquainted with Chibi and find out Chibi was sensitive to his environment?
4. How was Chibi different from your idea of what a small boy does at school?

Retelling: (through the reading activities). With partners, students role play events in the story and take turns being Chibi and a friendly new teacher.

Extended Activities: (beyond the reading activities).

1. Taking the role of a Chibi, invite children to tell a friend how they feel about school.
2. Have girls and boys retell the story, and somewhere, insert their name and personality with the words, "Suddenly, there I was...." Encourage them to see how the story changes as their personality helps the small boy or makes choices different from Chibi's.
3. Have children rewrite the story from the teacher's point of view. Discuss and imagine several ways (feelings, emotions) Chibi felt during his school years.
4. Have children interview someone with, "What was your schooling like?"
5. Invite children to dictate a letter to the author and tell parts they liked about the story.

Interdisciplinary Ideas

Social Studies: Discuss some of the behaviors Chibi showed in the story that may/may not differ from the children's perceptions (stereotype) of a young boy in school. Examples:

Discuss: "But slowpoke or not, day after day, Chibi came trudging to school. He always carried the same lunch, a rice ball wrapped in a radish leaf. Even when it rained or stormed he still came trudging along, wrapped in a raincoat made from dried zebra grass" (pp. 16–17).

Discuss: "Our new teacher was Mr. Isobe. He was a friendly man with a kind smile. Mr. Isobe often took his class to the hilltop behind the school. He was pleased to learn that Chibi knew all the places where the wild grapes and wild potatoes grew. He was amazed to find how much Chibi knew about all the flowers in our class garden. He liked Chibi's black-and-white drawings and tacked them up on the wall to be admired. He liked Chibi's own handwriting, which no one but Chibi could read, and he tacked that up on the wall. And he often spent time talking with Chibi when no one was around" (pp. 19–23).

Discuss: "...Mr. Isobe announced that Chibi was going to imitate the voices of crows. ...Then Mr. Isobe explained how Chibi had learned those calls—leaving his home for school at dawn, and arriving home at sunset, every day for six long years" (pp. 25, 30).

Discuss: "Chibi was the only one in our class honored for perfect attendance through all the six years" (p. 33).

Discuss: "... nobody called him Chibi any more. We all called him Crow Boy. 'Hi, Crow Boy!' Crow Boy would nod and smile as if he liked the name. And when his work was done he would buy a few things for his family. Then he would set off on the far sides of the mountain, stretching his growing shoulders proudly like a grown-up man. And from around the turn of the mountain road would come a crow call—the happy one" (pp. 35–37).

With children, discuss the idea that people often have preconceived ideas about other people different from themselves, and elicit from students a list of "ideas" that some people might use to type people from other countries— sometimes in a kind way and sometimes in an unkind way.

In a group discussion, ask the children to suggest placing the letter "R" (for rural child) after the ideas they believe people would find related to children who live in the country, mountains, rural areas. Ask the children to suggest placing the letter "C" (for a city child) after the ideas they believe people would find related to children who live in the cities, and urban areas.

Recreational Reading: Have children look for stories about characters—both female and male—and discuss the characters who changed their minds about others in the plot.

Science: Investigate the growth cycle of the wild plants that Chibi knew or the habits of crows, i.e., their looks, habitat, food, and so on.

Art: Invite children to draw a scene of how they think Chibi learned to make the voices of crows.

Math: Discuss ways to keep attendance in class to discover which student is "perfect" in attendance at the end of the year.

Relating math to natural history study, chart the stories about crows and other birds found by the children in the class book collection. Discuss if there are differences between the choices of the girls and boys.

205. *Flossie and the Fox* by Patricia McKissack. Ill. by Rachel Isadora. New York: Dial, 1986.

Focus on Modifying Gender Stereotypes: This is a spunky young girl who outwits a troublesome fox.

Overview: A young girl, Flossie Finley, is sent to take eggs to "Miz Viola at the McCutchin Place" and is warned about a dangerous fox; Flossie has never seen a fox and doesn't know what one looks like. 2–3.

New Vocabulary: aine, August, ceremony, creature, critter, curtsy, disremember, generation, particular, proof, rascal, recollect, slickster, smokehouse, Tennessee, terrified, tucked.

Materials: drawing paper, pencils, crayons, pictures of a fox

Motivation: (linking prior knowledge; "into" the reading activities).

1. Ask students to think of a way they would describe a fox if, like Flossie, they had never seen one. Have them quickly sketch their idea of a fox on paper. In small groups, ask them to tell their classmates why they drew their sketches the way the did.
2. Show students the picture of the fox in the book. Cluster their words to describe the fox on the chalkboard or overhead.
3. Ask children to think if they have ever changed their minds about a person or animal after getting to know them. Encourage them to share incidents that made them change their minds about the person/animal.
4. Write the word *scary* on the board. Have students turn to a partner and discuss, "One thing that I thought was scary was when . . ."

Purpose for Reading or Listening: "You are going to read (hear) a story about a young girl named Flossie Finley, who had never seen a fox before. She meets one when she takes eggs to Miz Viola at McCutchin's cabin. Read (listen) to find out how Flossie outwits—tricks—the fox when he meets her in the woods."

Discussion Questions: (through the reading activities).
1. What stories had Big Mama told Flossie about the fox?
2. Describe what you think Flossie thought when she saw the fox.
3. How do you think Flossie felt when she saw the animal (fox) sitting beside the road "like he was expectin' somebody?" What might *you* have said or done?
4. How did Flossie introduce herself to the fox? How did the fox introduce himself to Flossie?
5. How did Flossie try to get the fox to prove he was a fox?
6. When Flossie said "I don't believe you are a fox, that's what," what were Flossie's feelings? How would you have felt?
7. What would YOU mean if you said to someone, ". . . you sho' think a heap of yo'self"?
8. What do you think Flossie meant when she said to the fox, "You just an ol' confidencer"?
9. When Flossie and the fox came out of the woods, how did Flossie get him to turn back to the woods?

Retelling: (through the reading activities). Engage students in a role play of the story, with partners taking turns being Flossie and the fox.

Extended Activities: (beyond the reading activities).
1. Taking the role of Flossie, have the children tell Big Mama how the fox tried to frighten her and how she outwitted him.
2. Have girls and boys retell the story with their name and personality substituted for Flossie, with the words, "Suddenly, there I was looking at the fox, and . . . ." Encourage them to see how the story changes as their personality makes choices different from Flossie's.

3. Have children rewrite the story from Flossie's point of view. Help them to imagine that Flossie knew the fox was afraid of Mr. J.W. Mc-Cutchin's sharp-toothed hound.
4. Have the girls and boys interview someone being Flossie with, "What was your trip through the woods like?"
5. With children role-playing Miz Viola, engage them in writing a note asking for eggs and another note to thank Flossie for delivering the eggs to her house.

Interdisciplinary Ideas

Social Studies: Children may discuss the idea that Flossie was a problem-solver in this story. For example, the problem of thinking of a way to get the "best" of the fox (or any other dangerous wild animal) may be discussed. Talk about alternatives that girls and boys in the class might have tried in facing a similar problem. Discuss how these alternative ideas might have influenced Flossie and changed her actions in the story. Discuss the relief the little girl must have felt when she reached the cabin, and the frustration the fox must have felt when he failed at getting the eggs he wanted. Further, discuss some of the strengths Flossie showed in the story and record them for the students to see.

1. "Why come Mr. J.W. can't catch the fox with his dogs?" Flossie asked, putting a peach in her apron pocket to eat later (p. 5 unpaged).
Strength:
2. "What if I come upon a fox?" thought Flossie. "Oh well, a fox be just a fox. That aine so scary" (p. 7 unpaged).
Strength:
3. Flossie skipped right up to him and nodded a greeting the way she'd been taught to do. "Top of the morning to you, Little Missy," the critter replied. "And what is your name?" "I be Flossie Finley," she answered with a proper curtsy (p. 9 unpaged).
Strength:
4. Flossie rocked back on her heels then up on her toes, back and forward, back and forward . . . carefully studying the creature who was claiming to be a fox. "Nope," she said at last. "I just purely don't believe it" (p. 10 unpaged).
Strength:
5. "So, why should I be scared of you and I don't even-now know you a real fox for a fact?" Fox pulled himself tall. He cleared his throat. "Are you saying I must offer proof that I am a fox before you will be frightened of me?" "That's just what I'm saying" (p. 11 unpaged).
Strength:
6. "I have the proof," he said. "See, I have thick, luxurious fur. Feel for

yourself." Fox leaned over for Flossie to rub his back. "Ummm. Feels like rabbit fur to me," she say to Fox. "Shucks! You aine no fox. You a rabbit, all the time trying to fool me" (p. 14 unpaged).

Strength:

7. "You know," she finally said, smiling, "it don't make much difference what I think anymore." "What?" Fox asked. "Why?" "Cause there's one of Mr. J.W. McCutchin's hounds behind you. He's got sharp teeth and can run fast, too. And, by the way that hound's lookin', it's all over for you!" (p. 25 unpaged).

Strength:

Have children find books in the library that tell how others have been strong when they met "troublesome" animals in folk literature. As one example, the children may hear or read *The Gunniwolf* (Dutton, 1967) by Wilhelmina Harper.

Recreational Reading: Invite children to look for other stories about troublesome animals.

Science: Investigate foxes, i.e., their habitat, and so on.

Art: Ask the girls and boys to draw scenes of Flossie's walk in the woods.

Math: Chart the favorite animal in stories of all the children in the class. Discuss if there are differences between the choices of the girls and boys.

Music: Refer to the girl's song in Harper's *The Gunniwolf* and ask students to suggest musical tones for the words: "Kum-kwa, khi-wa, kum-kwa, khi-wa."

206. *Hansel and Gretel* by Grimm Brothers. Retold by Rika Lesser. Ill. by Paul O. Zelinsky. New York: Dodd, 1984.

Focus on Modifying Gender Stereotypes: Gretel rescues her brother.

Overview: Near a large wood, a poor woodcutter, who lived with his wife and two children by a former marriage, listened to his wife, who wanted to take the children to the thickest part of the woods and leave them. Despite attempts to leave the children in the woods, the children managed to find their way home. Left once again, the children wander three days and arrive at a cottage made of bread and cakes, with window panes of clear sugar. An old woman, really a witch who waylays children, fattens them up with milk, pancakes, sugar, apples, and nuts. Her plan is to eat the children, but Gretel foils her plan. This classic tale of an evil witch, a selfish mother, a weak father, and two resourceful children focuses on Gretel. Faced with the prospect of seeing if the oven was "hot enough," Gretel tricks the witch into showing her how to do it. Gretel gives her a push into the oven, shuts the iron door, and bolts it. She releases Hansel from his cage, and they collect the witch's pearls and precious stones. They return to their father, who has not had one happy hour since he left the children in the forest. 1–3.

New Vocabulary: woodcutter, woods, cottage, clear sugar.

Materials: writing materials, writing utensils, art paper, markers such as crayons or colored pencils.

Motivation: (linking prior knowledge; "into" the reading activities).

1. Ask the girls and boys to close their eyes and visualize "a cottage made of bread and cakes and window panes of clear sugar." Have them quickly sketch the cottage on paper. In small groups, ask them to tell their classmates what they like about the cottage and how it makes them feel.

2. Show children some of the illustrations of the story characters and the cottage.

3. Ask the girls and boys to think if they have ever had to help someone out of a dangerous situation (similar to releasing Hansel from his cage). Encourage them to share incidents.

4. Show the illustration of the cottage and write the word *cottage* on the board. Have students turn to partners and discuss, "One thing that I know about a cottage is. . . ."

Purpose for Reading or Listening: "You are going to read (hear) a story about a young girl who rescues her brother from danger. Read (listen) to find out how Gretel saves her brother Hansel."

Discussion Questions: (through the reading activities).

1. What attracted Hansel and Gretel to the cottage? What did the old woman do for the children?

2. Describe how you think a day in the lives of the two children at the cottage might have been as the old woman fed them milk, pancakes, sugar, apples, and nuts.

3. How did resourceful Gretel trick the old woman?

4. What would you do if you described someone like the old woman in the cottage made of bread and cakes?

5. If you had been there, how could you have helped Gretel?

Retelling: (through the reading activities). Retell this story again using some cue words to show the sequence of events: *first, second, third, finally.* With children, discuss some of the sequence of events:

1. Though Hansel scattered crumbs to make a trail to find their way back home, the birds ate them all. The children follow a little white bird whose song ended with chirps, as if to say, "Follow me! Follow Me!" What could Hansel have done differently? How could Gretel have helped?

2. The children found themselves at a tiny cottage that looked "good enough to eat." Its walls were made of gingerbread, its roof was made of cake. It was trimmed with cookies and candy, and its window-panes were pure transparent sugar. They began eating right away and heard a voice from the cottage:

Nibble, nibble, nottage,
Who's nibbling at my cottage?

3. A bent woman came out of the cottage. She had a sharp nose bent down to meet her bristly chin. She had folds and wrinkles in her face, and it looked like a shriveled pear. She had three teeth, two above and one below—all long and yellow. She said, "Come right in and stay with me. I'll take good care of you." Discuss with children the stereotype of the "old woman" as a witch character in folk tales.

4. The next morning, while the children were sleeping, the woman took Hansel into the backyard and locked him up in a goose-coop. She made Gretel cook each day and make fattening food for Hansel. Discuss what plans Gretel might be making.

5. One day, the old woman built a roaring fire for the stove and said, "Do you think it is hot enough to make bread, Gretel? Stick your head in the oven and see." But the same white bird that had led them began to sing a song: "Beware, Beware, Don't look in there." So Gretel said, "I don't know how. Could you show me?" The old woman said, "Just stick your head in and give a look around. Like this." The old one put her head into the oven, Gretel gave her a push, closed the oven door, and justice was done:
"The old one called and cried, and frizzled and fried, but no one heard. That was the end of her, and who cares?"

6. Gretel freed Hansel. The birds of the forest returned, and each had a pearl or gem and carried it down to the children. The little white bird said, "Thank you for the crumbs of bread. Here are some gems for you instead." Led by the white bird, Hansel and Gretel followed a familiar path back to their father's house, where they lived happily, for the hardhearted stepmother had become angry and put her things in a large red handkerchief and run away. Discuss ways Gretel broke the stereotype of girls (women) relying on boys (men) to escape danger.

Retell the story and mention: the names of the main characters, what the character wanted, what got in the way to keep the character from getting what was wanted, and then the way the problem was resolved.

Dictate the story by group participation. The teacher asks the students in one group to talk about information that tells about the character and to dictate it for a group story; a second group discusses facts about what the character wanted to do and dictates it; a third group discusses what got in the way of the character's goal and dictates the part; a fourth group discusses how the problem was resolved and dictates the part. The teacher records the dictated story and rereads it with the children.

Extended Activities: (beyond the reading activities).

1. Have the girls and boys draw the story with their persona (and a

friend's) substituted for Hansel and Gretel. Encourage them to see
how some of the events in the story will differ as each new character
makes choices different from those of Gretel and Hansel.
2. Have children rewrite the story from the sorrowful father's point of
   view. Help them to imagine the father's concern for the children.
3. Have the girls and boys write a letter to Gretel and Hansel telling them
   how the students feel about Gretel and Hansel's adventure and their
   safe return.

Interdisciplinary Ideas

Social Studies: "Saying No to Strangers." Engage the children in discussing what to do when meeting strangers—even an old woman in a cottage
made of bread and cakes.

With children, engage in an activity, "Justice." When the story tells of the
old woman's demise in this translation of the Grimms' tale, the story focuses
on justice:

> The Old One poked her horrid old head into the oven, Gretel gave her a push
> and a shove, closed the oven door, bolted it swiftly and ran away. The Old One
> called and cried, and frizzled and fried, but no one heard. That was the end
> of her, and who cares?

With the girls and boys, discuss times when they feel justice was done in
the classroom, at school, or other times, and discuss who had a role in seeing
that justice was done. Record their thoughts on the board or on a chart for
the classroom. Children may illustrate the chart with small original
illustrations.

Justice Chart

It's justice when. . .   It's not justice when. . .

People who have helped see that "Justice was done":

———————
———————

———————

Recreational Reading: Have children look for and read folk literature
where the main characters are resourceful, as Gretel was.

Science: Discuss what might have to be done to make windows of clear
sugar and list some of the contributions from science that would be needed
to do this. Also, discuss what materials can be used to build houses. What are
the advantages and disadvantages of each material?

Art: Ask the girls and boys to make their own illustrations of Gretel's resourceful act. Display.

Make gingerbread houses or sketch illustrations that children feel look like their visualization of the cottage in the tale.

Math: Review folk literature stories collected and identify the characters who perform the resourceful acts (female and male). List. Tally the characters on a chart.

Language Arts: Engage children in the activity, "Closing In on an Opening for a Tale That Modifies a Gender Stereotype," and in selecting another tale from folk literature that features modifications of the usual stereotypes of female or male characters.

Encourage the students to use an old folk tale beginning or ending—a story teller's coda—to open or close their story and to modify a gender stereotype:

Openings: "Once upon a time . . . " or "I will tell you the story I heard when I was little." or "Many years ago . . . " or "There was once . . . " or "There lived in ancient times . . . " or "This is the story that was told . . . " or "Know, O my brothers and sisters . . ." (or my sisters and brothers).

Endings: "There, that is a real story!" or "There runs a mouse: Whoever catches him/her may make a great, great cap out of his/her fur." or "You see, that's my story. I heard it when I was a child, and now you've heard it too, and know the tale of _____."

Option: "Comparing Versions"

With the girls and boys, look at other versions of the story to locate ways girls and women are portrayed. Consider "Hansel and Gretel" in *Tales from Grimm*, trans. by Wanda Gag (Coward-McCann, 1936), where Hansel is sympathetic to Gretel's crying and says, "Don't cry, little sister. Just wait until the moon is out; I'll find the way home."

207. *I Hate English!* by Ellen Levine. Ill. by Steve Bjorkman. New York: Scholastic, 1989.

Focus on Modifying Gender Stereotypes: Mei Mei is determined to not learn English; a caring female teacher helps Mei Mei feel comfortable about learning English at a Chinese Learning Center.

Overview: A young girl who loved to speak Chinese, Mei Mei, lived in Chinatown in New York and attended school where everything was done in English. Mei Mei hated English and wouldn't speak it because she thought English was a lonely language where each letter stood alone and made its own noise—different from Chinese where there were fast strokes, short strokes, long strokes in writing and Mei Mei could make the brush (or pen or pencil) fly in her hand. 2–3.

New Vocabulary: California, covered wagon, Chinese, Director, dragon dances, English, Hong Kong, Shek, Yee Fong dances, English, Hong Kong, Shek, Yee Fong.

Materials: paper, pencils, pens, illustrations from the book, chalk, chalkboard, supplementary reading books.

Motivation: (linking prior knowledge; "into" the reading activities).

1. Ask the girls and boys to close their eyes and visualize one thing that they say they "dislike." Have them quickly sketch the object of their dislike on paper. In small groups, ask them to tell their classmates why they dislike this object and how it makes them feel.

2. Show the children some of the illustrations of Mei Mei that show her dislike of English: her stubborn look (p. 3 unpaged); her lack of participation in class (p. 8 unpaged); her thoughts about the post office in New York (p. 11 unpaged); and her thoughts about the happening of a "terrible thing," e.g., a teacher who helped Mei Mei with English (p. 17 unpaged). Cluster the children's reactions to Mei Mei's attitude on the writing board or on transparency on the stage of the overhead. Solicit possible reasons why many children might hate English.

3. Ask the girls and boys to think if they have ever "hated" learning words in another language. Encourage them to share incidents that made them change their minds about the language.

Purpose for Reading or Listening: "You are going to read (hear) a story about a young girl from Hong Kong named Mei Mei who was determined not to speak English. Read (listen) to find out how Mei Mei became a friend of the teacher's and how the teacher, Nancy, helped her to overcome her objections to English."

Discussion Questions: (through the reading activities). Ask the children:

1. What reasons did Mei Mei have to dislike English? Would you agree or disagree with the reasons? Why did Mei Mei call English a lonely language?

2. Describe what you think a day in Mei Mei's life must have been when most of the time she did not understand English. What sort of problems, if any, could Mei Mei have had during a day at school? How could you have helped Mei Mei if you had been there?

3. Why did her cousin, Bing, take her to the Chinatown Learning Center for help? How do you think Mei Mei felt when she decided not to work at learning English?

4. Why did Mei Mei help others with arithmetic?

5. How did Mei Mei address her letters to friends in Hong Kong?

6. What were Mei Mei's feelings about English by the end of the story?

7. What would you do if you discovered someone like Mei Mei—girl or boy—who did not want to speak the language of the country in which she or he was living? How could you help the student?

8. What are some ways you can become a friend to the student who does not speak English?

Retelling: (through the reading activities). Ask the children to:

1. Retell this story again using some cue words to show sequencing: *first, second, third, finally.*
2. Retell the story and mention: the name of the main character, what the character wanted, what got in the way to keep the character from getting what was wanted, and then the way the problem was resolved.
3. Retell the story through group participation. The teacher asks the students in one group to find information that tells about the character and to write it down; a second group finds facts about what the character wanted to do and writes it; a third group finds sentences that tell what got in the way of the character's goal and writes them; a fourth group finds sentences that tell how the problem was resolved and writes them. The teacher collects the informational sheets and redistributes them to the groups. Working together and discussing the information, the members determine which of the story parts they have (character, goal, conflict, resolution) and report on the story parts in order to keep the sequence of the retelling. Of course, the members can add more information about their part.

Extended Activities: (beyond the reading activities).

1. Participating as an audience, have the girls and boys give a refrain in the background during an oral rereading. As a group, the children should decide on the refrain they want to say when Mei Mei's name is heard during an oral reading (perhaps Mei Mei's feeling of "I love Chinese! I love Chinese!") and when the teacher, Nancy, is mentioned (Forever talking English! Forever talking English!).
2. Have children rewrite the story with their names substituted for Mei Mei. Encourage them to see how some of the events in the story will differ as each one's character makes choices different from those of Mei Mei.
3. Ask the boys and girls to rewrite the story from the teacher's point of view. Help them to imagine the teacher's concern for Mei Mei.
4. Have children interview a friend who has had to learn a second language in addition to their first language. Listen to them as they point out comparisons of their first language and another language. Are there any words in one language for which there are no words in the other language?
5. Playing the role of Mei Mei, engage the children in writing a thank-you note to Nancy, and tell the teacher at the Chinatown Learning Center how Mei Mei feels one year later, as she thinks back to the day when the teacher engaged her in speaking English.

Interdisciplinary Ideas

Social Studies: "Sensitivity to Mei Mei and Other Newcomers." Engage the children in watching as many television programs as they can after school during a week. Have them pay special attention to any newcomers and the way they are portrayed on the program. Engage the children in doing "research" about each program they watch with a research form such as the one that follows:

Research with TV Programs

_____   _____
name   date

_____   _____
name of TV program   channel and date and time

Traditions and customs of newcomer presented:
_____

Observed in a TV program _____ Did not observe in a TV program_____

Discuss what portions of the program appeared to show the strengths of the newcomers and their contributions; talk about what appeared to be accurate and inaccurate.

Recreational Reading: Have the girls and boys look for and read folk literature from Mei Mei's cultural group.

Science: When are examples of contributions from science found in the illustrations of the story? List and discuss.

Art: Ask children to make a different type of book—a "regular" picture book or a "concertina" book—about the teacher and Mei Mei. To make a "concertina" book, the children fold or tape together the pages concertina style. To complete the book, the students draw illustrations on the title page, which says _Mei Mei's Story_, and on succeeding pages, the students illustrate the events that happened in _Mei Mei's_ life before and after she met the teacher at the Chinese Learning Center.

Math: Tally the responses related to what was observed in any TV program and not observed in a TV program from the TV research activity suggested earlier.

208. _Mirandy and Brother Wind_ by Patricia C. McKissack. Ill. by Jerry Pinckney. New York: Knopf, 1988.

Focus on Modifying Gender Stereotypes: Mirandy is anything but the stereotypical "passive" little girl character. She actively solves problems in her own way and refuses to give up.

Overview: Mirandy is determined to catch the wind to be her partner in the cakewalk, a traditional Southern dance rooted in African American culture. She tries a variety of strategies and finally succeeds. 2–3.

New Vocabulary: cakewalk, commenced, conjure, whitewashed, sassy, guarantee, moping, hedges, gait, flickering.

Materials: map or globe, writing board, or chalk board and chalk.

Motivation: (linking prior knowledge; "into" the reading activities).

1. Write the word *wind* in a bubble in the center of the board. Ask children to free-associate all the things that come to their mind when they hear this word. Example:

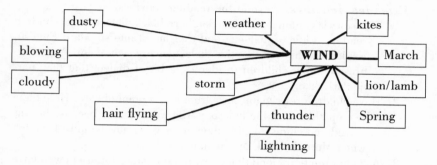

2. Ask children if it is possible to catch the wind. Why or why not? What ways might they think of to try and catch the wind?
3. The illustrations in *Mirandy and Brother Wind* are rich, eye-catching watercolors for which the illustrator received a Caldecott Honor Award. Show children the illustrations page by page and ask them to construct what they think is happening in each one.

Purpose for Reading or Listening: "You are about to read (hear) the story of a remarkable young girl who wanted very badly to win a dance contest. Read (listen) to find out how she did not give up and managed to reach her goal."

Discussion Questions: (through the reading activities).

1. Why did Mirandy think Brother Wind would be an ideal partner for the cakewalk?
2. What were the answers that were given to Mirandy as she tried to find out how to catch the wind?
3. Why did Ezel tell Mirandy he was going to ask Orlinda to be his partner?
4. Why did Mirandy decide to dance with Ezel after all?
5. What made Mirandy win the cakewalk?
6. What evidence do you have that Mirandy was a very determined young girl?
7. What did Grandmama Beaseley mean when she said, "Them chillin' is dancing with the wind"?

8. How did the conjure woman, Miss Poinsettia, help Mirandy?
9. How do you think the other little girls felt when they saw "clumsy" Ezel winning the cakewalk?
10. How would YOU have gotten yourself ready for the cakewalk? Who (or what) would you choose for a partner? Would you have consulted the conjure woman for advice? Why or why not?

Retelling: (through the reading activities). Have pairs of children take turns reading a page of text to each other. The "listener" then summarizes the text of that page and the reader adds to the listener's summary. The pairs switch roles on every page.

Extended Activities: (beyond the reading activities).

1. This story is written in obsolete Southern black dialect. Have children read each line of dialogue and translate it into standard English. Explain to children that this dialect is very rich, colorful, and expressive. Ask children to identify a bit of dialect that they particularly like.
2. Have children rewrite the story from Ezel's point of view. Help them to empathize with the little boy who was rejected because he was considered clumsy. Guide them to imagine how he must have felt when Mirandy stuck up for him.
3. Ask children to pretend that they are newspaper reporters who have been assigned to cover the cakewalk. Have them write a newspaper article that contains the essential elements of *who, what, why, where, when.* Let them read their newspaper articles to the class.
4. Have children role play this story, choosing children to reenact scenes such as: Mirandy asking Grandmama Beaseley, Ezel, Mr. Jessup, and the conjure woman how to catch the wind; Mirandy chasing the wind into the barn; the cakewalk.
5. Write an acceptance speech that Mirandy might have written as she graciously accepted her triple-decker cake award.

Interdisciplinary Ideas

Social Studies: Have children investigate the African American culture in the early 1900s, when this story takes place. Specifically, have them search for information about the flamboyant cakewalks.

Science: Have children research the meteorologic phenomenon of "wind." Why is it generally more windy in the spring? Before a storm? By a body of water?

Art: Using watercolors, invite children to paint their concepts of what "Brother Wind" would look like.

Math/Social Studies: Have children ask their parents (or adults in the home) what other states they have lived in during their lives. Make a list of the southern states. Chart the number of those who have lived in any of these states. Find these states on a map or globe.

209. *Miss Maggie* by Cynthia Rylant. Ill. by Thomas di Dirazia. New York: E.P. Dutton, 1983.

Focus on Modifying Gender Stereotypes: A young boy sensitive to the needs of an elderly woman; relationship with caring "other" person; positive vision of life.

Overview: A young boy, Nat, has heard stories about the old lady who lives in the log hut on his family's property; a big black snake is rumored to live with her. Nat initially fears Miss Maggie but overcomes his fear when she is in trouble. He develops a special relationship with her. 2–3.

New Vocabulary: trembled, rafters, cupboards, Guernsey, wrinkled, starling.

Materials: live snake, pictures of black snake or plastic snake, drawing paper, pencils, shoeboxes, pipe cleaners, art paper.

Motivation: (linking prior knowledge; "into" the reading activities).
1. Ask students to close their eyes and visualize one thing that makes them afraid. Have them quickly sketch the object of their fear on paper. In small groups, ask them to tell their classmates why they are afraid of the object and how it makes them feel.
2. Show students the snake. Cluster their reactions to the snake on chalkboard or overhead. Solicit possible reasons why many people fear snakes.
3. Ask children to think if they have ever been afraid of a person prior to getting to know them. Encourage them to share incidents that made them change their minds about the person.
4. Write the word *loneliness* on the board. Have students turn to a partner and discuss, "One thing that made me feel lonely was when . . ."

Purpose for Reading or Listening: "You are going to read (hear) a story about a young boy named Nat, who was very afraid of an old woman named Miss Maggie who lived alone in a little hut near his house. Read (listen) to find out how Nat became Miss Maggie's friend and how Nat helped her to overcome her loneliness."

Discussion Questions: (through the reading activities).
1. What stories had Nat heard about Miss Maggie and her hut? Were they true? Why did people tell these stories?
2. Describe how you think a day in Miss Maggie's life must have been before she became Nat's friend.
3. Why was Miss Maggie clutching the dead bird? How do you think she was feeling?

4. How do you think Nat felt when he saw Miss Maggie clutching the dead bird? What might *you* have said or done?
5. When was Nat no longer afraid of Miss Maggie? How did he lose his fear?
6. How did Nat and Miss Maggie become friends?
7. What were Nat's feelings about Miss Maggie by the end of the story?
8. How do you think Miss Maggie felt about Nat?
9. What would YOU do if you discovered someone like Miss Maggie living all alone without food or heat?
10. What are some ways you can become a friend to an older person?

Retelling: (through the reading activities). Pairs of students role play the story taking turns being Nat or Miss Maggie.

Extended Activities: (beyond the reading activities).
1. Taking the role of Nat, have children write a letter to Miss Maggie telling her how she previously frightened you and why. Explain what you learned about her and how much you care about her now.
2. Have children rewrite the story with their name and persona substituted for Nat's. Encourage them to see how the ending to the story differs as their character makes choices different from Nat's.
3. Have children rewrite the story from Miss Maggie's point of view. Help them to imagine that Miss Maggie is afraid of the little boy who is constantly peering in the windows.
4. Have children interview a grandparent or an elderly person living in a nearby nursing home. Questions can include, "Are you ever lonely? What is a day in your life like?" Help them to compare their lives with that of an elderly person.
5. Have children write a thank-you note to Nat from Miss Maggie telling Nat how she felt when he visited and found her alone holding the starling.

Interdisciplinary Ideas

Social Studies: Have children find books in the library that tell how elderly people are respected and treated in other cultures, e.g., Japanese, Chinese, Navajo Indian, etc.

Recreational Reading: Have children look for folklore about snakes. Discuss how snakes are considered in these legends. Why do they suppose this is so?

Science: Investigate the habits of nonpoisonous snakes, i.e., their diet, predators, habitat, etc. Have children make a poster explaining why these creatures have been unfairly maligned.

Art: Have children construct a diorama of Miss Maggie's log house in the middle of the pasture.

Math: Chart the number one fear of all the children in the class. Discuss if there are differences between the fears of the girls and boys. Brainstorm ways to overcome these fears.

210. *Pelle's New Suit* by Elsa Beskow. Ill. New York: Harper, 1929.

Focus on Modifying Gender Stereotypes: In this book of the late 20's, Pelle is a sensitive young boy who has a relationship with caring "other" persons.

Overview: In Sweden, Pelle shears a lamb's wool, pulls the weeds in his grandmother's garden while she cards the wool, tends his other grandmother's cows while she spins the yarn, rows to the store to buy some blue dye, and dyes the wool. He takes care of his little sister while his mother weaves the yarn into cloth. He rakes hay, brings in wood, and feeds the tailor's pigs while the tailor makes Pelle's suit. Pelle is considerate of others and says "Please" when making requests of his relatives and the tailor. He doesn't object or argue when Mother says ". . . take care of your little sister for me." K–1.

New Vocabulary: shears, lamb's wool, cards the wool, dye, weaves, tailor.

Materials: remnant of blue wool; pictures of people spinning, carding, weaving; art paper and markers or crayons or colored pencils.

Motivation: (linking prior knowledge; "into" the reading activities).
1. Ask students to close their eyes and visualize one time when they were helped by others to acquire something they wanted. Have them quickly sketch the object they wanted on paper. In small groups, ask them to tell their classmates what they wanted, who helped them, and how they felt when they acquired the object.
2. Engage the children in observing and touching the piece of blue wool. Cluster their reactions to the material on the board or overhead transparency. Solicit possible jobs that had to be done to make the piece of blue wool.
3. Ask children to think if they have ever helped another person acquire something she or he wanted. Encourage them to share incidents from their experience.
4. Write the word *Pelle* on the board and show Pelle's picture from the book. Have students turn to a partner and discuss, "One thing that I think of when I see Pelle is. . ."

Purpose for Reading or Listening: "You are going to read (hear) a story about a young boy named Pelle who wanted a new suit. Since Pelle lived in a time and place where there were no stores to buy a new suit, read (listen) to find out how Pelle got his new suit."

Discussion Questions: (through the reading activities).

1. What are some of the things that Pelle did to acquire his suit? Were they helpful to others? Why did he do these things?
2. Describe how you think a day in Pelle's life must have been after he got his new suit.
3. What were some of the things Pelle did to shear a lamb's wool? How do you think he learned to do this?
4. How do you think Pelle felt when he tended his grandmother's cows while she spun the yarn for the suit?
5. How do you think Pelle felt when he tended his little sister while his mother wove the yarn into cloth?
6. How did Pelle help the tailor while the tailor made his suit?
7. What were the ways Pelle showed he was polite and considerate?
8. How do you think Pelle felt about his new suit?
9. What would YOU do if you had to get a new suit the way Pelle did?
10. What are some ways you can be polite and considerate to others?

Retelling: (through the reading activities). Pairs of students role play the story taking turns being Pelle and the other characters—grandmother, sister, mother, tailor.

Extended Activities: (beyond the reading activities).

1. Taking the role of Pelle, have children review the illustrations and act out his motions in pantomime—shearing the wool, pulling the weeds, tending the cows, rowing to the store, caring for a little sister, raking hay, bringing in wood, and feeding the tailor's pigs.
2. Have the girls and boys rewrite the story with their names and today's setting to tell how they would acquire a new suit or dress. Encourage them to see how their story differs as their character is in a different time and place from Pelle's.
3. Have children discuss and dictate the story from another point of view—the mother's view, the little sister's view, the tailor's view.
4. Have the girls and boys discuss and dictate the story by switching the male character to female.
5. Have children interview a tailor. Questions can include, "How do you make a suit? What do you need to do? What tools do you use?" Help them to compare what the tailor says with what Pelle had to do.
6. Have the girls and boys design a poster (mural) to show the steps that one has to go through to make a suit from lamb's wool as Pelle did.

Interdisciplinary Ideas

Social Studies: Have children find books in the library that tell how clothing is made. Display Tomie De Paola's *Charlie Needs a Cloak* (Prentice-Hall, 1974) and Lauren Mills' *The Rag Coat* (Little, Brown, 1991).

Recreational Reading: Have children look for other stories with a setting in a country other than the United States.

Science: Investigate the characteristics of dye (use food coloring or egg coloring). Have children experiment with drops of food color in water in a glass container on the overhead stage, and use primary colors to make secondary ones, e.g., children may place three drops of red in the water, turn on the overhead light, then place three drops of yellow in the water, stir it, and observe the colors combining on the screen.

Art: Have girls and boys cut out paper shapes of "new suits" and "dresses."

Math: Chart the number one "wish" for an article of clothing of all the children in the class. Discuss if there are differences between the wishes of the girls and boys.

Language Arts: Engage the boys and girls in an activity, "Please do this for me," and with questions such as the ones that follow, encourage children to role play making requests of others, to show they can be polite as well as "give something back."

Discuss with children:

1. After looking at the illustration where Pelle shears the lamb, how many different descriptive words can you use to describe what you see in the illustration? In the illustration that shows Pelle pulling weeds in grandmother's carrot patch while she cards the wool? Children may participate in role play in various scenes. For instance, children may switch roles as Pelle asks, "Granny, dear, please card this wool for me"? Grandmother replies, "That I will, my dear . . . if you will pull the weeds in my carrot patch for me."

2. Consider role play for the following: *Scene #1:* Pelle asks his other grandmother to spin the wool into yarn. Grandmother says she will if he will tend the cows for her. *Scene #2:* Pelle asks his neighbor to give him some paint to color the yarn. Pelle learns he has to row to the store to buy some dye. *Scene #3:* Pelle dyes the wool himself until it is all blue. *Scene #4:* Pelle asks his mother to weave the yarn into cloth for him. Mother says she will if Pelle takes care of his little sister for her. *Scene #5:* Pelle asks the tailor to make a suit for him out of the cloth. The tailor says he will if Pelle will rake the hay, bring in the wood, and feed the pigs. *Scene #6:* Pelle puts on his new suit and visits his lamb to say, "Thank you very much for my new suit, little lamb." The lamb replies, "Ba-a-ah."

Extended Activity Units
for Grades 4–8

211. *Bridge to Terabithia* by Katherine Paterson. Ill. by Donna Diamond. New York: Thomas Y. Crowell, 1978.

Focus on Modifying Gender Stereotypes: relationship with caring "other" person; a very sensitive male has a gender unstereotypical hobby; the young girl is portrayed as the stronger of the two friends.

Overview: Jesse and Leslie are friends and create Terabithia, a magic kingdom in the woods where they are the lord and lady. When Leslie dies, Jesse copes by turning to the legacy that she has left him. 4–6.

New Vocabulary: hypocritical, proverbial, conspicuous, conceited, consolation, reassessing, siege, veiled speculation, foundling, garish, vanquished.

Materials: Songs: "Beautiful Balloon," "This Land Is Your Land," "Blowin' in the Wind," "Free to Be . . . You and Me"; newsprint, colored chalk.

Motivation: (linking prior knowledge; getting "into" the reading material).

    1. Write the word *kingdom* on the board. Web the concept on the blackboard or overhead, using children's free associations like so:

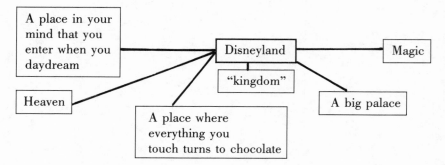

    2. Discuss "fear" with students. Explain that Jesse is afraid to swing across a creek on a rope when the creek is especially high. Ask them if they find that unusual. Ask them why they think Jesse is concerned about his fear and if any of them has ever been made fun of for being afraid of something. Discuss the positive aspects of fear—is it "healthy" to be afraid of something?

    3. Tell students that Jesse practiced all summer to become the fastest runner in his school, but then he was beaten by a girl. Ask them how they would feel about that girl. Do they think a friendship could ever develop between Jesse and the girl who beat him?

Purpose for Reading or Listening: "The book you are about to read (listen to) tells about an unlikely friendship between a ten year old girl and boy growing up in rural Virginia. Read (listen) to find out how they become friends and why they are important to one another."

Discussion Questions:
1. Why is Jesse so fond of his sister, May Belle?
2. Why does he resent his older sister?
3. Why didn't Jesse show his drawings to his Dad?
4. How did Leslie seem different from the other children Jesse knew?
5. Why had Leslie's family moved to the country?
6. How do Leslie and Jesse become friends?
7. Describe Terabithia. Why is it important to the two children?
8. Why can't Jesse accept that Leslie has died?
9. How does rescuing May Belle make Jesse feel better?
10. How had Leslie taught him to "stand up to his fear"?

Retelling: Have students pick a partner. Ask one child to tell the partner about Jesse's friendship with Leslie as Jesse might have explained it later on in life.

Extended Activities: (beyond the reading activities).
1. Have students rewrite the story as if Jesse had invited Leslie to accompany Miss Edmonds and him to the Smithsonian. Would Leslie have died? Would he have brought May Belle to Terabithia?
2. Ask students what they think Jesse will be like when he grows up. Will he be an artist? Will he still remember Leslie? Will he still have fear? Will he still be close to May Belle? Have students write a paragraph describing Jesse's life twenty years later.
3. Perhaps Jesse wishes he could have seen Leslie just one more time. Ask students to imagine what Jesse might have said to Leslie if he'd known he could have one last conversation with her. Have students present a dialogue of this conversation.

Interdisciplinary Ideas

Social Studies: In the story Leslie's parents would suddenly begin talking to Jesse about ". . . how to save the timber wolves or redwoods, or singing whales," but he knew nothing about these topics. In groups of three or four, have students select one of these issues, do research, and explain why the topic might have been a concern to Leslie's parents.

Social Studies/Language Arts: Discuss the dialect of rural Virginia as presented in this story, e.g., "You shouldn't ought to beat me in the head!" "You ain't got no money for school shopping!" Select some phrases from the text and have students convert them into standard English. Ask children why they think the author chose to use this nonstandard dialect in her text.

Art: Have students draw a picture of Terabithia as they imagine it, using colored chalk and newsprint, or toothpicks and glue.

Music: Teach students the songs that Miss Edmonds taught Jesse: "This Land Is Your Land," "Blowing in the Wind," "In My Beautiful Balloon," and "Free to Be . . . You and Me."

212. *My Name Is Not Angelica* by Scott O'Dell. Boston: Houghton
    Mifflin, 1989.

Focus on Modifying Gender Stereotypes: Raisha, a girl who is a
survivor, is captured in Africa and sold as a slave. She hates her new name
and slavery but is strong and wants to retaliate. She realizes, however, that
rash action is dangerous for her, and so she survives through other strategies.

Overview: In Barato, Africa, Konje, Raisha, and Dondo are captured at
a rival king's feast and sold as slaves. They are unloaded in St. Thomas (Danish
Virgin Islands), participate in the slave revolt on St. John (1733–34), see the
suicide leap by slaves into the sea, and hope for a better future. 4–8.

New Vocabulary: survivor, Barato, St. Thomas, St. John, Danish Virgin
Islands, revolt, Mary Point, Martinique.

Materials: chalk, chalkboard, paper, pencils or pens, related books for
further reading, African-American folk literature, materials for constructing a
mural.

Motivation: (linking prior knowledge; "into" the reading activities).

1. Ask students to imagine/sketch this scene: "You have been invited to
   enjoy a dinner and spend the night at the home of an acquaintance
   in a nearby town, when suddenly, while you are sleeping, you and
   two of your friends are dragged from your bed and put aboard a ship
   bound for another land." In small groups, ask them to tell their
   classmates their feelings about this scene and what they would have
   done in the situation.

2. Discuss the custom of each of the slaves receiving a new name when
   purchased by a planter and the ways each African responded to this
   captivity in the strange surroundings. Encourage them to locate incidents that show that Dondo was docile and obedient on the outside
   while angry inside; that Konje showed his kingly bearing and attitude
   and escaped to Mary Point, the gathering place for runaway slaves
   on the island; that Raisha hated slavery but realized the danger
   around her.

Purpose for Reading or Listening: "You are going to read (hear) a
story about a girl named Raisha who was renamed Angelica when she was sold
into slavery. Read (listen) to find out how Raisha changed her attitude from
one of despair (and jumping into the sea from Mary Point) to one of 'life
forever.' How did Konje's love help her make this decision?"

Discussion Questions: (through the reading activities).

1. In Africa, what trickery was played on Raisha, her family, and her
   friends at the rival king's feast?

2. Describe how you think a day in Raisha's life must have been before
   she became a slave.

3. How do you think Konje felt when he escaped to Mary Point, the

stronghold of the runaways on the island? What might *you* have said or done if you had been with him when he escaped?
4. Why did Raisha continue to work as a personal servant for Jenna van Prok and not escape? How did she finally escape?
5. What were Raisha's feelings about Konje by the end of the story? How do you think Konje felt about Raisha?
6. What are some ways you can help someone who may have no hope for a better life?

Retelling: (through the reading activities). Pairs of students role play the story taking turns being either Raisha or Konje.

Extended Activities: (beyond the reading activities).
1. Taking the role of Raisha, have students write a letter to smuggle back to her homeland telling about the day when Jost Van Prok, a planter of Hawks Nest on the island of St. John, purchased Konje, Dondo, and Raisha. Explain how Raisha felt and what actions she planned to take.
2. Have students take the role of a participant who was there to see the day when Captain Dumont arrived at Mary Point with the soldiers. Ask students to rewrite the event from their point of view.
3. Have students discuss the story from the point of view of Captain Dumont and the planters. Help them to imagine that the planters and the soldiers were afraid of the slaves in their revolt and needed the laborers to work in the fields.
4. Have students interview a student playing the role of Raisha. Questions can include, "What is a day in your life like? What are some of the things you do to survive?" Help students to compare their lives of freedom with that of another who is not free.
5. Have students write a letter to Konje from Raisha telling of her plans to escape.

Interdisciplinary Ideas

Social Studies: Suggest students find books in the library that tell how African Americans were treated in slavery.

Recreational Reading: Ask students to look for folklore about the desire of people to be free. Discuss how freedom is seen in these folktales and legends. Why do they suppose this is so? Select *The People Could Fly*, a collection of African-American folktales. The title tale tells of the ability of field laborers to fly away from the harsh life as slaves.

Science: Investigate the ways that people can send secret messages. Have students write expository paragraphs explaining the use of secret writing, secret codes, secret signals.

Art: Engage students in construction of a diorama of the capture of Raisha and her family and friends at the rival king's feast in Africa.

Math: Count the number of books the students find that tell about slavery. Graph the information in categories, e.g., informational books, historical fiction, and biographies.

213. *The Pigs Are Flying* by Emily Rodda. Ill. by Noela Young. New York: Greenwillow Books, 1986.

Focus on Modifying Gender Stereotypes: courage; ability to solve problems; Rachel is a very courageous little girl who solves problems in a rational, methodical way.

Overview: Rachel is bored and wishes something exciting would happen. She suddenly finds herself transported to a strange land where pigs fly and storms cause the inhabitants to behave strangely. 4–6.

New Vocabulary: succession, thunderous, hordes, nickered, dicey, documented, bilious, subsidy, scatty, reproachfully, affinity, queue.

Materials: butcher paper, tempera paint, information books on Australia and meteorology.

Motivation: (linking prior knowledge; getting "into" the reading activities).

1. Write on the blackboard the expression "It's raining cats and dogs." Ask students what the expression means. Have them guess where they think the expression might have come from. Ask them if they think the saying might be confusing to people who are just learning to speak English. Brainstorm some other phrases and English idioms that might be understood by limited English speakers.

2. Read students the book *Cloudy with a Chance of Meatballs* by Judi Barrett. Ask them to tell how they think they would feel if, in a storm, it were suddenly raining pancakes instead of water. What would be some advantages of this? Some disadvantages?

Purpose for Reading or Listening: "You are about to read (listen to) a story about a little girl who is just recovering from the flu. She is bored and wishes something exciting would happen. Read (listen) to find out what very unusual thing happens to Rachel."

Discussion Questions: (through the reading activities).

1. Why was Rachel feeling bored?
2. How did she feel when she found she was riding a unicorn?
3. What happened in a "Grunter"?
4. What was happening to Gloria?
5. How did Gloria return to Bert and Enid?
6. How had Alex returned to the outside?
7. How had Sandy caused Rachel's adventure to happen?
8. Why had they both brought UEF Force 10 back with them?

9. Do you think Rachel will ever go back to the Inside? Why or why not?
10. What would you do with the UEF Force 10?

Retelling: Have students pretend they are Rachel trying to tell her friends about her adventure as an Outsider. How would they persuade their friends that such an unlikely adventure had actually occurred?

Extended Activities: (beyond the reading activities).
1. Have students write the next chapter of the book, in which Rachel and Sandy return as Outsiders.
2. Ask students to write an invitation to Enid and Bert inviting them to the Outside to see what life is like.
3. Encourage students to write a diary of the strange events that occurred as Rachel or Alex would have experienced it.
4. Have students write the dialogue for a conversation among three pigs at the beginning of a storm.

Interdisciplinary Ideas

Social Studies: The author of this book, Emily Rodda, is from Australia. Hence, many of the expressions, e.g., "scatty," "dicey," "nickered," "queue," are different expressions. Have students make an American/Australian dictionary with their findings of differences between the two dialects. Have students research additional words and expressions that differ in the two dialects.

Language Arts/Economics: Have students, in small groups, decide how they would market bottles of UEF Force 10. Encourage them to write a one minute commercial to sell the product to the American public.

Art: Post butcher paper along the length of one wall. First using pencil sketches and then tempera paints, allow students to make a mural of pigs in a "grunter."

214. *Rose Blanche* by Robert Innocenti. New York: Stewart, Tabori & Chang, 1985/Creative Ed., 1986.

Focus on Modifying Gender Stereotypes: A girl, who is in every way a heroine, shows great bravery as well as selflessness and compassion in this moving story.

Overview: During World War II, a young German girl's curiosity leads her to discover something far more terrible than the day-to-day hardships and privations that she had been experiencing—she discovers a concentration camp full of cold, hungry children. 4–6.

New Vocabulary: holocaust, crocuses.

Materials: 3″×5″ cards, pictures from concentration camps, pastel chalks, construction paper, Vivaldi's *Four Seasons,* tape recorder.

Motivation: (linking prior knowledge; getting "into" the reading activities).

1. Write on the writing board the phrase "All tyrannies begin and end with thoughts uncritically accepted." From what students already know about Adolf Hitler and World War II, ask them how they think this quote relates to the actions of the Nazis in Germany in World War II.

2. Play a game called "Heroines" with students. On 3″×5″ cards, write the names of famous women who have done brave things and could be considered heroines, one per card. Tape a card to each child's back. By asking questions that could only be answered with "yes" or "no," have students try to identify the heroine on the card taped to their backs. Some possible heroines include:

Sally Ride	Indira Gandi	Golda Meir
Elizabeth Kenny	Corazon Aquino	Margaret Thatcher
Mother Teresa	Eleanor Roosevelt	Barbara Jordan
Harriet Tubman	Clara Barton	Pat Schroeder
Florence Nightingale	Maya Angelou	Shirley Chisholm

3. Encourage students to do research on the heroines with which they are unfamiliar.

4. Ask students to think back to a time when *they* did something brave or heroic in their lives. Have each student turn to a neighbor and relate that experience, beginning with, "I was a hero/heroine when _____."

Purpose for Reading or Listening: "You are going to read (hear) a story about a brave girl whose curiosity leads her to make a startling, horrific discovery. Read (listen) to find out what Rose Blanche does for which you would give her the title of 'heroine.'"

Discussion Questions: (through the reading activities).

1. How did Rose Blanche's life change when the soldiers came to town?

2. Why did Rose Blanche follow the little boy?

3. Would *you* have followed him? Why or why not?

4. Rose Blanche was stealing food from her house and sneaking out of school early to go to the camp. Were these actions right or wrong? Why do you think so?

5. Have *you* ever deliberately gone hungry so that someone else could eat? Can you imagine a situation where you would?

6. How do you think Rose Blanche felt when she saw the children getting thinner and thinner?

7. Why do you think Rose Blanche didn't tell her mother what she was doing?
8. Why did all of the people suddenly disappear? What had happened?
9. Why did the soldiers shoot Rose Blanche?
10. Why does this author begin the story in wintertime and end with vivid descriptions of springtime? Was this an effective technique?

Retelling: (through the reading activities). This story begins through the voice of Rose Blanche and then, halfway through, is told in the third person. At no time are Rose Blanche's feelings described. Have pairs of students reread the story one page at a time. As one page is completed by the reader, have the listener take the part of Rose Blanche and say, "I am feeling _____." Have the pairs of students alternate reading and responding in the voice of Rose Blanche.

Extended Activities: (beyond the reading activities).
1. Have students rewrite the story from the point of view of one of the hungry children in the concentration camp; from the point of view of Rose Blanche's brother; from the point of view of a Nazi soldier.
2. Instruct students to write an epitaph for Rose Blanche's grave that would appropriately summarize the brave circumstances of her death.
3. There is no dialogue in this book. Have students choose a scene from the book and create a conversation between the following people: Rose Blanche and her mother; Rose Blanche and one of the children in the camp; Rose Blanche and a soldier. Have groups of students present their dialogues to the rest of the class.

Interdisciplinary Ideas

Recreational Reading: Have students find books in the library about Hitler, Nazi Germany, and World War II. Ask them to write a paragraph about why they would or would not have liked to live in Germany at that time.

Social Studies: Bring in pictures of the holocaust and concentration camps. Encourage students to find out about the Jewish religion through research or by interviewing a Jewish person. Ask students why they think the Jews were killed.

Art: Ask students to close their eyes and listen to the final words from the book:
"The crocuses finally sprang up from the ground. The river swelled and overflowed its banks. Trees were green and full of birds. Spring sang." From this imagery, encourage students to draw a picture of springtime as the author describes it, using pastels and construction paper.

Music: Obtain a copy of Anton Vivaldi's *Four Seasons.* Play the sections entitled "Winter" and "Spring." After each, allow students to brainstorm some words and open-ended phrases that the music brings to their minds. Discuss how the composer makes the listener think of the appropriate season through his use of instruments, volume, tempo, etc.

215. *The Secret of Gumbo Grove* by Eleanora E. Tate. New York: Franklin Watts, 1987.

Focus on Modifying Gender Stereotypes: Raisin, a young girl who is interested in history and her cultural roots, is curious and solves the problem of discovering African Americans who did something "worth talking about."

Overview: With the help of her friends—Bunny, Sin-sin, Jeff, and Junebug—Raisin tracks down the mystery of a famous person buried in the cemetery of the New Africa No. 1 Missionary Baptist Church. Raisin is interested in history and talks to Miz Effie: "We read about people doing stuff in history class, but it was always about White people when it came to Calvary County. I asked Miz Gore, my teacher, how come we never studied about anybody Black, and she said nobody Black around here had ever done anything worth talking about." 4–6.

New Vocabulary: Harriet Tubman, Sojourner Truth, research, circa, historical.

Materials: paper, pencils or pens, chalk, chalkboard, poster board, painting materials, related books for further reading.

Motivation: (linking prior knowledge; "into" the reading activities).

1. Show students the book cover and elicit their reactions to the picture of Raisin and Miz Effie staring at the vine-covered tombstone in the cemetery at Gumbo Grove. Write their dictations in a word and phrase web on the writing board. Solicit possible reasons why Raisin and Miz Effie are there.

2. Ask students to think about information that one can collect from the cemetery, and allow time for students to tell about experiences related to searching for information about family, friends or acquaintances in a church or cemetery.

3. Display the word *secret* on the board, overhead, or chart, and ask students to provide a definition of the word and give examples after talking to a partner and discussing, "One thing I know about a secret is . . ."

Purpose for Reading or Listening: "You are going to read (hear) a story about a girl named Raisin who was interested in history and who wanted to solve a mystery about a famous person. Read (listen) to find out how Raisin and her friends discover the name of the famous person who is buried in the cemetery."

Discussion Questions: (through the reading activities).

1. What was Raisin, the main character, like in the story?
2. What did Raisin want to do?

3. What were some of the problems that kept Raisin from doing what she wanted to do?
4. How could you have helped Raisin?
5. What friends did Raisin have?
6. How was Raisin's problem solved?
7. What are some ways you can do your own research about a famous person who lived in your community?

Retelling: (through the reading activities). Pairs of students role play the story taking turns being Raisin or Miz Effie.

Extended Activities: (beyond the reading activities).

1. As Raisin's friend, have each student write an entry in a diary about Raisin and how she missed her chance to compete in the Miss Ebony Pageant. How did the friend feel and why? As Raisin's friend, explain what you learned from this experience.
2. Have students discuss heroes and heroines in their lives after discussing that Raisin thinks that Dickson is the biggest hero she has come close to in her life.
3. Back in the role as Raisin's friend, write a letter to another friend about the Alfronia Meriweather Community Service Award being presented to Raisin Stackhouse at the Calvary County Negro Business and Professional Women's Club. Be sure to say that the award was given in recognition of hard work, determination, and a commitment to preserving history in the community.

Interdisciplinary Ideas

Social Studies: Raisin shared her thoughts with the reader when she said, "I liked heroes. And I liked to feel good about what people did back in the old days, because it helped me go ahead and feel good about now. But lots of times the kids made fun of me because I talked about heroes like Harriet Tubman and Sojourner Truth. Some of the kids didn't even know who THEY were, and they were real famous" (p. 17).

Discuss with students "feeling good about what people did back in the old days," feeling "good about now," and the idea of getting rid of discrimination based on gender, prejudice against the female sex, or the stereotyping of males—sexism. As part of feeling "good about now," discuss some of the guidelines that have been developed to eliminate sexism in published materials:

1. Encourage students to write for a free copy of guidelines to combat sexism from such sources as a) National Council of Teachers of English, 111 Kenyon Road, Urbana, IL 61801; and b) McGraw-Hill Book Company.
2. Discuss ways that the rights of women and girls and men and boys have been limited by social customs and conditions of their time period.

3. Discuss the point of view that neither sex should be stereotyped or arbitrarily assigned to a secondary role (or a primary role). When talking about this point of view, mention: a) showing a wide range of professions and trades for both females and males; b) showing that both can be the ones to support a family; c) showing that job stereotypes can be broken and that both sexes are at all professional levels; d) showing that all have choices about marriage, working or not working, and job preferences; e) showing that all can have an interest in mathematics, mechanical skills, and sports, or in poetry, art, music, cooking, sewing, and child care; f) showing that all have *human* strengths and weaknesses (rather than feminine and masculine strengths and weaknesses); g) showing that *all* humans can be active, courageous, competent, decisive, persistent, serious, strong, and successful; h) showing that all should be treated with dignity, respect, and seriousness.

4. Give attention to career opportunities and engage students in preparing a set of posters for the room that announce:
   a. Something is important: human rights!
   b. Girls and boys are absolutely equal: we mean it!
   c. Anyone can do almost anything they want to—regardless of their sex.
   d. You'll see "human rights" in our class.

Language Arts: Suggest that students write the speech given by the president of the community when she gave Raisin the award.

Suggest that interested students select a story published earlier (in the 50s, 60s, and so on), read it, and record examples of inept wording related to portraying the roles of both females and males. For examples, certain words could be suggested by the student and substituted with terms acceptable in today's society:

Wording found	*Rewording suggested*
mankind	humanity, human beings, people
primitive man	prehistoric people, human beings
man's achievements	humans' achievements
the best man for the job	the best person for the job
manmade	constructed
manpower	human power, work force
congressman	congress member

Recreational Reading: Discuss with students the aspect of researching one's cultural heritage with folk literature: if Raisin wanted to know more about her African American cultural heritage, what folklore from Africa or from African-American groups elsewhere would be available for her to read? and what could Raisin learn from each story?

Selections for Review

Aardema, Verna. *Bringing the Rain to Kapiti Plain: A Nandi Tale.* Ill. Beatriz Vidal. Dial, 1981. Accumulating tale from Kenya.

Aardema, Verna. *Who's in Rabbit's House?* Ill. Leo and Diane Dillon. Dial, 1987. Repetitive story.

Aardema, Verna. *Why Mosquitoes Buzz in People's Ears.* Ill. Leo and Diane Dillon. Dial, 1975. Accumulating story.

Bryan, Ashley. *Turtle Knows Your Name.* Atheneum, 1989. West Indian folktale.

Carew, Jan. *Children of the Sun.* Ill. Leo and Diane Dillon. Little, Brown, 1980. Twin boys search for their values.

Diop, Birago, translator. *Mother Crocodile/Maman Calman.* Delacorte, 1981. An Ouolof tale from Senegal, West Africa, about Golo the monkey, who almost convinced the little crocodiles that Mother Crocodile was crazy because she kept telling stories from the past.

Fournier, Catharine, adapter. *The Coconut Thieves.* Scribner, 1964. African folktale where the small animals outwit the larger and stronger ones.

Graham, Lorenz. *God Wash the World and Start Again.* Crowell, 1970. Story of Noah and the ark told in the rhythmic English of the Liberian African.

Graham, Lorenz. *A Road Down in the Sea.* Crowell, 1970. Moses leads the Hebrew people out of Egypt in this spoken song.

Grifalconi, Ann. *The Village of Round and Square Houses.* Ill. Little, Brown, 1986. A "Why" tale from Cameroon.

Guirma, Frederic. *Princess of the Full Moon.* Macmillan, 1970. An African folktale about a beautiful and selfish African girl who wants to marry the richest and most handsome prince in the land.

Guy, Rosa. *Mother Crocodile.* Ill. John Steptoe. Delacorte, 1981. West African folktale from Senegal with theme of following elders' advice.

Kirn, Ann. *Beeswax Catches a Thief.* Norton, 1968. Adapted from a Congo folktale where Beeswax, the turtle, is the hero, and the villain is a jackal.

Lexau, Joan M. *Crocodile and Hen.* Harper & Row, 1969. An African folktale from Bokongo, Africa, that tells why crocodiles do not eat hens. Traditional folktale about a turtle who outwits his enemies and can be seen as a prototype of the B'rer Rabbit folklore.

Rowe, A.K. *The Clever Turtle.* Prentice-Hall, 1969.

Williams, Sheron. *And in the Beginning. . .* Ill. Robert Roth. Atheneum, 1991. In this African creation tale, Mahtimi, the Blessed One, creates a man from the soil of Kilimanjaro. He is Kwanza, the First One, who explores the world. When he returns, he finds Mahtimi has created others with red skin, long hair, and blue eyes, and he is jealous.

Anthologies also provide a range of stories for recreational reading:

African Tales: Folklore of the Central African Republic. Ill. Rodney Wimer. Telcraft, 1992. Tere, a supernatural figure, is in several of these expressive tales from the Mandjia and Banda people of the Central African Republic.

Bryan, Ashley. *Beat the Story-Drum, Pum-Pum.* Atheneum, 1980. Collection of tales.

Science: What references are made in the story to contributions of engineers and other scientists? Record and list some of the contributions found in the story and research some facts about the contribution in other sources:

Contribution of engineers and other scientists: pickup truck (p. 11). Some facts about the reference (What scientific contributions/engineering contributions fostered the development of the truck?):

_____

_____

Sources used:

_____

_____

Gumbo Limbo Soda Fountain and Cafe (p. 12).
Some facts about the reference:

_____

_____

Sources used:

_____

_____

Two airplanes flew low, trailing banners (p. 13).
Some facts about the reference:

_____

_____

Sources used:

_____

_____

Panama Jack Suntan Lotion (p. 13).
Some facts about the reference:

_____

_____

Sources used:

_____

_____

Hotels, restaurants, and beachwear shops (p. 13).
Some facts about the reference:

_____

_____

Sources used:

_____

People who worked all night cleaning up hotels and condos (p. 13).
Some facts about the reference:

_____

_____

Sources used:

_____

"We rattled across the wood bridge spanning the Fifteenth Street drainage ditch and turned onto Cypress Swamp Road" (p. 14).
Some facts about the reference:

_____

_____

Sources used:

_____

Strom Thurmond Highway (p. 15).
Some facts about the reference:

_____

_____

Sources used:

_____

Other:

Art: Ask students to think of one thing they like or do not like about the way the illustrator drew the scene on the cover of the book.

Have students construct a large poster showing the changes they would make for the book's cover.

Math: Using other realistic fiction books in a display, ask students to graph the types of characters—women and girls, men and boys. Discuss some of the strengths of the characters.

Index

References are to entry numbers, not pages.